LUCRETIA MOTT

LUCRETIA COFFIN MOTT, 1793–1880

(From the Kyle painting owned by Mrs. Alan Valentine)

Lucretia Mott

By

OTELIA CROMWELL

HARVARD UNIVERSITY PRESS

Cambridge, Massachusetts

1958

IN MEMORIAM

Winifred McGuinn Lewis

PREFACE

In 1821, before Lucretia Mott was thirty years old, she was designated as minister in the Society of Friends. Recognized for her exemplary character and her eloquence, she soon became not only a respected Quaker minister but one of the leaders in the reform movements of the nineteenth century. As a public speaker she declared that her religious convictions were founded on intelligent interpretation of the Bible and independence of thought and that her pleas for human brotherhood and world peace were expressions of her convictions. Leadership was accorded her not through any ambitions or strivings of her own but through recognition of an inspired talent consecrated to righteous ends. Believing that sectarian dogmatism, human slavery, the inequalities suffered by women, intemperance, and war were social wrongs resulting from confused thinking about religious and social relationships, she pleaded for freedom of thought, even as she advocated an unflinching and consistent opposition to all forms of injustice.

By the middle of the nineteenth century, Lucretia Mott had become a person eagerly sought by reformers as the main speaker on their programs, and her participation was generally announced in headlines. Many orthodox believers regarded her and denounced her as a heretic; and she did indeed oppose many of the tenets of formalized religion. But by liberals, homage was paid to her force of conviction, her sincerity, her gentleness, and her love of humanity. In public tributes appearing after her death, she was cited as "the greatest American woman" and "the noblest of them all."

With the exception of the letters included in Anna Davis Hallowell's valuable biography, *James and Lucretia Mott, Life and Letters,* primary sources for a study of Lucretia Mott's early life seem limited to the impersonal though reliable evidences of official documents. These include the Quaker and Real Estate Records of Nantucket, Boston's Real Estate Records, "Taking Books," and early School Reports, the Yearbooks of Nine Partners Boarding School, and the Minutes of the Friends' Meetings of Nantucket and New York State.

But fuller and richer are authentic data revealing in greater clarity her maturity and later years. There is at hand the Diary she wrote during a visit of three months to Great Britain in 1840. To this memoir may be added the correspondence with her family and friends, Minutes of significant organizations, Quaker records, and phonographic reports, as well as brief or extended summaries of her speeches. Available also are the diaries and biographies of several of her contemporaries as well as the official records of certain organizations.

For much encouragement I am happy to express my gratitude to descendants of William Lloyd Garrison and to members of Lucretia Mott's family. By Miss Eleanor Garrison I was permitted to examine the unpublished "William Lloyd Garrison Family Papers," which were entrusted to Mrs. Dorothy Porter, Curator of the Moorland Collection of Howard University, before they became a part of the Sophia Smith Collection of Smith College. From Mrs. Lucretia Mott Churchill I received the gift of several of Lucretia Mott's manuscript letters and Mrs. Hallowell's interleaved copy of *James and Lucretia Mott*. I am indebted also for suggestions and encouragement to Mr. Lloyd M. Garrison, Miss Fanny Garrison, Mr. Charles Osborne, Miss Lucy Davis, Mrs. Lucretia M. Gilchrist, and the late Oswald Garrison Villard. Not the least of my indebtedness to the family is due to Mrs. Alan Valentine who allowed Mr. Hertzel Brown to make for the frontispiece a photograph of the Kyle painting. I am obliged to Professor Henry Cadbury of Harvard University for pointing out much relevant source material; to Professor Thomas E. Drake of Haverford College; and to Dr. Frederick Tolles, Librarian of the Friends Historical Library of Swarthmore College, for the reading of certain chapters of the manuscript; to Professor Oscar Handlin of Harvard University and to Professor Charles W. Thomas of the City College of the District of Columbia, for valuable suggestions; and to Mr. Thomas A. de Valcourt for information concerning *A Review of Dana's Philadelphia Lecture.*

I am obligated also to directors and staff members of the Boston Public Library, the Massachusetts Historical Society, the Library of Harvard University, the Nantucket Historical Association, the Athenaeum in Nantucket, the New York Historical Society, the Astor Lenox and Tilden Foundations and the Countee Cullen Branch of the New York Public Library, the Fifteenth Street Meeting House, the Arch Street Center, the Worcester Historical Association, the Sophia Smith Collection of Smith College, the Library of Cornell University, the Historical Society of Pennsylvania, the Nantucket Historical Association, the Library Company of Philadelphia, the Friends Historical Library of Swarthmore College, the Library of Haverford College, the Baltimore Yearly Meeting, and the Library of Congress.

From Mr. Leo J. Sullivan and Mr. William Fitzgerald, Registrars of Suffolk Registry of Deeds, I secured copies of the deeds relevant to the transfers of Thomas Coffin's real estate in Boston, and permission to visit the vaults under Boston's City Hall where I had opportunity to study Boston's *Taking Books,* the old census records of the city. In Nantucket, I was allowed by the Recorder of Deeds to examine the real estate records of the town. Through Dr. William E. Gardner, who gave me many directions in Nantucket, I met Mrs. Cyrus Barnes who permitted me to make a leisurely examination of the Coffin home in Nantucket. Mrs. James T. Irish of the Board of Managers of the Stephen Smith Home for the Aged furthered my inquiries in regard to Lucretia Mott's connection with the Home. In Philadelphia, also, I received guidance from Mr. and Mrs. William Cash of Fairview. And by no means the least of my significant and happy experiences was the visit to Oakwood School where Mr. Reagan, Principal, and Miss Craig, Assistant Principal, showed me the old records of Nine Partners Boarding School.

Permissions to use manuscript material were granted by Mr. Howard H. Brinton, Director, Arch Street Center; Mr. Richmond P. Miller, Vice-President, Atwater Kent Museum; Dr. Zoltán Haraszti through Miss Harriet Swift of the Boston Public Library; Mr. Joseph B. Rounds, Director, Buffalo Public Library; Mr. S. A. McCarthy, Director, Cornell University Library; Mr. Walter W. Merrill, Director, Essex Institute; Professor Thomas E. Drake, Haverford College; Mr. William H. Bond, Curator of Manuscripts, Houghton Library, Harvard University; Mr. Stephen T. Riley, Librarian, Massachusetts Historical Society; Miss Ruth C. Craig, Assistant Principal, Oakwood School; Mr. R. N. Williams II, Curator, Pennsylvania Historical Society; Mrs. Margaret S. Grierson, Executive Secretary, Sophia Smith Collection, Smith College, and Miss Eleanor Garrison; Mr. Hobart C. Jackson, Administrator, Stephen Smith Home for the Aged, Philadelphia; Mr. Wayne S. Germaine, the Library of Syracuse University; Dr. Frederick B. Tolles, Librarian, Swarthmore College; Miss Ethel M. Fair, Curator of Manuscripts, Vassar College Library; Miss Katherine Reid, Librarian, Worcester Historical Society; Mr. Shirley F. Ebinger, Columbia University Press; and Mr. Edward S.

PREFACE

Forbes, Director of Ralph Waldo Emerson Memorial Association. Permissions to quote copyrighted material were granted by Mr. Philip D. Jordan and the University of Minnesota Press; Professor Ralph Rusk, Columbia University; Houghton Mifflin; and Professor Robert Samuel Fletcher, Oberlin College. For constructive criticism and sustained patience I am obligated to Miss Ann Louise Coffin of the Harvard University Press. And not to be forgotten is the expert typing of Miss Cordelia Key and Mr. Roger Kyles.

Over the years the interest taken in the study by my family — Mary Lucy and John Cromwell and Henry and Adelaide Hill — has been a sustained help.

O. C.

CONTENTS

LUCRETIA MOTT

"All these subjects of reform are kindred in their nature, and giving to each its proper consideration, will tend to strengthen and nerve the mind for all . . ."

LUCRETIA MOTT

Chapter One

ISLAND HERITAGE

On May 6, 1877, Alfred H. Love [1] noted in his Diary that Lucretia Mott had been present at that day's meeting of the Pennsylvania Peace Society held in Warminster. He mentioned the tribute made to Lucretia's endurance under attacks of criticism; to her power's having been compared to the fortitude of Joseph when "his bow abode in strength and the arms of his hands were made strong by the hands of the mighty God of Jacob." Then Love added:

Lucretia followed & said When a little girl this was the first quotation she heard at meeting which affected her. She went home & felt it was for her that she must do her part & conform to Friends & although she never dressed much & had not much dress to change, for she had not taste enough still she had on bright blue bows on her shoes & these she cut off & from that to other things she gave up.

Lucretia did not indicate the exact time or place of this childhood resolution. In all likelihood it occurred on Nantucket. It has been said that she had the opportunity to listen to Elizabeth Coggeshall's preaching when this widely traveled Quaker minister came to Nantucket in 1797 shortly before she sailed on a religious visit to "Friends in England, Ireland and the Continent of Europe." [2] Too much need not be made of any possible effect Elizabeth Coggeshall may have had on Lucretia, for in 1797 the child was but four years old. But she was seven when Rebecca Jones, a Quaker minister from Pennsylvania, together with "a detachment" held appointed meetings on the Island. [3] It is possible that the preaching of Rebecca Jones or of one of her fellow ministers influenced Lucretia Coffin to make her earliest conscious concession to Quaker practices, to undergo a significant religious experience, that she remembered when she was well over eighty.

In the closing years of the eighteenth century, Nantucket, an island lying southward from Cape Cod about thirty miles, was largely swamp meadowland, dense marshes, and windswept moors that all but encircled a little hamlet on the western shore. Sherburne, or Nantucket Town, as the hamlet was eventually to be called, sheltered a mixed group of people. Among them were descendants of the shrewd pioneers, purchasers of the territory from Thomas Macy whose ownership had been obtained from the agents of the absentee English proprietors. Security for the pioneers in their new home was then doubly assured through an agreement with the Indians.[4]

In the hundred years following these transactions, other settlers claimed the island as their home. The lure of whaling had attracted to the neighborhood a motley sprinkling of sailors from Prince Edward Island, the Azores, and other foreign ports; from time to time a few Indians strolled from the outlying wastelands into Sherburne; and Quakers found in the place a haven from persecution. Living close together in Sherburne or scattered over the unfertile stretches of land across the eastern wilds where the cattle and sheep grazed, these divergent Nantucketers found in the island a strong welding bond. Forced into mutual trust by the common problems and dangers of frontier life, they had learned to respect one another, to live together in harmony and good will.

Through industry, hardihood, and thrift, a stark unpromising territory, divided originally by "shares" among the first settlers, had grown into a settlement built up mainly in four-square, broad-timbered homesteads and less pretentious, plain-boarded or shingled cottages. Here and there among these cottages were single-room dwellings, expanded often by unconventional additions in the rear; the prosperity, however, of several Nantucketers was evident in a few beautiful spacious residences. Practically all these dwellings, however, seemed to have borrowed a uniformly grayish coloring from the lowering moor and the encircling waters.

By 1800 Sherburne had added to its dwelling houses a "Town House," "shops of goods," meeting houses put up by the Presbyterians, the Baptists, and the Quakers, a few private schools, the quarters of the tradesmen, and a combination jail and workhouse which was almost always untenanted.

But whaling was the mainspring of Nantucket. To help promote this industry all Nantucketers lent a hand: many men were kept busy; young boys became apprentices in the crafts of rope twisting and barrel making, as they were trained to watch the bubbling whale oils in the refining trypots; and almost all the Nantucket children, girls as well as boys, were inducted into some of the mysteries of candle making. Nantucketers took these industries seriously, for although the whalers were venturesome and courageous, the roots of whaling were on the island itself. The skillful, steady Nantucket craftsmen, the sheep and cattle grazers, the shop-keepers, the gardeners and road menders had their interest in and responsibility for the success of the men throwing the harpoons.[5]

In its remoteness from the mainland, Nantucket had escaped the actual physical ravages of the American Revolution. But, in spite of the efforts of the islanders to preserve their neutrality, whaling had been grievously imperiled and curtailed by privateers. When peace, however, had been declared between Great Britain and her former colonies, Nantucket housewives could not welcome their husbands home to tranquil living, for the whalers resumed their adventurous calling and whaleboats again threaded their way among the perilous shoals of Nantucket's landlocked harbor or set sail from the less dangerous port of neighboring Woods Hole on Cape Cod.

Among these eighteenth-century whalers was Thomas Coffin, customarily called "Thomas Coffin junior" to distinguish him from his grandfather, who also bore the name Thomas. Descended from Tristram Coffin, one of the purchasers of the island, Thomas Coffin, Jr. was the son of Benjamin and Deborah Coffin. In 1789, he married Anna Folger, a descendant of Peter Folger, another first settler.

According to "A Record of the Births, Deaths, Receptions, Disownments & Renewals, Alphabetically Arranged, in the Society of Friends On the Island of Nantucket," Thomas and Anna Coffin had seven children between 1790 and 1804, of whom Lucretia, born January 3, 1793, was the second.[6] As one of her descendants [7] puts it, "Grandmother was in the sixth generation from Tristram Coffin and in the seventh generation from Peter Folger." Among those sharing this ancestry was Peter Folger's grandson, Benjamin Franklin, to whom Lucretia liked to refer as "Cousin Benjamin."

Lucretia would have been hard put to name her Nantucket connections. One of her favorite reminiscences was of an incident that occurred on a boat between Woods Hole and Nantucket, when she was making one of her frequent journeys to her birthplace. As she records the experience in a letter written in 1869 to her daughter Martha, she found herself seated on the boat next to a Mrs. Chadwick of Brooklyn, a Nantucketer herself returning to the island for the first time in thirty years. Lucretia soon engaged her neighbor in a friendly chat:

"Name Coffin," she began.

"So was mine," responded Mrs. Chadwick.

"Folger on the mother's side," Lucretia again.

"So was mine," was the answer.

"76 yrs. old."

"So am I."

She concluded by declaring that she had discovered so many incredible coincidences of background that she felt "almost related" to the stranger.[8]

When the Nantucket whalers set to sea again after the Revolutionary War, young Thomas Coffin had become master of his own vessel, the "Trial."[9] Following his calling, the master of the "Trial" was away from Nantucket for long periods of time. Of his experiences in foreign ports or of his success as a whaler, or "trader," there seems to be little recorded. But official documents in Nantucket are not silent on Thomas Coffin's standing in the community, his business integrity, and his concern for his family. In these records there is evidence of Thomas Coffin's ownership of several pieces of property. These holdings are described as "real estate and pasture lands for sheep" in addition to the parcel of ground in "the Fishlot shares" at "Scool Street," purchased in 1797 by Thomas Coffin from William Folger. This property was increased in size by an adjoining strip of land acquired from the aforesaid William Folger in 1800.[10] In the meantime he continued to enjoy the respect of his fellow-townsmen, for on December 7, 1797, "Thomas Coffin Junior of Nantucket" was given power of attorney, "Full and whole strength power and authority" by Stephen Waterman.[11]

But Thomas Coffin was more than the astute, highly respected businessman, or rather his successful ventures in business redounded to the comfort and happiness of his family. Direct evidence seems lacking as to just where Thomas and Anna Coffin lived prior to 1797, but in that year on the land bought from William Folger, Thomas Coffin built a dwelling, a solidly constructed, broad-timbered house of ample spaces and simple lines. It was the home of a man holding firmly the conviction that nothing was too good for his family, and that the best was cheapest in the end; it was the beautiful home of a man of sound judgment and conservative taste.

Set just above the sea-scented marshland leading to the south shore, the Coffin home was only a step or two below the main street, and very close to one of Nantucket's two Quaker meeting houses, the South Meeting House. When Anna Coffin on one of her husband's long sea voyages chose to open a "shop of Goods," the narrow room opening from the left of the center hall and facing School Street seemed designed for her purpose without dwarfing the needs of the household. Opposite this converted shop was the large oak-paneled, oak-raftered living room where the family and their friends were wont to gather around the wide deep fireplace.

Disinterested writers of fact and fiction have been enthusiastic in extolling the virtues of the Nantucket housewife. The Quaker John Woolman, so mild in disposition that he was permitted to carry his message against slavery right into the very heart of the South without giving offense, had, at one time, "drawings in his mind" to include Nantucket among the number of places he selected for his missions. When he reached the island, he made a special visit to the "Women Friends in their monthly Meeting of business."[12] Not insignificant as a tribute to the women of Nantucket are his references to the responsibilities so capably borne by these women in the education of their children and in the maintenance of the welfare of the family in the absence of the husbands at sea.

Anna Coffin may have been the prototype for John Woolman's picture of the Nantucket housewife; for in words used by Lucretia in 1853, there is more than an echo of Woolman's opinion:

On the island of Nantucket, for I was born on that Island — I can remember how our mothers were employed while our fathers were at sea. The mothers with their children around — 'twas not customary to have nurses then — kept small groceries and sold provisions that they might make something in the absence of their husbands. At that time it required some money and some courage to get to Boston. They were obliged to go to that city, make their trades, exchange their oils and candles for dry goods, and all the varieties of a country store, set their own price, keep their own accounts; and with all this, have very little help in the family to which they must discharge their duties. Look at the heads of those women, they can mingle with men; they are not triflers; they have intelligent subjects of conversation.[13]

Thomas Coffin's confidence in his wife is shown by his giving her, according to the Nantucket Court Records, power of attorney to be used during his absences from Nantucket. The same source also reveals that at the turn of the century, the family's legal papers bore the signatures of Thomas and Anna Coffin instead of the "Thomas Coffin junr Trader" of earlier years.[14]

The memory of Anna Coffin's wit and wisdom, her versatility, and the sheer vitality of her character, was kept green by her children throughout their lives, and allusions to "Mother's ways" were constantly recurring. To Martha, the youngest daughter, the ceaseless round of household tasks was heavy sledding, and she gladly reverted to her mother's sanity:

You don't catch me apologizing for rooms not in perfect order or windows less clear than crystal, she declared once to her sister Lucretia, for if I keep still it will not be noticed and I have no more idea than Mother of calling attention to defects or omissions.

I should like to see, she wrote, the old Clock of Grandfather's that Mother used to tell us of . . . I should like to see . . . those rosebushes down to Newtorn from which Mother used to buy very full bloom roses at a penny apiece . . . And that pump . . . if it is in existence . . . that Aunt Barker was mortified for Mother to pump so strong at.

I have been reading your last letter all over to try & make it seem like a new one but it wouldn't — that is an enviable talent of Mother's that can make a letter seem as interesting after the fortieth perusal as at first. She generally manages to find something "she hadn't noticed before," the thirty-ninth time.[15]

A day in the Coffin home began at an early hour; in winter the children dressed by candlelight to begin their chores. While Sarah helped to dress the younger children, Lucretia was laying the table, bringing in water from the neighborhood pump, and darting here and there almost under her mother's heels. Breakfast over and dishes washed, the older children left for school while Anna Coffin kept her shop between household duties and the care of her younger children. After school, Lucretia took her turn at minding the shop for her mother between hours of learning to mend, darn, make over garments, and cut scraps into strips to be woven into floor mats and carpet lengths. Moreover, as a Nantucket child, she could hardly have escaped an initiation into the process of candle dipping. Lucretia Mott's "traveling pockets" — the ingeniously contrived bags of gingham fashioned to hold a traveler's valuables — evince skill in fine needlework, a skill bespeaking early training and long practice in sewing. Dexterity in knitting followed at a time when machine-woven stockings and gloves were practically unknown. She learned to cook and enjoy dishes she described as "Indian pudding with milk and eggs," "real Nantucket Indian dumpling," "pig sauce, indigenous to this island," "Stewd cranby so rich & sweet," "veal pie," "Cod fish," "berry pudding," and other Nantucket food.

The girls were trained not only to become careful housekeep-
ers but to regard good housekeeping with wholesome respect.
Such expertness did Lucretia achieve in the performance of the
numberless duties involved in the daily routine that she reflected
all through her life the results of her early apprenticeship. "A
clean hearth" was not inspired in the expectation of a game of
whist, but Lucretia Mott's fireside was one secret of her magnetism, one evidence of her belief that the open fire sparked a note
of welcome as it promoted the complete happiness of the family
circle and a background for the hospitality dear to her heart. A
meticulously regulated home was also one of her ideals. Such a
master hand in housekeeping did she become that in later years
her established order was never disturbed even when she was engaged in an incredibly strenuous public life. Indeed, she seemed
to find a certain satisfaction in the performance of household tasks
even when she had outside assistance for this work. As late as 1853,
at the height of her career as a public speaker, Theodore Parker
evidently had Lucretia in mind when he referred to "the most
distinguished preacher [among the Quakers as] a woman who
adorns her domestic calling as housekeeper, wife, and mother,
with the same womanly dignity and sweetness which mark her
public deportment." [16]

Few details of Lucretia's early schooling seem to have been
brought to light. Public schools were not established in Nantucket
until 1818. But, during the earliest years of the settlement, Dame
Schools, Infant Schools, Sewing Schools, and the so-called Cent
Schools had been maintained for the children of the islanders. In
the Cent Schools children paid for their instruction by depositing
a penny on the teacher's desk. And not to be forgotten is the fact,
as stated in the records of the Monthly Meeting of Women Friends
of Nantucket for 1798, that education under the supervision of
the Meeting was provided for the Quaker children, sewing and
knitting being "admitted into the exercise at the School when requested by the Parents." [17]

Lucretia learned to write by the "Copy-book" method, a twofold device that promoted habit in the correct formation of letters,
while at the same time a pious sentiment was hammered on the
mind and heart of the learner. The precise, legible, but not in-
flexible style of handwriting mastered by Lucretia and retained
throughout her life may be one effect of the Nantucket schooling.
And perhaps the memorizing of certain precepts embraced in the
methods of the early schoolmasters could account also for some

of the traits of her character. About a year before her death, in writing to Alexander M. Ross of Montreal, a fellow abolitionist, she recommended that Dr. Ross's little boy commit to memory this maxim:

> Learn to avoid what thou believst is sin
> Mind what reproves or justifies within
> No act is good, that dost disturb thy peace
> Or can be bad which makes true joy increase.[18]

"These lines," she confided in the message she wrote the child, "were set for me as copies in learning to write when nine or ten years old — I have never seen the book since from which they were taken but they were fixed in my memory."

One may not ignore the possibility of Lucretia's having received indirect instruction from other sources, notably, from *A Looking Glass for the Times,* a long didactic poem written in 1676 by her ancestor Peter Folger. This work, compact as it is of pictures of the persecutions of the Quakers and of reflections on the sins of oppression, the virtues of peace, and the guidance of the Light Within, could have been choice reading for the serious-minded girl; thus it may be no coincidence that the Psalmist's solemn pronouncement, "I am for Peace," a declaration repeated by Peter Folger in the closing lines of the *Looking Glass,* was also one of Lucretia Mott's favorite maxims. Of course, she may have chosen the words from her own study of the Bible; but the possibility of her selecting the line from Folger's poem need not be rejected. Throughout her life Lucretia showed a preference for serious literature. Novels, romantic poetry, indeed the entire realm of fiction rarely found an echo in her heart. She missed the relaxation that comes through the imagination stimulated by vicarious pleasures, but apparently she did not need a force from without herself to renew purpose and energy and power for the sober duties of life.

But the days of Lucretia's childhood were not gloomy ones. She and her sister Elizabeth, "Lucretia's twin," found it no chore to race home from school to "keep the shop" before supper, or to venture over the breezy moors toward "Sconset Way," the hamlet of Sciasconset at the extreme eastern point of Nantucket. On errands for their mother to "the main street" the two little girls made occasional detours to peer into the workshops near the wharf, the "centers of industry" of Nantucket. Included among these "centers" were the eight or ten "rope walks" or cordage factories, the coopers' shops in which pine strippings were fashioned into barrel staves, and the foundries piled up with black kettles and boathooks and harpoons. Lucretia and Elizabeth lingered long over these workshops where the needs of the long voyages were made or repaired or sold or bartered. What a fascinating sight these busy centers must have been for two little girls! And no child could have resisted the adventure of scampering up the strong, oaken staircase leading to the roomy attic of the Coffin home on Fair Street, for in the attic one could play for hours under the huge rafters of the roof or climb to the scuttle itself to peer out across the neighboring chimneys to the broad waters of Nantucket Sound.

Lucretia had a cheerful disposition and was inclined to talk overmuch, as her discreet mother often warned her. "Long tongue" was Anna Coffin's name for her second daughter,[19] a name that in a way was prophetic of the fluency Lucretia Mott attained as a public speaker in the years ahead. At times she was prone to tease, and she was known to be an adroit mimic, displaying a childlike gaiety which developed into the pervasive wit of her maturity. In the evenings there were recreations at home: jackstraws, spelling contests, feats of memorizing verses from the Bible, and reciting the multiplication tables forward and backward. Life was well-ordered and pleasant and, though the tones were serious, no one was unhappy.

But a change of fortune struck the family when Thomas Coffin, in a voyage up the west coast of South America, fell into a dispute with certain Spaniards, a dispute forcing him to leave his ship, the beloved "Trial," at Valparaiso. This brush with the law dampened his ardor for a maritime life, and though he reached home safely he made no more whaling voyages. For a year or two he lived on in Nantucket making evidently a comfortable living. The fact that in 1798 he bought pasture land from his brother suggests not merely the ex-whaler's ability to make a living on shore but his financial competence.

During the years that followed he may have found still other ways on Nantucket of adding to his income. On this the record is apparently silent, but it is known that in 1804, the Coffins sold the house on Fair Street to Anna Coffin's sister, "Phebe Hussey . . . of Nantucket and her children." The deed of this last transaction, dated October 22, 1804, was signed by "Thomas Coffin Junr. and Anna Coffin." [20]

In a letter written in 1868 to her cousin Mary Hussey Earle,

Lucretia Mott was explicit as to the time of the moving to Boston: "Thy next question," she asked Mary Earle, " 'what year did my parents remove to Boston.' Ans. in 7 Mo. 1804." Then she added that, although she could not remember the exact date of the death of Mary Earle's father, she had "a distinct recollection of the sad news coming." It was her belief that the date was 1802. She could not recall the details connected with Mrs. Earle's converting the front parlor of the Coffin house into a shop, but she had no misgivings as to the data concerning her own family. As she said, "From memory with data to corroborate I can tell the year of every important event in our family — & of many of the transpirings of the country from the beginning of this century — & rather before." [21]

The Quaker "Record" of Nantucket lists the date of the approved removal certificate for "Thomas Coffin and Anna his wife, with their children, viz. Sarah, Lucretia, Elizabeth, Thomas Mayhew, Mary and Lydia" as of August 2, 1804. Moreover, advertisement of prospective merchandising by Thomas Coffin in Boston appeared in the *Columbian Centinel,* an early nineteenth-century Boston newspaper, on March 12, and 28, 1804; and on April 4, 11, 14, 18, 21, 1804.

Did Thomas Coffin in the spring of 1804 establish his business in Boston before moving his family from Nantucket in the middle of the summer? Or did he think it prudent to come to Boston "to look over" things before subjecting his family to the uncertainties of life in a new environment? Words in a letter written to the Motts by Lucretia's cousin and close friend, Nathaniel Barney, on April 7, 1861, point to the possibility of Lucretia's having left the island, probably for a short visit, before the summer of 1804. "It is drawing to 60 years," wrote Nathaniel Barney in 1861, "since thou, Lucretia & I amused ourselves in playing upon a 'Traveling Map' at uncle Rotch's in Bedford." [22] Lucretia may have accompanied her father on a trip to Boston several years before the family left Nantucket, or Nathaniel Barney's memory may have been untrustworthy.

The departure for a new home did not, however, sever the ties that bound Lucretia Mott to her birthplace. In her maturity she was to cherish memories of "Nantucket ways." Sometimes these memories provoked thrusts of merriment from the wits in the family. After Nantucket was virtually destroyed by fire in 1846, one in-law even suggested that it might be possible to rebuild Nantucket from the funds derived from the sale of a book compiled of the sayings relating to the virtues of the island.[23] But Lucretia took her Nantucket in serious affection and continued to recall the days of the former prosperity of the island. Although she saw that the sterility of the soil, the migrations to California, the decline of whaling shattered all hopes of a return of the good old days of the past, each visit, indeed the mere mention of Nantucket, awakened in her a nostalgia of mingled emotions. The island remained a measuring stick: "What," she asked on learning that a friend had postponed starting out on a business trip until his wife was over her confinement, "would Nantucket say for husband not to sail when the ship was ready?" Again, sensitive doubtless to the sallies of wit leveled at the unbroken constancy of the wedded companionship of James and Lucretia Mott, she countered, "Natives would think it odd for husbands *not* to be as ready as wives to visit."

Again and again she was to bring her children to Nantucket that they too could be impressed with Nantucket hospitality and general good will, the solid comfort of the island life, the pervasive friendliness and informality, and with what she described as the "expanse of land & roads without fences or trees." She liked to go out to 'Sconset to visit relatives and friends; and time and again she loitered on the south shore to marvel at the "sublime surf & breakers." It was her belief that social relations and happy times were more enduring in Nantucket than elsewhere; and she enjoyed those homecomings as her spirit was kindled in the warm atmosphere of her birthplace.

Chapter Two

BOSTON INTERLUDE

Certain notices in the *Columbian Centinel* announced Thomas Coffin's trading as conducted by himself alone, "Thomas Coffin jun"; others, "Sumner and Coffin," indicated a partnership in the business. In Boston's "Taking Books," the musty volumes in the vaults of Boston City Hall, which preserve the census of the citizens residing in Boston during the nineteenth century by ward, name, occupation, and real and personal property holdings, the names of Jesse Sumner and Thomas Coffin appear with pertinent identifications. There seems to be in these books no additional information. Perhaps Thomas Coffin used Sumner as a silent partner because he himself had resided in the town for too short a period of time to secure under his own name a license for trading.

Sumner and Coffin carried a wide selection of stock, not only "in store" but at times "complete cargo" of specified schooners "on landing" or "afloat." A fairly comprehensive list of the merchandise included candles and oils, sugars, flour, wines and spirits, teas and coffee, cotton, linen, carpets and tiles, rosin, turpentine, and indigo. They also sold "boat passage" to Nantucket, and extended their activity to a mild sort of banking as the firm advertised for sale "Exchange on London at 30 days sight." [1] Accustomed to the limited lines of wares in Anna Coffin's converted shop, Lucretia must have been transfixed in wonderment if she ever saw her father's warehouse on the wharfs of Boston.

In his new home the talents of the erstwhile Nantucket whaler paid off so handsomely that within two years after his arrival, he owned real estate described as "5400." In this same year of 1806, according to the Suffolk Registry of Deeds, testimony is given that, "Thomas Coffin, Junior of said Boston, Merchant" purchased from "William Sutton Skinner of Boston" a new brick dwelling house on Round Lane, costing $5600, a considerable sum to be paid for a family house at the beginning of the nineteenth century. [2]

Nantucket has cherished the tradition that Thomas Coffin moved to Boston that his children, Sarah, Lucretia, Elizabeth, and Thomas Mayhew, might have opportunity for a better education than the island offered. On arriving in Boston, he placed the children in a private school only to send them to the public schools later. This change he made in his steadfast belief that private schools were undemocratic as they tended to foster feelings of pride and superiority in their students.[3]

In the early years of the nineteenth century the city of Boston provided public education for children from seven to fourteen years of age. This education comprised instruction in "reading schools" and in "writing schools," the divisions being shifted alternately into morning and afternoon sessions. Girls and boys were taught in separate groups. Here could be enrolled children who had already begun their educational pilgrimage under the guidance of "dames," the women who taught the rudiments of spelling and writing in their homes.

In the Free Schools of Boston the studies were not outlined by grades or by topics and much was left to "the discretion of the master." Yet, as textbooks were rigorously prescribed and instruction was presumed to be thorough, the town's provision for the education of its young citizens was no hit-or-miss affair. Enrolled in one of these schools, Lucretia could have read chosen excerpts from the prescribed anthologies, the *Beauties of the Bible,* the *Child's Companion,* the *Children's Friend,* selections savoring of ethics and piety. Provisions for instruction in arithmetic and English grammar were frankly pointed and thorough and uncompromising. The exercises in "parsing," spelling, word and sentence analysis, and "false syntex" stressed in Murray's *Grammar,* even in the *Abridgment* of the text, left no loophole for evasions or shallow teaching. "Equal equality," as the *Educational Reports of Boston* assured the citizens, was promised for all children; but boys had the opportunity of year-round instruction, while girls were allotted only a six-month's term, their session extending from April 20 to October 20.[4]

Inasmuch as, prior to 1817, records for the attendance of pupils in Boston's schools were not kept, an official account of Lucretia's attendance is not available. When the eleven-year-old Lucretia started to school in Boston, she was evidently far enough advanced to enter one of the Free Schools to receive instruction in reading, English grammar, geography, and arithmetic. For a time she was evidently sent to one of these schools. At the longest, however, her Boston training must have been limited to one year, for, when she was thirteen years old her parents decided that she deserved and should have further education.

The selection of a school involved weighty consideration. The school chosen must offer solid training, for Lucretia had shown unusual ability; its location must not be too far from Boston; expense was a problem; finally, it was not only desirable but indeed necessary to make sure that the atmosphere of the school was serious, with Quaker ideals.

An answer to their prayers seemed the Nine Partners Boarding School, a Friends' academy in southeastern New York.

Admission to Nine Partners having been obtained, Lucretia and her father made the momentous journey from Boston to New York. Although they may have traveled in a private conveyance, another way for reaching New York from Boston existed. This was the tri-weekly stage. If they went by stage, a new experience began for the young Lucretia, when with her meager wardrobe packed in the corded box, she boarded the cumbersome stage at "Daggett's Inn, Market Square," Boston, at four o'clock one morning. Traveling by easy stages the passengers on the "New York Mail Stage" skirted Sudbury, Shrewsbury, Worcester, and Brookfield before stopping at Wilbraham for change of horses. Reinforced, the stage passed through Springfield and then on to Suffield, "to distribute the mails." Touching Hartford and New Haven the stage moved onward to New York. This thirty-hour ride was advertised in 1806 as "the fast route" between Boston and New York.[5]

Chapter Three

NINE PARTNERS BOARDING SCHOOL

The name "Nine Partners" derives from the compact made by nine men who, as partners mutually bound "in equal ownership and responsibility," settled on a tract of land in southeastern New York near present-day Poughkeepsie.[1] In the late eighteenth century many Quakers lived in this settlement. Desiring a "guarded education" for their children, these settlers appealed to their supervisory body, the New York Yearly Meeting for permission to establish in the vicinity a boarding school. Authority obtained for the Institution, a committee was immediately appointed to make plans for carrying out the idea. On this committee was Elias Hicks, the noted Quaker, who was later regarded as the inspiration of the so-called Hicksites; another member was James Mott,[2] the grandfather of Lucretia's future husband.

In inviting James Mott to be a member of the advisory committee for the proposed school and in appointing him later as the superintendent, the New York Yearly Meeting paid due regard to a direct relationship between the educational tone of a school and its administrative officers. Mott, who maintained his connection with the school from its earliest days, was esteemed for his lofty principles and solid understanding. He was a born preacher, a writer of several treatises on educational theory and practice, and an inspired educator. In the advice he gave to the New York Yearly Meeting for the establishment of the proposed academy and later in his position as superintendent of the established institution, he set and helped to mold sound fundamental principles for the young school. Emphasizing the advantages of appealing to the reason of children, of teaching by example, of adjuring threats, scoldings, arbitrary punishment, and undue severity, he held views that were advanced for the time; but it was found that he could and did carry out his theories of education in a practical way. "The right education of children," he was said to believe, "was the most certain means, under the Divine blessing, of promoting the reformation of the world." [3]

Following the recommendation made by the committee, the affiliated Quakers drew up plans for the establishment of an academy in Dutchess County, New York. The site chosen was located in the settlement known as "Nine Partners." Legal papers were signed, and then plans to carry out the project moved so rapidly that in 1796 the doors of Nine Partners Boarding School were opened. The new institution was housed in a large building located "on the main road, half way between the Hudson River and New England" and about three miles from the city of Poughkeepsie. Among the substantial homes of the well-to-do, influential Friends in the vicinity, this structure was considered "the noblest building of all." Large and square, it provided comfortable if austere living quarters for the boys and for the girls. And although the school was coeducational in principle, the sexes were kept separate in all classes of instruction.[4]

As revealed in the yellowed records of Nine Partners School, the chief aim was to provide "a thorough academic course." Beginning studies were outlined as "Reading, Writing & Accounts together with English Grammar," "Branches of the Mathematics," and "Business & Domestic Employment." Emphasis was placed on the fact that the program was to be planned under the direction of the Committee with "the ability of the child and the principles of Quakerism in mind." Thus an efficient plan was outlined for providing a religious education gauged to the talents of the child and the career he might follow. Extra charges were made for instruction in subjects described as "the more advanced branches of Literature."

The outlines of studies were supplemented by formal regulations as to the clothing or dress permitted in the school. Some of the items listed as advisable for the girls were "1 or 2 plain bonnets, 1 cloak (not silk) . . . 2 stuff or gingham gowns suitable for the season made plain . . . 2 or 3 night caps . . . 3 or 4 long check aprons . . . 1 pr of scissors & a paper of pins." Then a rule, unequivocal as to purpose, provided that "Each child should also bring . . . a piece of cloth, thread & yarn for mending." Moreover, parents received this final warning: "If the clothing sent be not plain or require much washing it is to be returned or colored, or altered at the parents' expense. All the clothing sent to be strong and substantial." [5]

Reading was taught through Priscilla Wakefield's *Mental Improvement or The Beauties and Wonders of Instructive Conversations*.[6] This reader was such a popular medium of instruction that, after its first printing in London in 1795, edition after edition was in demand for more than a generation. In this textbook Lucretia and the other children were introduced by the "Series of Instructive Conversations" to a "Mr. and Mrs. Harcourt" and their children. This family group was presented through "Dialogues" which combined discussions of the natural resources, the economic order, and the social life of the entire globe. No region was omitted; nor was any opportunity lost for instilling principles of ethics and enforcing concrete examples of conduct. Models of behavior were these Harcourt children, as they were instructed by their parents to "read, draw, walk and accustom" themselves to observe everything minutely. The dangers of life, especially the hazards encountered by less fortunate people living in rigorous climates were kept constantly before the children, who were thus taught to regard highly the comforts of life provided by their parents and the civilization of their country. At the same time they were led to be humble, compassionate, and self-controlled.

These dialogues and other readings at Nine Partners Lucretia Mott never forgot. Years later on an occasion when she was endeavoring to convince the Pennsylvania Anti-Slavery Association that a boycott of the products of slave labor was the most effective weapon to use against slavery, the conversations of the Harcourt family were recalled:

I knew that in the boarding school where I had received such education as was then customary, we had the middle passage, the slave ship presented to us, and the appeals from Clarkson's works for the abolition of the slave trade, which were presented to all the children of the school.[7]

But Nine Partners offered other reading matter than that of Priscilla Wakefield's "Conversations." From the beginning "instruction in the more advanced branches of literature," had been specifically provided.[8] Whether the poetry read was solely didactic or not, the lines that Lucretia cherished in memory were chosen not from Shakespeare and Spenser and Milton nor from the newer poets Burns and Blake, Coleridge and the young Wordsworth, but came almost exclusively from the moralizing poets, the "graveyard school" of the eighteenth century. Despite the fact that Lucretia could barely carry a tune, she had an unfailing sense of rhythm and an acute musical ear. The imagery and melody of pure lyrics left her unmoved, but she treasured lines of didactic poetry from the transitional poets of the eighteenth century whose humanitarian moods struck a responsive note in her soul.

Lucretia's reading preferences for didactic poetry, philosophy, and economics, for social theory, history, and religion, may or may not have stemmed from directive forces or "courses" in her formal education. It is true that Nine Partners Boarding School did indeed offer its students a sound academic course. It is equally clear that in its administrators and teachers the standards of the school were high, comparing favorably with other early nineteenth-century academies. That the curriculum was seemingly meager, innocent of much of the richness in the way of elective courses and the activities of a later day does not necessarily bespeak inadequacy or shallowness. Rather the reverse. Emphasis being upon fundamentals, drills in essentials seemed to develop in the students breadth of intelligence and power of judgment. On the other hand, the readings that Lucretia eventually liked could easily have been her own selection, chosen independently without any guidance from the classroom.

At the end of two years in Nine Partners, Lucretia was regarded as the best student among the advanced girls in the academy, and no record indicates that she was outdistanced by any of the boys. As a reward for excellence in studies and character, "Thomas Coffin's daughter," as the school's records designate her,[9] was made an "assistant teacher," to help Deborah Rogers, who taught "Reading, Grammar and Arithmetick," and was offered a permanent position on the staff. The promotion brought Lucretia no financial compensation, the Report of the Committee held at Nine Partners on August 8, 1808, specifically stating that Thomas Coffin's daughter had been designated as an "assistant to Deborah without salary." At this time the "average number of Scholars" in the school was "about 58," with the principal or "Superintendent" receiving £150 per year, the assistant principal, one "James Mott Jun" receiving £100; but the woman assistant Deborah Rogers was given the yearly bounty of £20.

Lucretia's promotion was a recognition of her ability and a tribute to the preparatory education she had received, particularly in Nantucket, for she had studied one year only in Boston. Yet, while grateful for the recognition of her talents, the young girl must have resented the fact that the compensation paid the women teachers at the school was less than that paid the men. Years later she spoke of the [10] Nantucket women as being able to "mingle with men," women who were no "triflers," who had "intelligent subjects of conversation," but who had to receive less compensation than men for equal labor. Her sense of fairness would allow her to accept the fact that as an apprentice teacher she was employed without salary. She may not have resented the customary differences between the compensation given to men and to women for work equal in every way; but in her maturity, she referred again and again to discriminations against women as she had noted them in her youth. In Nine Partners School the double standard of remuneration was observed in a classic illustration. James Mott, Jr., a mere youth comparatively, commanded by reason of his sex a higher salary than Deborah Rogers, a seasoned female teacher and officer of the administration, could obtain.

But in Lucretia's own case there were compensations. By a special arrangement, she was permitted to join several teachers in a class for private instruction in French, a subject to be introduced in the years ahead in the girls' school conducted in Philadelphia by Lucretia's cousin, Rebecca Bunker, with Lucretia's assistance. A member of the privileged group at Nine Partners, Lucretia found herself not only beginning to study a foreign language and enjoying full faculty status but thrown into a more liberal social circle than the "guarded education" allowed generally.

As the informal meetings of the French class led to closer personal associations and new friendships, Thomas Coffin's daughter became acquainted with James Mott, Jr., an instructor at Nine Partners.[11]

A tall, blond young man, James Mott, Jr. was the son of Adam and Anne Mott, and the grandson of the James Mott to whom the New York Yearly Meeting had turned for guidance in the establishment of Nine Partners Boarding School. He was a descendant of two branches of a family of Friends, living in eastern New York, principally on Long Island, and among his ancestors were ministers and other notable Quakers. Sent to Nine Partners School when he was nine years old, he had been from the first a thoughtful student. As he grew older he made such progress in his studies and developed such dignity and responsibility that by the time Lucretia Coffin entered the academy he, at seventeen, had become one of the teachers. In fact, he was the ranking teacher of the school, second only to the superintendent. The gravity, reserve, and dignity of James Mott, Jr. recalled, it was said, traits of his noble grandfather, the elder James Mott.

Perhaps it was this serious strain in the character of the younger man, the contrast of his reserve to the vivacity of Lucretia Coffin, that drew the two young people together. Attraction almost immediately became complete understanding; and, during Lucretia's last years at Nine Partners, a strong tie of affection and mutual trust developed between her and the young James Mott.

When Lucretia Coffin was seventeen years old, her formal schooling was considered "finished," and her days at the academy came to a close. This education was comparable, as she herself described it, to what was "customary for the times." "For the times" she had been prepared for what the future might require of her; and in her life in that future lay, in part, the answer as to what the value of this education was. At the moment, though, the vista, if not prophetic, must have been rosy. Was she not really "grown up"? Was there not magic in the prospect of leaving the confined borders of school to live in new, entirely unfamiliar surroundings? Was there not another little sister to meet? [12] And was she not beloved by young James Mott, who had won her heart?

But the influence of the years in Nantucket, Boston, and Dutchess County never disappeared. On Nantucket she had observed men and women of different religious and social groups living in peace and harmony in a working democracy which recognized the rights of all. Through the stringent economy of the island, she had learned to exercise and respect labor and thrift. From a prudent mother she had acquired habits of industry and thrift and a sense of responsibility. Life on Nantucket had also imposed respect for the rights of others.

From her earliest years she had observed women active in the wear and tear of life: shouldering the burdens of housework, bearing and rearing children, mastering the details of business, teaching school. She had noticed that women had met these onerous tasks in a competent way. But in Boston, where girls had to be satisfied with a shorter school term than that provided for boys, she had come to grips with discrimination on account of sex. She may not have noted the injustice of this custom. At Nine Partners School she was a witness of discrimination in remuneration for employment. In these early years her sympathies had been awakened for the victims of any imposed injustice, particularly for the human beings held in the bondage of American slavery. Above all she had accepted literally and without question the obligations of the members of her faith to live in simplicity and integrity.

She may have taken herself rather seriously, but an innate sense of humor and a consistent humility of spirit protected her from becoming self-righteous or irritatingly superior. When she left Nine Partners she was a petite, brown-haired girl whose gentle mouth and merry dark eyes almost obscured the firm lines of her countenance. Up to this time, the experiences of her life had combined to make her a versatile, observant, sympathetic, and just person. One may readily believe that she had adopted lofty principles, but there seems to be little to justify the conclusion that at this time Lucretia Mott envisioned the role of leadership which lay ahead of her.

Chapter Four

WIDENING PATHS

Thomas Coffin had provided a comfortable home for his family in Boston; moreover his success was so assured that he had been able to send two of his daughters to a good boarding school. Yet, in spite of this prosperity, life in Boston could not have been completely satisfying, for after a few years he was seized with a desire to move again. It has been said that he was urged to enter the "cut nail business" with a relative who had prospered in this line of industry at French Creek near Philadelphia. On the other hand, it is entirely possible that the smooth tenor of inland life began to pall on the man who had spent so many years at sea. Perhaps the family had been made unhappy in Boston's chilly attitude toward Quakers. At all events, in 1809 Thomas Coffin weighed anchor again, and moved to Pennsylvania where Quakers lived in a congenial atmosphere.

Settling in Philadelphia was mainly a process of moving from one section of the city to another. These changes of residence by the Coffins are evidenced in the records of the different groups of Philadelphia Quakers classified as "Monthly Meetings" and organized on the principle of residential boundaries.

That the family, including Lucretia, had reached Philadelphia early in 1809 is evidenced by the minutes of a "Monthly Meeting of Women Friends of Phila. held the 23rd of the 2nd mo. 1809." The relevant entry reads, "The following certificates were read and accepted . . . one from Salem mo. Meeting held at Lynn the 9th of 2nd Month for Thomas Coffin, Anne his wife, and their Children Sarah, Lucretia, Elizabeth, Mary, Thomas Mayhew and Martha." [1] At first the family united with the Southern District Monthly Meeting, as the home, in one of the red brick houses on South Second Street, near Walnut Street, was within the boundaries set up for the Southern Meeting. Later their religious membership was transferred to the Western Meeting, then to the Philadelphia or Central Meeting, then back to the Southern Meeting. [2]

For the Coffins, the important fact was that, after the separations of boarding-school days, all its members were reunited. Lucretia particularly had the added joy of beginning to know her youngest sister, little Martha, born while Lucretia was away at

Nine Partners School. At this time neither she nor Martha probably realized that the tie between them was to develop into one of
the most important experiences of their lives.

A few years passed, and the separations began anew as Martha
was sent away to boarding school at Kimberton, the family boarding school kept by the daughters of Emmor Kimber, a well-known
Quaker schoolmaster.[3] In their rambling home in Chester County,
Abby Kimber and her sisters emphasized in their school the mildness and gentleness which their father substituted for conventional
severity and strictness in education. Martha Coffin's mentality
could have developed in any school; but to the wholesome influence of Kimberton may be partially traced her breadth of outlook,
her sanity, and her sense of humor. From Martha's presence at this
school Lucretia may have been given the opportunity to meet the
Kimbers' cousin, Sarah Pugh, as well as the daughters of Emmor
Kimber. A talented young woman was Sarah Pugh to whom Lucretia Mott would have been drawn inevitably. Like the Kimbers
and Lucretia, she was a Quaker schoolteacher, but instead of being
associated with others she maintained her own school. Eventually
a triumvirate of close friendship was developed among Lucretia
Mott, Sarah Pugh, and Abby Kimber. Beginning with mutual attraction and shared experiences, this friendship was cemented by
affection and trust, respect and understanding.

With the exception of the year in Boston, Lucretia Coffin had
lived up to this time far from the busy walks of man. Now in
1809 she came to America's largest city — a city limited in breadth,
it is true, as its east and west boundaries were fixed by two rivers,
but measureless apparently in its extent from north to south. The
new home teemed with the bustle of business. Wherever one
turned there were rows and rows of red brick, white shuttered
homes all built on straight streets set up one foot above the pas-
sageway for the carriages and carts and drays. After the tortuous
windings of the lanes of Boston, after the wide stretches of countryside near Nine Partners School, Lucretia must have been
amazed at Philadelphia's narrow straight streets that crossed other
narrow straight streets in a regularity that inspired Emerson's calling the city "the fair geometrical town." [4]

New also to this young girl from New England were the sights
and sounds of the city: the cook shop where turtle soup was made
in full view of the passers-by, the stacks of South Jersey vegetables
and fruits that almost crowded out her father's business quarters
on Dock Street, the musical cries of the street venders: "Pepper-

pot, smoking hot." At the market she must have met adventure, edging her way among stalls piled high with poultry, cheese, butter, and eggs from the farms of neighboring Chester, Lancaster, and Bucks counties. On her route home she could but marvel that the rush of business along the Delaware River and through High Street had suddenly and surprisingly given way to groups of serene family homes. From the first, born housekeeper that she was, Lucretia felt drawn to housewives apparently obligated to renew daily with brush and soap and water the immaculate whiteness of marble steps and house facings spattered by mud from the "canals" of the busy highways.[5]

In due time Lucretia accepted Philadelphia as the abode of restrained, dignified, conservative people; a day came when she declared that she not only ate scrapple — that Pennsylvania concoction of corn meal and pork drippings — but that she liked it "rich"; [6] as she learned to understand Philadelphia with its crosscurrents of social, religious, and business interests, she held in affection the city where she was to live for over fifty years among her family and friends.

Shortly after Lucretia reached her new home, James Mott gave up his teaching career at Nine Partners School and left New York for Philadelphia. In the quiet youth, Thomas and Anna Coffin recognized stable qualities that made it no problem for them to approve the affection between him and their second daughter. Needing assistance in his rapidly growing business, Thomas Coffin found it agreeable to offer Lucretia's suitor a position in the Philadelphia establishment advertized as "Coffin, Thos. commission merchant, 42 Dock." [7]

As the spring of 1811 approached, while the Coffins were living on South Second Street, Lucretia Coffin and James Mott received parental consent to their engagement. The steps for marriages between Friends were then taken. At first the couple made applications to their Meetings; examination according to Quaker Discipline followed; then permission to proceed with the marriage was given.[8] After these steps, "James Mott and Lucretia Coffin appeared in a public meeting of the said people, held in their meeting house on Pine Street in Philadelphia aforesaid," joined hands and repeated the vows of the marriage ceremony of Friends. The marriage certificate was then signed by the couple, by the members of the two families who were present — a numerous gathering of Motts, Coffins, Folgers, and Macys — and by a large number of friends. Among the 175 signers of the Wedding Certificate were the well-known Quakers Nicholas Waln and John Cox.[9]

At the beginning of their married life James and Lucretia Mott set up housekeeping in the home of Lucretia's parents on South Second Street. Here they remained a few months before settling in modest quarters of their own, first on Union Street, and, later on South Fourth Street.[10] During this period James Mott continued as a merchant of the firm, now registered as "Coffin and Mott, Merchants," and still located on Dock Street.[11]

As few men engaged in business during the second decade of the nineteenth century escaped the effect of the economic depression following the War of 1812, the Coffins and the Motts lived in a state of financial instability for several years.[12] Hoping to better their condition Thomas Coffin and his wife tried their fortunes in Ohio, only to return to Philadelphia when the Ohio experiment proved an illusion. James attempted to make a living by working in the cotton mill of his uncle Richard Mott at Mamaroneck, New York. It was there that Lucretia found time to bind with her neat stitches the "peace almanacs," issued by her uncle. In the years to come she frequently referred to her uncle's endeavor to spread the doctrine of world peace through the publication of calendars, embellished with maxims that preached love and harmony.[13] Finding the Mamaroneck venture unprofitable, James Mott went to New York City where he worked as a bank clerk. But, learning finally that the problem of making money was as acute in other areas as it was in Philadelphia, he decided to return, and it was this city that gave him the opportunity to build up an independent business in foreign and domestic staples.

While James Mott was endeavoring to provide for his family, Lucretia decided to put her shoulder to the wheel; and, although in a short time she became the mother of two small children, Anna and Thomas, she began to look around for an opening in teaching. Good fortune answered her needs as the Women Friends of Philadelphia for the Southern District had just decided that "the Select School for girls" under their sponsorship needed more than one teacher. "In pursuance of their views in this respect they engaged two well-qualified Friends under whose superintendence the various branches of useful learning were taught." [14] The minutes of this Monthly Meeting record that Rebecca Bunker, Lucretia's cousin, was the teacher in charge of the school; and there is evidence that Lucretia was the other instructor.

Writing to his parents, on April 1, 1817, James Mott notes that "Lucretia and Rebecca Bunker commenced their school two weeks since," [15] but a more intimate picture of this teaching venture is drawn by Lucretia herself in a postscript to her husband's letter. The school, she wrote, was located so far from her home that a long walk was imposed twice a day. The inconvenience, however, of eating a cold dinner in the brief recess between the morning and afternoon sessions was not regarded by the two young teachers as a hardship; buoyed up by the indications of an increased enrollment, they remained in sanguine mood. And they had the satisfaction of recording in a very short time an enrollment of forty children. Moreover, each child was paying the seemingly adequate compensation of seven dollars a quarter for tuition. Best of all, the school was being regarded as one of the better institutions of its type in Philadelphia, offering French to a select few of its students. But soon Lucretia's teaching experience was brought to a close in 1818 by the birth of her third child.

Lucretia Mott was now an extremely busy wife and mother. Between the rounds of sweeping and dusting, making beds and cooking, washing and drying dishes, she found herself answering the call of many other duties. In cutting and making garments, in mending, patching and making-over, she was confronted with a never-to-be-finished occupation; while as a frugal housewife she was constantly besieged with the endless duty of darning. Some time was given to knitting, a pleasanter occupation, for while knitting one could read and think about her reading, a pleasure that sewing usually forbade. While knitting, she taught her children "their letters" and simple sums. But she was never too occupied to forego almost daily association with her parents and her sisters and brother; thus the ties of the Coffin family remained unweakened by the separations and establishment of new homes in the wake of marriages.

Sorrow scarred these early days in Philadelphia. In 1815 Lucretia lost her father and in 1817 her son Thomas. In 1824 two sisters, Sarah Coffin and Mary Coffin Temple, died. This double blow was followed by the separation caused when Lucretia's youngest sister, Martha Coffin, married Peter Pelham and departed for a home in the South. After a brief married life, Martha became a widow and returned to Philadelphia; but in 1829 she married David Wright, a rising young lawyer practicing in western New York.[16] At this time Anna Coffin began the practice of having the family write letters which soon became an institution to be en-

joyed through the years. These unique "family sheets" comprise
hundreds of delightful "round robins," that, starting in Philadelphia or Auburn or Nantucket or London or some other place
of permanent or transitory residence for a member of the family,
inevitably reached each and all, and thus kept the hearthstone
intact.

In the spring of 1826, Lucretia "prepared" her daughter Anna
to enter Westtown boarding school, "the excellent Friends Academy," established in Westtown, Pennsylvania, in 1799. At the same
time Maria, the second daughter, learned "to write and cipher at
cousin Rebecca's School," this Select School for Girls having continued to win the approval of the Women Friends for the Southern District. After a few weeks Maria was reported by Lucretia as
enjoying her lessons at "Cousin Rebecca's," and Anna from various accounts was giving marked evidence of her ability and progress at Westtown.

Despite the exacting cares of her own household, relieved only
occasionally by the treasured moments for reading and meditation,
Lucretia began to realize that her family responsibilities were
gradually lessening, that she had more free time. Then it was that
she began to broaden the scope of her vision, to extend her interests beyond her home, to make practical application of her accepted principles of human love. At first, she was challenged by
the idea of starting a so-called "Fragment Society," one of the
groups designed to relieve the poor by providing an income for
indigent women through handwork performed in a comfortable
environment. Such an organization (the Female Society for the
Relief and Employment of the Poor) had been established in
Philadelphia in 1795 through the efforts of Anne Parrish. The
minutes of this Society do not list the name of Lucretia Mott
among its members, although an active worker, recorded as "Eliza
Coffin," was probably Lucretia's sister.[17]

The Female Society's program of assistance to "suffering Fellow Creatures . . . without distinction of Nation or Colour,"
however, seems to accord with what Lucretia had in mind when,
desiring to be guided by the experience of others, she brought up
to her mother-in-law the subject of forming "a fragment society."
Evidently this desire came to naught, for a week or two after Lucretia had appealed to Anne Mott for guidance on the subject of
"fragment societies," James Mott informed his parents that his
wife felt that she could relieve distress as easily by her own un-

aided efforts as by associating with others, especially with those given too much to what he designated as "gossip."

Between household chores, Lucretia had begun her lifelong habit of intensive reading, supplementing the very serious reading of her school days with a systematic study of the Bible. As Martha put it, "Sister L. became addicted to keeping the Testament in the foot of the cradle to read every odd minute." [18]

This thoughtful reading of the Old Testament and the New Testament led to meditation, then to studied reflection upon the incidents and ideas, the dignity and beauty of the Scriptures. Although her faith in the principles of Christianity remained unshaken, reflection upon the Scriptures led her to the study of Quaker thought and practice as found in the *Journal of George Fox,* in Robert Barclay's *Apology* and in William Penn's *No Cross No Crown.* At this time she added John Woolman's *Journal* and Robert Southey's *Life of Wesley* as well as readings in political economy, history, and philosophy. The *Life of Wesley* as she wrote her grandfather, was to her "An interesting work, though some parts we thought might have been omitted, such as the supernatural appearances. The author appears as much attached to the doctrines of the Episcopal Church, as some of us Quakers are to ours." [19] These serious works Lucretia Mott found stimulating, even though her sister decried Lucretia's choice of authors and subjects. But while Martha reveled in the novels of Scott and Dickens and in the poetry of Byron, she conceded: "My sister's intellect being of so much higher order she could take to profound literature 'as a cat laps milk' and she falls into the very common error of judging other people's minds by her own." [20]

In the hope, evidently, of deriving help on the bringing up of her own family, she read and reread the grandfather's treatise *"On the Education of Children";* even if she had already accepted sane theories on the training of children, she found much benefit in James Mott's advocacy of rational guidance as sound pedagogical policy.

To these writings may be added the *Vindication of the Rights of Women* by Mary Wollstonecraft that had appeared in 1792, barely a year before the birth of Lucretia Coffin. The *Vindication* argued the case for an enlarged education for women, an education that would enable women to weigh essential values and to focus the understanding upon issues of right and wrong. When Lucretia Mott was middle-aged, she assured one of the leaders in the struggle for Woman's Rights, that she had kept Mary Wollstonecraft's *Vindication* "on the center table" in her home for forty years, only lending the book from time to time to her friends when she "could find readers." [21]

By virtue of Lucretia's faithful memory, she retained not merely the ideas, but the exact words of chosen passages — book, chapter, and verse. After the reading was put aside she was in no danger of forgetting or misinterpreting a thought, for she could recall the precise language of the writer. This gift accounted for her storehouse of apt quotations from the English Bible, from Fox and Penn and Barclay. And because her memory never betrayed her she was able to silence opponents relying, perhaps innocently, on inaccurate references.

In the letter of the law alone she was wont to take no refuge. The Report of one meeting of the Woman's Rights Movement notes that a gentleman in the audience "sought to embarrass Lucretia Mott by injecting Scriptural quotations into the discussion." "All scripture is given by inspiration of God," he said, "and is profitable . . ." To this seemingly redoubtable argument, Lucretia replied, "If thou will look at that passage thou will see that the 'is' is italicised, which signified that it is put in by the translators. The passage should read 'All scripture, given by inspiration of God is profitable,' etc. At a proper time I would like to discuss the subject with thee." Needless to say, her critic was silenced.[22]

Her familiarity with the Bible, with the thought of theologians and philosophers was sound preparation for a life as preacher and advocate of the rights of man. Perhaps it was at this period of her life that she began her habit of taking notes on her reading. This habit she referred to in a letter written on April 26, 1847, to Richard and Hannah Webb, her friends in Dublin: "I wish I could show you my notes, they form 3 little volumes, S. Pugh has hers also & we are going to compare them some day, when Abby has gone & we haven't your letters to read, nor ours to write." [23] (One would give much to see these "3 little volumes.")

In the early 1820's, as the business of Lucretia Mott's husband became more prosperous, she was able to lighten her household duties. The children required less care, and it became relatively easy for her to be away from home, even for long periods of time. Soon her voice was heard more frequently in public assemblies.

Chapter Five

REVOLT AND FAITH

Shortly before her death, Lucretia Mott made an explicit statement as to the time of her first public speech. These were her words:

A prayer offered in 12th st. Mg. in 1818 — As all our efforts to resist temptation, and overcome the world prove fruitless, unless aided by the Holy Spirit, enable us to approach preservation from all evil, that we may be wholly devoted to thee and Thy glorious cause.[1]

This "prayer" seems to be the only record of Lucretia Mott's early public utterances. But her memory of the time may be considered trustworthy, for it was in 1818 that the elder James Mott, writing to his son Adam, referred to Lucretia's having entered "the preaching line." [2] Of great significance is the theme of the invocation, which — while a confession of man's helplessness in his own powers and a solemn entreaty for God's protective support in the complexities of life — indicates a complete and unquestioning faith in God's omnipotence.

In this same year a tribute to Lucretia's religious standing was made by Sarah Zane, a well-known Philadelphia Quaker. Sarah Zane was accustomed to travel widely on religious visits not only in Pennsylvania but far and near in Maryland, Virginia, and eastern Ohio. On several occasions she went to Winchester, Virginia. A woman of wealth, she presented land in Winchester to the "Friends of Center" for a Meeting house, gave "to the citizens of Winchester" money for a "volunteer fire company," and became the donor of such extensive and generous private benefactions that the arrival of her coach in Winchester always caused much rejoicing among the poor and afflicted.[3]

Under the guidance then of this notable woman, Lucretia Mott is said to have made what was possibly her first religious journey, the precursor of many travels she was to take during the coming years, usually in the company of her husband. Writing home, she described the scenery in the neighborhood of Harpers Ferry as "romantic," and the condition of the slaves she saw working on the Virginia farms she called "affecting." She was told, she wrote, that the tolerance of the Virginia slaveholders was the cause of the apparent contentment of the slaves. This letter also included the names of the places Lucretia visited and a reference to the length of time she was away from home.[4]

A few years after her return from Virginia, the Monthly Meeting of Women Friends for the Western District of Philadelphia took a step that indicated beyond a doubt that Lucretia Mott had not only done much public speaking, but that she was highly regarded by Quakers. This action of the Meeting was a statement of belief in the essential integrity of Lucretia Mott's living as well as a testimony to the more specific attribute, "a gift in the ministry committed to her." Through this gift, as the minutes read, Lucretia Mott had shown "in her public appearances" qualities that proved that she was worthy to be a Minister in the Society of Friends. Beyond a doubt the action expressed an abounding faith in the soundness of Lucretia's Quakerism, a staunch belief that she would live up to the regulations of the Discipline. Following customary procedure, the Women Friends "prepared a Minuit expressive thereof," which, having been signed by the clerk of the Meeting, was sent for approval to the Quarterly Meeting of Ministers and Elders, the body having the final decision on the designation. The concordance of the Quarterly Meeting followed.[5]

Although it is quite likely that Lucretia followed up the prayer uttered in the Twelfth Street Meeting House with much more public speaking, the date 1821 marks the factual inauguration of her ministry in the Society of Friends.

Friends are not inducted into the ministry of the Society by a ceremony of ordination following specific training, but the ministers have a respected status comparable to that conferred on ministers in other denominations, except that these leaders of the Society receive no salary. With the elders — who do not preach — the ministers are responsible for the spiritual welfare of the Meeting; in their living they must be examples of integrity; they may advise and even reform according to the rules of the Book of Discipline, the compilation of "Friends' principles of belief and practice"; but they are explicitly warned not to be guilty of faulty inferences in the interpretation of the Scriptures. Restrained by the letter of the Discipline only, the ministers are virtually independent; but should controversial issues growing out of the doctrines of Friends arise, they are apt to become involved.

When Lucretia Mott was thus officially recognized by the Society of Friends as having "a gift in the ministry," she became clothed with the dignity and responsibilities of a Quaker minister.

Barely twenty-eight years old, this young woman was elevated to a position of great responsibility, honor, and trust.

Among the regulations in the Discipline of the early nineteenth century, was a provision covering the marriages of Friends with persons not in membership with the Society, such marriages being designated as "outgoings" or "marrying out." The guilt of outgoing incurred disownment; and, more than this, Quaker parents condoning marriages of their children with non-Friends were adjudged guilty of the technical error of "conniving"; thus they were likewise subject to disownment.

Shortly after Lucretia Mott became a minister she discovered that her allegiance to the Discipline was sorely challenged by an action taken by the Philadelphia Monthly Meeting of Women Friends in a case growing out of an "outgoing in marriage." The specific dereliction involved the action of Rebecca Paul, a widow and a member in good standing in the Philadelphia Monthly Meeting of Women Friends. In June 1822, Rebecca Paul was brought before the Preparative Meeting for "conniving" at the marriage of a daughter with a non-Friend. Rebecca made no denial of her approval of the marriage, no widow being apt to frown on an exemplary young man who shows intention of marrying one of her daughters. But after the Women Friends had "several interviews" with Rebecca Paul (the consideration of the case extended from June 27, 1822, through January 30, 1823), the widow received little sympathy from the Meeting. Obeying literally the dictates of the Discipline, these judges "weightily considered the case of Rebecca Paul . . . [and] decided upon issuing a testimony of disownment." The petitioner, however, was informed that she had the "privilege of appeal." [6]

When Lucretia Mott learned that the Monthly Meeting had disowned Rebecca Paul, she became so perturbed over the case that she wrote a letter of protest to the elder James Mott, her husband's grandfather, pointing out particularly the fact that the son-in-law of Rebecca Paul had applied for membership in the Society of Friends only to have his application rejected. "Cannot you enlightened ones," she asked him, "set us a good example by making some improvement in the Discipline relative to outgoings in marriage. . . . What is to be done in such cases?" [7]

What indeed should be done? Lucretia was disturbed at what seemed to her a grave injustice, a condition leading to the unhappiness of several people. Beyond this, she thought that more than the well-being of the family of Rebecca Paul was at stake. She became concerned as to the principles involved in the authoritative force of the rules of the Discipline, rules too that were not always specific as to the nature of offenses under regulation.

In answer to her questions, the elder James Mott brought Lucretia small comfort for he confessed that he himself was "not enlightened enough" to arrive at a solution of the problem of "outgoings in marriage." He felt that the practice of Friends in regard to these "outgoings" called for newer directions than the stipulated regulations of the Discipline offered. Indeed the subject of "outgoings" seemed so weighty to James Mott that he concluded his answer to Lucretia's question in these words: "It is wrong now, but how to make it right, wiser heads than mine are required."

Thus in 1823, barely two years after Lucretia Mott's promotion to the Ministry, a symbol of the Society's faith in the utter soundness of her Quakerism, she indicated her disapproval of one tenet of the Discipline. Uncertainty remains as to whether she was at this time disturbed by other restrictions. The question also arises as to whether she voiced her inner disturbances beyond the confines of her family. Meanwhile she continued her preaching, emphasizing "practical Christianity."

During the 1820's Friends living in or near Philadelphia experienced the climax of an unrest which had been growing steadily for many years. Among the causes provoking the agitation were a decline in the spiritual faith, simplicity, and piety of the early Quakers, influences of the Evangelicism of the eighteenth century, aversion to the power residing in the authoritative body of the Society, and personal antagonisms. These were the remote causes of the rift; but in the final outcome the points at issue were summarized as the Divinity of Jesus, the Inspiration of the Scriptures, and the Atonement. At the Yearly Meeting of 1827, the opposing forces clashed into action, resulting in a division of the Society into two groups, the Orthodox and the Hicksites. Both groups called themselves Quakers. Although Elias Hicks was frequently in and out of Philadelphia in the 1820's, he himself assumed no leadership of the division of Quakers designated by his name.

Between 1823 and 1825, when the tension was growing increasingly bitter, a series of letters, signed respectively by "Paul" and "Amicus," had appeared in the *Berean,* a periodical published at Wilmington, Delaware. In these letters, the three points: the Divinity of Jesus, the Atonement, and the Inspiration of the Scriptures, were the issues of argument, showing that the Friends had become, as it were, "a house divided against itself." In 1842 writing to Richard Webb, whom she met in London, Lucretia said:

When you have read the controversy between Paul & Amicus, we should like to have your opinion of the work. It was first published in the "Berean," a periodical edited in Wilmington Del. by Dr. Gibbons, Benjm. Ferris & a number of (?) Friends of talents & worth as well as of liberal views. "Amicus" was Benjm. Ferris. He told us that every answer to "Paul" was written after his family had retired for the night — that frequently when he went to put his effusions into the Office, it was daylight. He never submitted one of them to the criticism of his friends & never had any objection made to them. After the controversy was ended, the "Mg. for Sufferings" issued a kind of disclaimer of it or protest against it — at the suggestion of Jonan. Evans — the Pope of that day, because it had not been submitted to their orthodox tribunal, previously to its publication according to the "good" order prescribed in the Discipline. This occurred about a year or two before the "Separation." In 1828 (?) or 9 (?) our friends did not relish a reproof from that quarter. All the Editors of that paper, were on *our* side when the division took place.[8]

Expressions on the disputed topics were voiced at meetings held in Philadelphia at Pine Street Meeting House, at Twelfth Street Meeting, at Cherry Street, at Key's Alley, Green Street, and Carpenters' Hall, not to mention assemblies in the adjacent counties. At these gatherings Elias Hicks was perhaps the most prominent speaker, but other Quakers have left records of their own thought and emotions on the controversy. In the contemporary accounts of the speeches made by these Friends there seem to be no words of Lucretia Mott, no records of Lucretia Mott's voice being raised in the controversy.[9]

This does not mean that she was silent. On one occasion when she was warned against criticizing the Monthly Meeting, she reminded her accusers that at the time of the Separation they were all outspoken in judgment against what she called "our Orthodox Hierarchy." On the other hand, in a letter written to the Philadelphian, A. S. Lippincott, in 1842, she emphasized her aversion to engaging in verbal controversy over the rift of 1839 which had caused a division in the antislavery ranks. This rift of 1839, she declared, was similar in its origin to the religious troubles that had divided the Quakers of an earlier decade into two bodies; in the religious controversy, as she assured Mr. Lippincott, "many had found it necessary to defend their simple faith by replies to Orthodox accusations," but she stated that she herself had "never felt much interest in those controversies." [10]

Prominent among the Quakers living in the Middle West were Joseph Dugdale of Green Plain, Ohio, his wife Ruth, and Sarah Dugdale, another member of the family. A year or two after writing to Lippincott, Lucretia shared her feeling on divisions in the Society of Friends with Sarah Dugdale,

I have not been able to see that another division & reorganization will afford more than a temporary remedy for the evils under which we are laboring. While our present Discipline remains as it is, giving power to a few over the ministry, we may expect such results to follow. A radical change is called for . . . What then is the right step to pursue? It may be well for Friends to confer together and report the results of such conferences.[11]

But with or without Lucretia Mott's expressed participation, the fires of dissension had been fanned and the rift resulted in many unhappy conditions. Families had become hopelessly divided, friendships strained or broken, personal animosities engendered, and even plans for the schooling of children had been altered. The effect on education touched the Motts, who in 1827 removed Anna, their fourteen-year-old daughter, from the Orthodox School at Westtown where she had been reported as doing "well in her studies." The most bitter experience of all to the peace-loving Quakers was a lawsuit, "Stacy Decow and Joseph Hendrickson vs. Thomas L. Shotwell," instituted over certain meeting houses used by the Society as a whole before the strife.[12] According to the deposition made by Joseph Hendrickson at the trial, the "Orthodox party" claimed to hold the "three prominent points of doctrine" of "the ancient Society of Friends." Forty years later, when disputes among some liberals gave rise to the Progressive Friends, Lucretia Mott wrote, "It is hard to have two such ordeals to pass through in one short generation." Although evidence seems to be lacking as to any specific or direct words she may have spoken as early as 1827 on the three disputed points, no doubt remains as to which side she took in the controversy. A mild and gentle person, she was, however, firm in her convictions and in her power to adhere to a decision involving action based on principle. In this religious controversy, she joined the Hicksite side and thus brought upon herself the stigma of unbelief in the "three doctrines of faith."

Many Friends choosing the Hicksite side of the controversy were disowned summarily by the Orthodox Friends, but action involving the separation of James and Lucretia Mott proceeded with no apparent haste. As one member of the Orthodox group was quoted as saying years afterward: "When this Separation took place, there were two persons they were sorely grieved to part with and Lucretia Mott was one of them." [13]

The Court Proceedings — "Decow and Hendrickson vs. Shotwell" — contain no reference to James Mott or to Lucretia, although many of their associates in Philadelphia Yearly Meeting were brought into the testimony.

After identifying themselves for a short while with Abington Meeting, a Meeting set up originally in 1683 and at the time of the Separation friendly to the Hicksite group, James and Lucretia Mott joined Cherry Street Meeting, a constituent member of Abington Meeting. Lucretia Mott's continued activity in the concerns of her Meetings is borne out by the Minutes of the Hicksite Philadelphia Yearly Meeting of Women Friends, which show that during the years 1827–1830 she was steadily a Representative from the Quarter of Abington to the Yearly Meeting and that she served on the committee to write the friendly letters of greetings sent by the Meeting to women Friends in New York, Baltimore and "other Yearly Meetings as best Wisdom may direct." [14]

Shortly after the Separation, the non-Orthodox group of Friends in Philadelphia felt the desire to apprise the London Yearly Meeting of the dissension, the significant correspondence being printed in the *Journal* of John Comly, one of the clerks of the Philadelphia Yearly Meeting of 1830. At one time during this exchange of letters Lucretia Mott was Clerk to the Women's Meeting.[15]

In these printed documents concerning the case, John Comly includes a letter signed by him and Lucretia Mott. This letter repudiated any guilt of heresy among the non-Orthodox Friends comprising this Philadelphia Yearly Meeting, or any dereliction "from the principles laid down by our blessed Lord." At the same time the claim was made that the Meeting had been condemned by the London Meeting on unproved charges of infidelity and deism. Fervent belief was expressed in the "history of the birth, life, acts, death, and resurrection of the holy Jesus as in the volumes of the book it is written of him," and the "divinity of the author of the gospel of Christ" was acknowledged. A goodly portion of the letter is an expression of loyalty on the part of this Philadelphia Yearly Meeting to the faith and principles of primitive Quakerism, in particular; and reference is made to the Separation as having been engendered not so much in "difference of opinion on doctrinal points as in a disposition apparent in some to exercise an oppressive authority in the church." No mention is made of a vicarious atonement.

The sentiments and tone of this letter created such an unfavorable reaction among English Friends that it is said that the letter was returned marked "mendacity" and a strong resentment was harbored against this Philadelphia Yearly Meeting and the Meeting's clerks, John Comly and Lucretia Mott. Indeed it was believed that the English Friends went so far as to place the major burden of the guilt upon the shoulders of Lucretia Mott.[16]

From the number and the significance of the offices held by Lucretia Mott in the Meetings one may see that her interests in the official affairs of her faith continued and that she was accorded no limited measure of responsibility and regard. Between 1830 and 1840 she was requisitioned constantly to assist in the conduct of the regular procedures of the Meetings: for five years she was Clerk to the Women's Yearly Meeting, for two years she was treasurer, she was almost regularly a representative to her Philadelphia Yearly Meeting from the Quarterly Meeting of Abington, and she continued to be placed on committees chosen to write messages of greetings to Women's Meetings in New York, Indiana, Ohio, and Baltimore.

In addition to her participation in these regularly recurring activities of the Society she was frequently designated to contribute her thought and imagination to other important matters. When in 1833 the Yearly Meeting of Women Friends, "in collaboration with Men Friends," sponsored an elaborate survey of the schools "under the care of the monthly and preparative Meetings" in the district of the Yearly Meeting, Lucretia Mott was called on to assist in the investigation. This committee went about its labors with such thoroughness that two years of unabated attention passed before the final report was completed. Significant among the topics stressed in the report were courses of instruction and the need of inducements to the training of teachers. Other items in this advanced study of education included buildings, textbooks, libraries, general ideals of education, and types of schools described as "manaul labor schools" and "family schools taught by females." The cooperation between teacher and parents was advocated and also the need of keeping "the Quarterlies, Monthlies and Preparatives" closely interested in "the guarded education of the youth." [17]

Among the constituent members of the Yearly Meeting were groups of Quakers from Chester and Lancaster counties organized as the Caln Quarter. In the opinion of this group Quaker religion could not and should not support a toleration of human slavery. Becoming disturbingly exercised over the question of American slavery, the Caln Quarter in 1836 brought to the Yearly Meeting the suggestion that an effort should be made to encourage Friends to abstain whenever possible from the produce of slave labor. As Clerk of the Meeting Lucretia Mott signed the endorsement of this proposition; and whatever her opinion was or was not as to the sentiments in the letter of 1830 to the London Friends, there is no doubt that she was in hearty accord with the proposal from Caln.

In the 1830's Lucretia Mott's independence of thought was becoming known beyond the circles of the Religious Society of Friends. To many, particularly young people, she was looked upon as a fount of wisdom and as a woman capable of giving guidance to those beset by religious problems. Among her young friends at the time was James Miller McKim of Carlisle, Pennsylvania. In his maturity McKim was one of the leading spirits of the antislavery crusade, not only in the Pennsylvania Branch of the Anti-Slavery Society, but in the national body as well. He was a thoughtful, fearless writer, and a spirited and convincing public speaker.

In 1833 Miller McKim was a young graduate of Dickinson College. Harassed at the moment by grave problems of dogma and religious doubt, he was in a state of extreme spiritual unrest which caused him to question the wisdom of the choice of his life's work — the Presbyterian ministry. Needing guidance, he sought out Lucretia Mott and almost immediately became an intimate member of the Mott family circle. Wise teacher that she was, Lucretia sought to divert the youth for a time from his religious dilemma by helping him to a way to practical righteousness. Consequently, he was soon taking part in the campaign against slavery as organized in Philadelphia and in other places in eastern Pennsylvania. Further guidance followed in enlightened responses to his questionings about his religious misgivings. The Bible, she advised him, should be read with an open mind in the search for the essential meanings and the general spirit of the Scriptures. "One should not become puzzled and perplexed," she declared, by isolated passages that "do violence to the noble gift of reason divinely bestowed upon us," but one should cherish his own ability to think for himself. This was the cardinal principle that she kept before Miller McKim at the beginning of their friendship.

In her own reading she had derived immeasurable satisfaction from Noah Worcester's *Causes and Evils of Contentions Unveiled in Letters to Christians,* a study of religion that presents as its main thesis the author's belief that the determining source of disunity among Christians, the cause of dissent, creeds, and sects, is the fact that authoritative dogma has developed from the interpretation of Scriptures as made by man. When Miller McKim therefore turned to her for guidance, she advised him to read "Causes and Contentions," as she usually designated the work. At the same time she cautioned him to hold steadfast to his convictions even though they might not be hers or Worcester's. But she was not evasive. On the subject of the inspiration of the Scriptures she maintained that although she had no desire to shake his faith in what he considered the "infallibly inspired doctrines," she could not understand why so much difference of opinion on an "infallible subject" continued to rear its head. And she told him that she believed that what she designated as "the uncertain ocean of natural religion" was as infallible as the truth of the Scriptures. After all, as she concluded this discussion, "the cardinal values were Righteousness, Goodness, and Truth." Then, too, she recommended to Miller McKim, but advisedly, the reading of John Woolman; for although she praised John Woolman's picture of the early Quakers, her vigorous rationalism protested what she termed "the visionary part" of Woolman's writings.

At this time she would not answer McKim's queries as to Unitarianism, but directed her questioner to seek advice from William Henry Furness, the Unitarian minister who was then making his home in Philadelphia. But a year or two later, when McKim again brought up the subject, she declared that Unitarianism seemed "to be almost without a system — having rejected those which they regarded unscriptural and 'destitute of the vitality of the religion of Christ & not in their stead substituting any creed or system." "If they are found fulfilling the law of practical righteousness" she continued, "I can recognize this as the 'Religion' of the New Testament. Whether this be the case I have not sufficient evidence in their fruits to enable me to judge." [18]

In 1838 John Greenleaf Whittier, who was in Philadelphia editing the *Pennsylvania Freeman,* was a frequent visitor in the Mott home. From him Lucretia attempted to secure light for McKim but met with little success. "I did not read thy remarks to him," she reported to McKim, "he is quite interesting in conversation if you will give him time to say all he has on his mind — you will observe how slow of speech he is, tho not of a stammering tongue. I should like for you to compare 'sentiments,' thou may find his views about square with thine of a 'liberal and rational orthodoxy.' I know not — having had little conversation with him on subjects of religion." [19]

To her, a consistent religion must find its basis in reason. But reason, followed logically to its first principles, led to unrestricted liberalism — to justice; and utter justice took one a step toward another grievance — the rights for women. After telling Miller McKim that a conference on the Indian question was to be held with the Secretary of War to which delegates from both branches of the Society were to be sent, she protested that no women were to be at the conference.

One of the earliest references to Lucretia Mott's speeches was made by the Orthodox Quaker Arnold Buffum, an importer and maker of hats, "satin Beavers on linen foundations" being his specialty. Living in Boston in 1832, Buffum had been chosen as the first president of the New England Anti-Slavery Society, but in 1836 he had moved his business to Philadelphia. From his new home he wrote to the *Liberator* on October 15, 1836, that he had heard an address to "colored citizens" delivered by Lucretia Mott in the Cherry Street Meeting House. "The meeting was opened," he wrote, "with a fervent address to the Throne of Grace after which Lucretia addressed the assembly for about an hour, in a strain of eloquence breathing an ardent solicitude for the temporal, moral, and spiritual improvement of that class of our citizens, for whom the meeting was appointed. . . . I said in my heart it is good for me to be here." But in his Orthodoxy, he added; "I do not attend that meeting, nor unite in sentiment on some doctrinal points with the speaker yet I do love that religion which like that of the good Samaritan manifests itself in doing good."

Another picture of Lucretia Mott in the 1830's may be traced to Harriet Martineau, the gifted English writer, who, visiting America in 1836, recorded her impressions of the country in a delightful travelogue, *Retrospect of Western Travel*. When Miss Martineau reached Philadelphia, she attended a Quaker marriage "at the Cherry Street Church belonging to the Hicksites." She observed,

A Quaker friend of mine, a frequent preacher suggested a few days previously that a seat had better be reserved for me near the speakers that I might have a chance of hearing "in case there should be communications."

Communications, indeed, became a part of the ceremony, discourses which evidently bored the English guest. But Harriet Martineau continued,

What a contrast was the brief discourse of my Quaker friend which
followed: Her noble countenance was radiant as the morning; her soft
voice though low, was so firm that she was heard to the farthest corner,
and her little sermon as philosophical as it was devout; Send forth thy
light and thy truth was her text. She spoke gratefully of intellectual
light as a guide to the spiritual truth, and anticipated and prayed for
an ultimate universal diffusing of both.[20]

Although the "Quaker friend" was not named, the allusion seems
to point to Lucretia Mott.

William Lloyd Garrison described a sermon preached by Lucretia Mott in the 1830's:

She dwelt with emphasis and power upon the wide difference which
exists between a ceremonial religion and practical godliness . . . She
urged upon all the duty of actively laboring in the reforms of the age,
especially that of anti-slavery — no matter what it might cost, no matter
from what quarter it might be condemned, whether from the high seats
of any ecclesiastical conclave. Her position on that occasion was one of
great moral sublimity, showing that she was wholly dead to that fear
of men which bringeth a snare.[21]

As a rule she maintained a benign attitude toward those who
disagreed with her; she could and did listen to her opponents with
unruffled mien while she defended her views with strength as well
as patience. But her gentleness involved no turning of the other
cheek. As one wit of the time portrayed her:

> Lucretia Mott
> Like the serpent and the dove,
> Thou hast wisdom and love;
> Thy faith by thy deeds is shown forth.
> Thy liberal mind
> Chains of sect cannot bind;
> Thy sect is the righteous of earth.[22]

At the moment direct criticism of her outspoken religious convictions was not silent. She wrote Miller McKim,

We find there are some fears in that quarter as elsewhere, lest our
testimony to a free gospel ministry should be violated by such intimate
intercourse with the ministers of other Societies. John Comly was in
the city while we were gone & complained to one of our friends that

a member of Cherry St. Meeting had sent a "hireling minister" into their neighborhood — If he would come and give us an opportunity to answer for ourselves *I* would like it better.[23]

Disapproval of her beliefs, however, did not content itself with words alone. In March 1840, Lucretia Mott with a group of Quakers, including Daniel Neall of Philadelphia and his young wife, went into Delaware, as the *Delaware State Journal* of March 3, 1840, reported: "for the purpose of visiting their friends, attending the 'Southern Quarterly Meeting' and appointing some meetings within its limits. They had proceeded satisfactorily to themselves; and so far as they know, to their friends having public meetings at Camden, Dover [in the Court House] and at Little Creek." While the members of this party were seated quietly in the home of Michael Offly, a Quaker living two miles distant from Smyrna, some twenty or thirty men entered the house and took Neall away, the other Friends following the mob in a carriage. Neall was tarred and feathered. In the printed account of the outrage, the charge was made that the mobsters, representing "some of the respectable inhabitants of the place, might have been dissuaded from their purpose, had they not pledged themselves to those acting behind the scene to carry certain threats into execution."

Widespread alarm followed this attack and, in answer to inquiries made by friends in Massachusetts, Lucretia wrote:

The scene was truly awful at the time. Dr. Neall's new wife was not inured to mobs as some of us are — she shook as with an ague fit from head to foot. I plead hard with them to take me as I was the offender — if offense had been committed & give him up to his wife — but they declined saying "you are a woman and we have nothing to say to you," to wh. I answered "I ask no courtesy at your hands on account of my sex," but they had heard of him before as of Penna. Hall. Our presence and remonstrances no doubt moderated their purpose.[24]

Continuing the account of this experience with mob violence, she told how the attackers seemed satisfied to put only a light coat of tar on Daniel Neall, and to add a few feathers before making their victim ride on a rail obtained from a fence near the scene. She concluded,

It was really a respectable mob, & I rejoiced to have no feeling in my heart toward them other than pity & love for the lads standg. around who listened to all I said.

But a year or two later, when Lucretia Mott and her husband were at Smyrna for a First-Day Meeting, one of the linch-pins was removed from their carriage. The carriage was repaired, but the landlord of the tavern refused to serve dinner to the Motts.[25]

Although her freedom from personal resentment against her attackers was never marred by sanctimoniousness, yet her piety went to such lengths at times that she must have been an irritating person to live with. Theater-going was one of the sins of the world she frowned on, and such was the veneration accorded her by her immediate family that her wishes were law; not, however, without protest. Martha Wright wrote to her husband on one of her visits to Philadelphia,

Some evening while Sister L. is absent Mary Ann Barber & I, Thomas & Mr. Hearn are going to the theatre. I mentioned it to Sister L. not dreaming but that she would be willing that such as were unenlightened should indulge moderately in such things until they could themselves see the enormity of it; but to use rather an undignified expression I had to haul in my horns she made such a fuss. She told Anna to be sure not to let us go while she was away — still she said that I had not considered what a nice chance her absence would give us and it seemed to me very much like the friends saying "there hangs the key, behind the door, but I shan't give it to thee."

In the same letter Martha throws light on another aspect of Lucretia Mott's Quakerism:

She [Sister L.] was so dissatisfied with my red handkerchief that she insisted on presenting me with white one which brother Benjamin pronounced an improvement. I have no objections as long as the expense is not mine, to being friendified to their heart's content.[26]

But the sincerity of "Sister L." was never questioned nor, apparently, her right to make the rules for the household.

Chapter Six

SOCIAL REFORM

At the Philadelphia Yearly Meeting of 1835, it was decided to send a Protest to Congress against the admission of Arkansas to the Union. The reason for this Protest was stated: "The Religious Society of Friends for a long course of years have held an unwavering testimony against Slavery." Delegated to represent the Meeting were "Jos. Parrish, Clerk of the Men's Meeting" and "Lucretia Mott, Clerk of the Women's Meeting." Endorsed, however, above the signature of "W. Buchanan," the appeal was "laid on the table of the Senate on April 25, 1836." [1]

This "unwavering testimony," beginning as sorrowful denunciations against slavery,[2] had reached formal protest shortly after the middle of the eighteenth century in the decision of the Philadelphia Yearly Meeting "to exclude any one who bought or sold slaves from participation in the business affairs of the church." [3] An eloquent example of the Quaker opposition to slavery in the eighteenth century was furnished by John Woolman. In his *Journal*, completed just before his death in 1772, Woolman wrote that he had abstained consistently and absolutely from using the fruits of slave labor because he held the faith that slavery "was not right." This conviction led him, at times a scrivener as well as a tailor, to excuse himself from writing wills when the property held by the testator included slaves. As he refused the remunerative employment he was wont to say, "I cannot write thy will without breaking my own peace." When traveling among slaveholders, Woolman even went so far as to leave "pieces of silver" to his hosts for the compensation of their slaves. Solutions to end slavery had thus taken the form of concrete plans. But all to little purpose: America slumbered on, and slavery remained strongly intrenched.

The last quarter of the eighteenth century, however, was marked almost everywhere by a striving against imposed bonds of repression, against authoritative restrictions in art and literature, in social conventions, in religion, and in constituted authority. It was the Romantic Age, a springtime when man strove to burst all shackles to realize his innate right to be free. Before this onslaught of resistance to authority established governments crumbled and revolt raised its head as Revolution in France and America. But when the newly born American republic faced the problem of adopting a Constitution, the inconsistency of free men holding slaves in legal bondage became disturbingly apparent. Agitators against slavery took heart; the words of John Woolman were recalled; antislavery associations were organized; and certain Northern states enacted statutes prohibiting slavery within their borders.

The emancipation of slaves here and there and the enactment of emancipation ordinances by a few states eased, in a sense, the American conscience. The acute need, however, of bettering conditions of American living exerted a greater challenge to the thought and resourcefulness of America's strongest men than did eleemosynary appeals. To legislators the pressing economic problems left by the War of 1812 constituted a more logical appeal than the consideration of theories of abstract justice. These theories, also, if put into actual practice would not only wipe out the main source of the income of Southern planters but would also lay inroads on the coffers of Northern merchants and industralists.

The plan to stifle slavery at its source had been found in the theories and practices of John Woolman. In the first part of the nineteenth century Woolman's mantle seemed to have fallen upon Elias Hicks. But the restrained proposals of Woolman were a far cry from the violent denunciations of Hicks. Indeed the conviction was widely held that Hicks' uncompromising attitude on the evil of slavery was a greater affront to his hearers in Philadelphia and elsewhere than his so-called heretical opinions. Moreover, the inauguration of an attack on slavery directly through the purse strings of the slaveholder and indirectly through the financial interests of many Northerners was not generally acceptable to some so-called strong abolitionists.

In the 1820's, James Mott was a thriving Philadelphia commission merchant, having developed a profitable business of his own since he entered the mercantile world as assistant to his wife's father. As "Mott, James and Co. Mers. 45 N. Front, h 14 Sansom," he conducted an active trade, particularly in cotton from the slave states. It took but a short time to convince him that the sincerity of his principles of justice was challenged by his commerce in cotton. Before long he eliminated the import of all cotton goods — cotton batting, hanks of spun threads, woven goods — and restricted his merchandise to different forms of wool. After making this change, he became a member of the Free Produce Society in Philadelphia, an all-male group. Lucretia, however, endorsed heartily her husband's decision.[4]

Even the Mott children took part in Free Produce by accepting,
though perhaps wryly, the substitutes for sugar from the slave
states. Not a little merriment was afforded at the children's parties in the Mott household by artificially sweetened candy contained in little nuggets called "prize packages." The "prize packages" were covered with wrappings concealing mottoes. To reach
the candy one had to read the motto. "Our young people," as
Lucretia described the device to Miller McKim in a letter dated
April 8, 1834,⁵ "have had some amusement in composing anti-
slavery couplets to fold in 'free sweets' in order to win a premium
offered for the best — we obtained about 150 which have found
ready sale at Sleeper's Free Store — among them are the following:

> Take this, my friend, you need not fear to eat
> No slave hath toiled to cultivate the sweet.
>
> Sweet as these sweets are, yet sweeter still
> The soil that Freemen tread and Freemen till.
>
> Fair Crandall's firmness merits acclaim
> Her foes may blush, and will, for shame."

Among the pioneers in the reawakening of the 1830's against
slavery were men whose names are landmarks in American history,
crusaders, however, who did not always agree as to methods of
solving America's problem. Arthur and Lewis Tappan of New
York were enthusiastic antislavery advocates. They contributed
their unswerving purpose and immense wealth to the support of
the Colonization Society, the group organized to purchase slaves
from the Southern plantations for transportation as colonists to
Africa. The Gradualists, opposing immediate emancipation as an
unpracticable and unworkable plan, were in favor of approaching
the solution slowly; while a radical view was taken by men and
women who saw one solution only, the immediate and complete
freedom for the slave.

Among the advocates of immediate emancipation was William
Lloyd Garrison of Massachusetts. Convinced of the rightness of his
stand, Garrison had scant patience with fainthearted compromise.
Like the Tappans he began his opposition to slavery as a member
of the Colonization Society; but when he became convinced that
Colonization was not the answer, he formulated his objections in
a Treatise, *Thoughts on African Colonization,* published in 1830.
In these *Thoughts* he repudiated the Colonization Society for what
he termed its evasiveness of the cardinal issues of slavery, its unwillingness to interfere with the property rights of slaveholders,

and its lack of any aim to attempt emancipation. Moreover, he charged that the Society had no desire to improve the "moral, intellectual and political" condition of the Negro.[6] Immediate Emancipation was his goal, and he turned his pen to the support of Abolition. Many of the antislavery pioneers disapproved of Garrison's views and his method of expressing them, but his sincerity, his integrity, and his significance at the moment of the organization of the American Anti-Slavery Society — the writing of the Society's Declaration of Principles was entrusted to him — are matters of fact.

Almost at the beginning of his career he was imprisoned for writing a castigating editorial against Francis Todd, who was engaged in the coastwise transport of slaves from Massachusetts to the South.[7] Released from jail, Garrison began his life's Crusade — an uncompromising attack on slavery. The medium of his onslaught was the *Liberator,* the defiant antislavery weekly, which was to endure for thirty-five years. The words on its masthead, "My Country is the World, My Countrymen are all Mankind," indicate the area of his vision; and his policy was declared in the first issue: "I am in earnest; I will not equivocate; I will not excuse; I will not retreat a single inch; and I will be heard."

Consistent in the desire to achieve principles of absolute justice, Garrison gave sympathetic and unequivocal support to the Woman's Rights Movement. This attitude was not shared by all abolitionists, and it explains in some measure the allegiance to Garrison of many pioneers among the movement for Woman's Rights.

Garrison became acquainted with the Motts about the time of his starting the *Liberator*. After a score of years, in a letter written from Philadelphia to his paper, he recalled the genuine hospitality he had always enjoyed in the Mott home:

I was indebted to those inestimable friends, James and Lucretia Mott, for a homelike reception, affectionate and delightful. My obligations to them, ever since our acquaintance more than nineteen years ago, have been constantly accumulating, and my regard for them amounts to unfeigned veneration. When I was a mere novice in the anti-slavery cause, long before I became identified with it, they were active co-workers with the intrepid pioneer, Benjamin Lundy, for the abolition of slavery.[8]

Under Garrison's leadership the New England Anti-Slavery Society was organized in 1832. Scarcely more than a year later a convention of sixty-two delegates from antislavery societies met in Philadelphia to form a national body. The convention, of course, included no women; but on the second day of the proceedings, after women had been permitted to take seats in the gallery, Lucretia Mott, her mother, and some other Philadelphia women were emboldened to come to the gathering.

Lucretia, speaking at the thirtieth anniversary of the Society, remembered the circumstances:

It was after the Convention had gathered the second day, that the invitation was sent out. Thomas Whitson came to our house with an invitation to women to come there as spectators or as listeners. I felt such a desire that others than those assembled at our house should hear, that I wanted to go here and there, and notify persons to go; but I was asked not to use up the whole morning in notifying others, for we must try and be there ourselves.[9]

On the other hand, Martha Wright, visiting her family in Philadelphia in 1833, referred jokingly to her sister's joyful acceptance of the invitation to the Convention to form "a Society favorable to immediate emancipation and opposed to Colonization." In Martha's words, Lucretia, her mother, and her daughter acknowledged the invitation by "clapping on their bonnets," and hurrying off to the Convention.[10]

At the door of the hall the visitors were ushered into the assembly, politely seated and, in their reserved seats, permitted to listen to the proceedings. In the course of the morning when the gathering became perplexed as to the wording of a phrase in the Convention's Declaration of Sentiments, Lucretia timidly arose to offer a suggestion. For a moment she hesitated to speak; but, encouraged by the president, Beriah Green, she suggested that the words, "according to Scripture" should be included in the document to indicate divine authority for the imputation of guilt which the Convention placed upon slaveholders. This proposal was opposed by Garrison, who was convinced that the allegation against slavery should be supported not by divine guidance but by reason and logic. But the Convention, while giving women no vote, was wise enough to accept Lucretia's advice, though it has been suggested that the opposition of Garrison, who was already antagonizing some antislavery leaders, may have influenced the assembly to accept Lucretia's suggestion.

Despite the demonstrated ability of a woman to offer wise counsel, the gathering felt no compunctions about its exclusion of women, and the women bowed to the dictates of the day. No objections were raised to the assumed superiority of the men, even though Article IV of the Constitution of the Society conferred the privilege of membership and voting upon any person, not a slaveholder, who paid the dues of the association. Women were not regarded as "persons." The organization also commended the establishment of "Ladies Anti-Slavery Societies," stating that "all ladies of the land" were "respectfully and earnestly invited" by the Convention to organize Anti-Slavery Societies in "every State, County and Town in the Union." Two provisions for the organization of Auxiliary societies were made; one for "the ladies" and the other for "the youth of the country male and females." Efforts to further the antislavery cause that had already been made by the women were acknowledged as "harbingers of a brighter day."

The organization of the countrywide association gave immediate impulse to the formation of subsidiary bodies, those significant for Lucretia Mott being the Philadelphia Female Anti-Slavery Society and the National Anti-Slavery Convention of American Women. Before many of the delegates to the National Convention had reached their homes, the Philadelphia Female Anti-Slavery Society was formally organized.[11]

Heading the list of the signers of the Constitution of this group is the name of Lucretia Mott.

Among the more than sixty women active at the start or shortly thereafter were two of Lucretia Mott's closest Philadelphia friends, Sarah Pugh and Mary Grew. Other early members were Lucretia's pioneering companions at the inauguration of the National Anti-Slavery Society: Esther Moore, Sydney Ann Lewis, and Lydia White. Both Sydney Ann Lewis and Lydia White kept stores for the sale of Free-Produce wares, Lydia White's store being for years well-known not only in Philadelphia but in New England and the Middle West.

Signers also of the Charter of the Philadelphia Female Anti-Slavery Society were several Negro women, foremost among whom was Sarah Douglas, the Philadelphia schoolteacher. For years her school was under the sponsorship of the Philadelphia Female Anti-Slavery Society, while she herself was not merely an officer but an active promoter of the organization's program. The young Forten girls — Charlotte, Margaretta, and Sarah Louise — had inherited antislavery zeal from their father James Forten, a prosperous Philadelphia sailmaker. In a comfortable home on Lombard Street near Ninth the Forten family lived in a gracious way, but for years the head of the home had used his wealth and intelligence mainly to promote antislavery sentiment in Philadelphia and throughout Pennsylvania.

Robert Purvis, the son of a wealthy Charlestonian and a free Negro woman, had settled in the suburbs of Philadelphia after being educated in New England. In his chosen home he lived as a country gentleman, raising flowers and choice vegetables that frequently took blue ribbons at the county fair. But abolition was his main concern, and soon he and his wife joined the antislavery group in Philadelphia. It was a matter of no surprise to find Hattie Purvis among the women who founded the Philadelphia Female Anti-Slavery Society.

The devotion of the Mott family to any cause close to the mother's heart was evident in the membership of Lucretia's oldest daughters, Anna Mott Hopper and Maria Mott Davis.

Naturally, the Society felt its first obligation was the furtherance of the principles and aims of the parent body, the National Anti-Slavery Society. Contributions were therefore made to the National body, the National program was endorsed, and petitions were sent to Congress for the abolition of slavery in the District of Columbia and the territories. The Society also endeavored to widen the circulation of antislavery literature by promoting the sales of "tracts and other papers throughout the city" and the adjacent counties.

After endorsing the proposals of the National body, the Philadelphia Female Anti-Slavery Society, at the suggestion of Lucretia Mott, took a stand on the subject of Free Produce. This action endorsed a Constitutional Amendment which provided that the Society should at all times and on all occasions give their preference to Free Produce over the products of slavery. Believing that the refusal to purchase and use the exports from the slave states was one of the most efficient means of abolishing slavery, these women brought their principles into forthright procedure. They went further on this unpopular subject of Free Produce by endeavoring, in 1837, to secure free cotton goods from Port au Prince, Haiti.

From time to time from the organization of the National Anti-Slavery Society to the Civil War, Lucretia Mott endeavored to secure the Anti-Slavery Society's support of the principle, "No business with slaveholders." But the National body would not endorse a measure leading to action which could affect the income of the individual members of the Society.

A unique work of the Philadelphia Female Anti-Slavery Society was its furtherance of a plan of social work to promote the
morale, living conditions, and general welfare of the colored people of Philadelphia. The first application of this endeavor was the
Society's assuming the sponsorship of Sarah Douglas' school for
Negro children. Then, a committee, under the chairmanship of
Lucretia Mott's daughter Anna, divided the city into charted sections and investigated the areas in a systematic manner comparable to the formalized method of social-service agencies of later
years.

On one of the visits made by Lydia Maria Child from her
Northampton home to Philadelphia, she extolled the Philadelphia
Female Anti-Slavery Society in a letter to Maria W. Chapman of
Boston, advising that it might be profitable for the New England
Anti-Slavery Society to study the program of the Philadelphia Society. "The name of the president," concluded Mrs. Child's letter,
"is Mrs. Sidney [sic] Ann Lewis; the Secretary Mrs. Lucretia Mott
— both of the Society of Friends." [12] A talented woman was Mrs.
Chapman, whose literary ability enabled her to edit the autobiography of Harriet Martineau. Moreover she was the acknowledged
leader of the groups of antislavery women in New England.

Lucretia Mott's name is not only the first signature to the Constitution of the Philadelphia Society, but with the exception of one
year during the life span of the organization she was a member of
the Board of Managers, being either duly elected or in an ex
officio position as president. She was chairman or a member of
almost every important committee, and each meeting found her
advocating or supporting some measure or program of practical
action. A study of the Minutes of the Philadelphia Female Anti-
Slavery Society reveals that no other member was as consistently
prominent in the ventures of the organization as was Lucretia
Mott.[13] This activity is easily understood, for she was not only a
natural leader, but in Philadelphia she was at home in the midst
of her family and understanding friends. Here she could bring
into full play her belief that "faith without works is dead."

In her speech at the Third Decade of the National Anti-Slavery
Society, Lucretia acknowledged the humble beginnings of the
Philadelphia Female Anti-Slavery Society.

It has been honestly confessed that there was not, at that time, a
conception of the rights of women. Indeed, women little knew their
influence, or the proper exercise of their own rights. I remember that

it was urged upon us immediately after that Convention to form a Female Anti-Slavery Society; and at that time I had no idea of the meaning of preambles and resolutions and votings. Women had never been in any assemblies of the kind. I had only attended one Convention — a Convention of colored people in this State — before that; and that was the first time, in my life I had ever heard a vote taken, being accustomed to our Quaker way of getting the prevailing sentiment of the meeting.[14]

The organization of the National Anti-Slavery Society promoted, it is true, numbers of branch associations; but a rising tide of antipathy against emancipation as well as a growing resentment of the presence of free Negroes in the North gave vent to outbursts of lawlessness in several places.

In Boston, Garrison was led through the city with a rope around his neck. That he escaped lynching was due to the fact that his friends succeeded in harboring him in the Boston jail until he could be spirited secretly out of the city. In New York violence was directed against the Tappans although the lawlessness was enkindled in the Bowery theater where Edwin Forrest was acting. Before the mob vented its fury on Negro churches, schools, and dwellings, the warehouses and homes of the Tappans narrowly escaped complete destruction. No lives were lost in New York, but the damage to property was disastrous. For three evenings in this same summer of 1834, mob violence raged in South Philadelphia.

Another outrage occurred in Canterbury, Connecticut, where a young Quaker schoolteacher, Prudence Crandall, conducted a successful school. However, when she decided to enroll two little Negro girls, the other pupils were withdrawn by their parents. Prudence Crandall determined, however, to stand by her Quaker principles; she would maintain her school for "Young ladies and little misses of color" as her resolution was advertised in the *Liberator;* and the novel experiment was soon started. Immediately the citizens of Canterbury became fanatic, and when the new pupils appeared in the streets of Canterbury, they were insulted, refuse was poured down the well in the schoolyard, and the house itself was daubed with filth. Merchants of Canterbury refused to trade with the teacher, the pupils were not permitted to worship in the churches, and an attempt was made to set the school on fire. Finally Prudence Crandall was arrested on the charge of "harboring vagrants."

Arthur Tappan came to the rescue of the Quaker schoolteacher by offering bond; and eminent legal counsel was furnished. But when the persecutors were forced to base their attack on a technicality, the case was ended. Then Prudence Crandall realized the futility of an attempt to continue her school in Connecticut. Plans were therefore put in progress to secure a new location, Philadelphia being one of the places considered for continuing the venture.

At this point Lucretia Mott stepped into the picture. As she wrote to Miller McKim on September 25, 1834:

Prudence Crandall and her husband have passed a week in our city since their marriage — they had previously visited New York and Boston with a view to decide in which of these places they should open a school for colored girls, having determined no longer to conflict with the iniquitous law of Connecticut — Esther Moore was much pleased with the prospect — she and myself called with Prudence on about 50 families of our most reputable colored people, and engaged a sufficient number to warrant her beginning here — but there was so much opposition to the attempt, at this time, by a few of our *prudent* abolitionists, that she was induced to return to Canterbury and wait till after our elections when it is probably [sic] they will all remove here — It appears by the papers that fresh insults awaited them there.[15]

Less violent but not insignificant as opposition to antislavery was a controversy that broke out in Lane Theological Seminary in Cincinnati. In the spring of 1834 certain students of the institution, concerned over the fact that a strong approval of Colonization had developed in the Seminary, decided to hold a debate on the problem of slavery. They desired to show whether the best interests of the slaves lay in the plans of the Colonization Society or in forthright abolition. As the majority of the Seminarians at the time were in their late twenties or early thirties, they had given mature and considered thought to the menace of slavery. Theodore Weld, pioneer in the controversy, was ably supported by classmates who, having lived in the South, brought convincing testimony of outrages they had witnessed in their own homes. After eighteen nights of serious, unemotional speeches, a vote disclosed that an overwhelming majority of the students were convinced that immediate action should be taken on the problem of slavery. Furthermore, the solution supported was not Colonization but abolition.[16]

This radicalism met strong punitive measures from the authorities at Lane, who prohibited all public assemblies at the institution except for purely academic exercises. Accepting the ultimatum, a majority of the students left Lane Seminary for other institutions. The most significant outcome was a large financial grant made by Arthur Tappan for the development of the theological department of Oberlin College with no restrictions as to the race of the students. The "account from Lane Seminary, near Cincinnati," wrote Lucretia Mott to Miller McKim, "thou hast no doubt seen in the Liberator and been cheered as we were with the result." A month later she had more definite news: "Two young Theological students from the Lane Seminary — Thome and Stanton, also passed thro' the City — delegates to the great anti-slavery Mg. in New York. We passed an evening with them and Wm. L. Garrison & Phelps of Boston, at our friend Jas. Forten's and were highly interested in their relation of circumstances. The cause is certainly making rapid progress — we may yet live to see the desire of our souls with regard to this oppressed people." [17]

Lucretia Mott was not silent on the riots of 1834. On September 25 of that year she wrote to Miller McKim,

The late outrages in this and other places were as thou supposed the absorbing topics for a time and painfully so to abolitionists — some sympathy was felt for the poor unoffending sufferers, by the Citizens generally — tho' very few took the pains to go "down town" to witness for themselves the injury done to their property. Repeated attempts were made on the part of their few friends to get together a town Meeting before they succeeded — and at last it was not as they could have wished. Thou hast doubtless noticed their proceedings as published in the papers, and may feel some surprise to see J. Mott's name attached to such a "report of the causes," etc. — but he had so much of it stricken out before it was adopted far more objectionable than the part retained, that he thought it best to suffer his name to be appended to it, believing he might be useful in making collections, distributions, etc. . . .

We hope a sum will be collected sufficient to repair their losses. My Husband and self were absent from the city at the time of the riots — having gone to Chester County to attend a Quarterly Meeting also a Meeting of the Clarkson Anti-Slavery Society 40 miles distant.

Then, referring to the Columbia riot, she added:

The shameful conduct at Columbia has aroused the indignation of the friends of the people of colour in the surrounding country, and they are giving them the preference as hired labourers. We heard of one manufacturer who sent to Columbia for 20 of them to employ in his Mill. Thus we have reason to believe that all these things may be to their ultimate benefit — altho "meant for evil" it may be turned to their good — but some of us have feared that our progress is too long

delayed by the threats and conduct of our adversaries. We are standing still — there has not been a public address, either in this City or
New York since the memorable 4th of July — and the Meetings of our
societies have been but poorly attended, tis true many were out of
town, and we may hope now the warm weather is past, there will be a
revival . . . I have received a letter from a newly formed Female
Anti-Slavery Society in New Hampshire asking information of our
doings, which I have answered at full length.[18]

When plans were made for the formation of a Pennsylvania
Branch of the Anti-Slavery Society, patterned after the National
Society, James Mott was one of the "upward of Twelve Hundred
gentlemen from various parts of the State" who signed the Call
and became one of the charter members. Like the parent body the
Pennsylvania Branch hailed "with great encouragement" the anti-
slavery efforts of women, "the mighty sum of female influence in
behalf of oppressed humanity." Yet for two years it refused to take
women into membership. Once the bars against sex were lowered,
Lucretia Mott became one of the most energetic workers in the
association, being almost continuously a member of the executive committee, attending practically all the meetings, contributing
to the funds of the association, and never failing to raise her voice
in defense of her strong convictions.

She was one of the leaders in the Anti-Slavery Convention of
American Women that was inaugurated at an assembly held in
New York, May 9–12, 1837.[19] Brought together to adopt a liberal
program were more than one hundred women representing ten
states. Among these delegates were Sarah and Angelina Grimké,
daughters of a wealthy South Carolina slaveholder. The Grimké
sisters had left their home to engage in an active crusade against
restrictions suffered by women and against American slavery. Both
women were convincing speakers, inspiring their audiences in
private homes when the platforms of churches and other places
were closed to women who dared raise their voices in public gatherings. Second only to the Grimkés as a convincing speaker was
Abby Kelly, who with Maria Weston Chapman and her sister, Ann
Warren Weston, was sent from Massachusetts. And of course there
were Lydia Maria Child and Lucretia Mott.

To the surprise of no one Lucretia Mott introduced a resolution advocating Free Produce; but the *Proceedings* of the organization includes no statement as to the adoption of this resolution.

Philadelphia was chosen by the Convention for its meeting
place in 1838.

Sometime before this meeting a group of Philadelphians, forming a joint-stock company, set about the raising of funds for a suitable building "wherein the principles of Liberty, and Equality of Civil Rights could be freely discussed and the evils of Slavery fearlessly portrayed." By the spring of 1838, the projected edifice, Pennsylvania Hall, was erected on "Delaware Sixth Street" between Mulberry and Sassafras streets, that is, on North Sixth Street above Arch Street, just in front of the Arch Street Theatre. No efforts had been spared to make Pennsylvania Hall an ornament to the city as well as a solid, sturdy edifice, consisting of several ground-floor rooms, suitable for offices and small conferences, and a main auditorium offering space for about three thousand persons.

On the first day appointed for the program the dedicatory address was an ode by Whittier entitled "Pennsylvania Hall." In these lines the poet prophesied that the new edifice would be

> . . . a fair field, where mind may close with mind,
> Free as the sunshine and the chainless wind;
> Where the high trust is fixed on Truth alone,
> And bonds and fetters from the soul are thrown;
> Where wealth and rank and worldly pomp, and might,
> Yield to the presence of the Truth and Right.

As the ode was being read little attention was paid to a brick-bat thrown at the window; and on the next day conferences of several organizations — the Free-Produce Convention, the Methodist Anti-Slavery Society, the Pennsylvania State Anti-Slavery Association — proceeded as scheduled. On Wednesday, however, during the opening session of the Convention of American Women, a furious disturbance was created by rioters; but despite the disorder, the women caried out their program.

At least two reports picture the role of Lucretia Mott in this Convention of American Women.[20] Mary S. Parker, the Secretary of the Boston Female Anti-Slavery Society, wrote, "Lucretia Mott exhorted the members of the Convention to be steadfast and solemn in the prosecution of the business for which they were assembled." But Sarah G. Buffum of Fall River has left a more detailed account of Lucretia's activity. After giving a summary of the speeches of Maria W. Chapman, Angelina Grimké, and Abby Kelly, Miss Buffum wrote that the next address was "by Lucretia Mott of Philadelphia, a woman of pleasing manners, apparently united with a firm mind, and a very meek devotional spirit." Continuing, Miss Buffum said:

She spoke of our being "a little disturbed last evening by the tu-
multous sea of human passions around us," but she thought it would
soon rock itself to rest, and then it would be permitted that we speak
forth the words of truth and soberness. She alluded very beautifully to
the first promulgation of the gospel; to the courage, calmness, and
perserverance of the early disciples; and then exhorted us most affec-
tionately to copy their example, to cherish a meek and quiet spirit, and
by all means to preserve love and harmony among ourselves. This session of the Convention was more interesting than the former one. . .

On returning to the Hall on Thursday, 4 o'clock, P.M., we found
the number and noise of the mob much increased. . . At this meeting
Mrs. Mott presented a message to the Convention, I think, from the
President of the Association which owns the Hall, desiring the Convention to recommend to their colored sisters not to attend the meeting to be held in the Hall this evening, because they would be more
exposed than the others, as the mob seemed to direct their malice
particularly toward the colored people. Mrs. Mott said that while she
presented this request, she wished to express her own opinion which
was, that our colored friends ought not to absent themselves from the
meeting this evening. She hoped no person would be alarmed by a
little *appearance* of danger. . . . For herself, she felt so desirous to be
present that she would request to be excused from the Business Committee. A vote was taken to excuse Mrs. Mott for this evening from
the Committee. . . Our conversation was interrupted before 9 o'clock
by the cry of "Fire!" Pennsylvania Hall was in flames. The mob had
accomplished the work by breaking in the door and deliberately kin-
dling a fire in the house — in view of the City of Philadelphia! We
walked out to witness the speedy destruction of that beautiful building which the diligent axe and hammer had been, for months, patiently rearing.

After the Hall had been set on fire, Lucretia joined a large
group of friends gathered at the Mott home on North Ninth
Street. Chief among the out-of-town guests were Maria W. Chapman of Boston and her sister Ann W. Weston, who joined the Philadelphians Sarah Pugh, Miller McKim, and Charles C. Burleigh.
Charles Burleigh, originally from Plainfield, Connecticut, was,
with his brother William, an enthusiastic member of the anti-
slavery cause; shortly before the dedication of Pennsylvania Hall
he had made his headquarters in Philadelphia and, as a matter
of course, had become a member of the Mott circle. When the
rioters poured through Race Street after the conflagration, the
huddled watchers in North Ninth Street feared an onslaught, especially, as Thomas Mott rushed in with the cry "They're coming." But, at the corner of Ninth and Race streets, a friend of the

Motts placed himself at the head of the mob calling out "On to the Motts," then deliberately led it away from the Motts' home.

At the time of the burning of Pennsylvania Hall, Edward M. Davis, husband of Lucretia's daughter Maria, was in Paris; and it is in a letter to him that Charles Burleigh writes of the riot:

In the *Freeman* you will find an address of the Ex. Com. to the people of Pennsylvania, giving an account of the riot and destruction of the Hall. It is from three pens. Whittier wrote what I have marked with two parallel lines drawn across; Brother W., what is marked with one, Whittier and myself together, what is marked with two lines crossing each other, and all that is unmarked is from my own pen. I mention this because I thought you might feel some curiosity to know who was the author of the address.

After this key to the collaborated authorship of the *Freeman's* account which described the events of the night as they affected the Motts, he continued,

We sat in calm expectation of their advance upon us, hearing every few minutes by voice of our friends who were on the alert, what progress was made, what points were occupied and what movements were going on. At length, however, as the main body seemed to have broken and to a great degree scattered, we concluded that we were to escape a visit that night at least and retired to rest.[21]

In her address to the Convention the next morning, Lucretia, as reported again by Miss Buffum,

spoke on the subject of the riot with the true eloquence of nature. She described her emotions last evening when she heard that the mob was directing their steps towards her house. "It was," said she, "a searching time. I had often thought how I should sustain myself if called to pass such an ordeal. I hope I speak it not in the spirit of boasting when I tell you, my sisters, I believe I was strengthened by God. I felt at the moment that I was willing to suffer whatever the cause required. My best feelings acquit me of shrinking back in the hour of danger. But the mob was not suffered to molest us, and I feel thankful that we slept a few hours in tranquility and peace."

Undaunted by opposition, the Convention concluded its labors according to prescribed schedule, duly meeting on the next day after the fire in Sarah Pugh's schoolhouse. All the planned items were dispatched; and the Convention, not frightened perceptibly by the hostility of the Quaker City, voted to hold its next meeting, May 1839, in Philadelphia. Lucretia Mott then closed the sessions with prayer.

News of the burning of Pennsylvania Hall was flashed throughout all sections of the country, creating an aftermath of publicity
that included not only the actual occurrences of the disaster but
a picturesque summary of fact and fancy. The charge was made
that the Philadelphia Fire Department exerted its efforts to prevent the fire from spreading to the adjoining building while the
flames were allowed full play on Pennsylvania Hall. One account
claimed,

The city was delivered over last night to the tender mercies of a
mob, and therefore we may be thankful that the affair ended with the
loss of property without the loss of life. Open incendiarism and mur-
der go generally hand in hand — but they were separated last night, no
thanks to the Police, which we must be permitted to say was wholly
remiss in its duty. . . The Mayor at an early hour went to the prem-
ises and locked the door, to prevent a discussion which was actually
designed to take place in the evening. Nothing more than this, we are
told, was done to save the honor of the City, and assert the majesty of
the laws. Legal interference walked in at the eleventh hour, to be
ousted by the mob at the twelfth.[22]

The Philadelphia Riot of 1834 was evidence of strong anti-
Negro sentiment among a large part of the population of the
Quaker City. The very need for a building open to reformers be-
speaks the attitude of many Philadelphians. On the defensive,
spokesmen for the city claimed that the Abolitionists themselves,
in associating openly with their Negro friends, were responsible
in part for the reactionary position charged to the rioters. And
the unpopularity of "Woman's Rights" in Philadelphia had stirred
up strong feeling against the Convention. One account of the burning of Pennsylvania Hall was concluded in these words:

Least of all have American females cause to complain of the position custom has assigned them. The kindness and attention they receive — the gallantry universally shown them — not the least worthy
for being often uncouth — should teach them one and all to appreciate
their social position without looking for immoderate or strange privileges or applauding and running after public Reformers from their
own sex. Instead of attending useless discussions and listening to
itinerant lecturers, let them read at home.[23]

Beyond her speeches in the Convention, Lucretia Mott seems
to have taken no part in this maelstrom. But William Ellery
Channing, in deploring the outrage to Jonathan Phillips, singled
out Whittier and Lucretia Mott as being present at the time of
the storm and fury. He wrote,

In that crowd was Lucretia Mott, that beautiful example of womanhood. Who that has heard the tones of her voice and looked on the mild radiance of her benign and intelligent countenance can endure the thought that such a woman was driven by a mob from a spot to which she had gone as she religiously believed on a mission of Christian sympathy.[24]

As the 1839 meeting of the Anti-Slavery Convention of American Women approached, Isaac Roach was Mayor of Philadelphia. Fearing a recurrence of mob violence, Mayor Roach went to Lucretia Mott, whom he must have regarded as of great influence. After routine questions as to the probable size of the coming Convention, the time chosen for the meetings, and the place of assembly, he then arrived at what was undoubtedly the real cause of his visit. He asked,

Does the Convention expect colored women to attend the meetings, and if colored women are present, will they mingle on terms of equality with the white delegates?

He then suggested that meetings should be held in the easily guarded Clarkson Hall, that evening meetings should be omitted and that "unnecessary walking with colored people" should be avoided. In the words of the secretary,

Undismayed Lucretia Mott told Mayor Roach: first, that Clarkson Hall on account of its inadequate lighting arrangements was not designed for evenings meetings; then that, as she had been in the habit of walking with colored people as occasion offered, she would continue to follow her habit in that practice; and finally that as she expected to have house guests "of that complexion," she would in all probability accompany her guests to and from the Convention.[25]

The 1839 meetings were undisturbed.

Closely connected with the antislavery movement as an organization of social reform was the New England Non-Resistance Society, established in Boston, in September 1838, by a group of Abolitionists. Its charter members included William Lloyd Garrison, Samuel J. May, Henry C. Wright, Adin Ballou, and three younger men recently recruited to the cause — Edmund Quincy of Massachusetts, the son of Harvard's President Josiah Quincy, Amos Walker of Connecticut, and Oliver Johnson of New York. In the "Declaration of Sentiments" adopted by the Non-Resistance Society, emphasis was placed on the repudiation of all forms of physical force as weapons to maintain public or private safety, not only in attack but in defense. Defensive warfare, therefore, came under the ban of the Non-Resistants. Holding this extreme position the Non-Resistants denied the right of any retaliatory justice and the claim of any allegiance to governments enforcing principles of redress for public or private injuries. All persons regardless of sex, color, or race were eligible for membership, and among the charter members were Maria W. Chapman and Lydia Maria Child.

The first anniversary meeting of the Non-Resistance Society was in Boston in September 1839. Lucretia Mott was present.

At the gathering this Resolution was offered: "that the only basis upon which a reformatory Society can stand and effect its work in the hearts of men, is a sacred respect for the right of opinion." During the protracted discussion that followed, Lucretia Mott pointed out the distinction between "opinions" and "the right of opinion." She asserted,

The right we cannot deny, and ought to respect though the opinion may be such as we disapprove. . . Once let it be laid down that an *opinion* is necessary to salvation and tolerance becomes inconsistent. But I dislike the word toleration, it does not convey the right idea. It is not yielded in the most orthodox sects that the members may adopt various opinions as to the mode of being in a future state of existence. So it might be with regard to other differences of opinion; and it is a most important thing that it should be so in our present association. This resolution, — involving a respect for the right of opinion — if heartily adopted, will bring good out of all our discussions. It will, like the philosopher's stone transmute base metal into gold.

When Stephen S. Foster (Stephen Symonds Foster, the Abolitionist) declared that the adoption of the resolution would be impracticable in the face of the assertion that ninety-nine hundredths of the Massachusetts Anti-Slavery Society did not believe in nonresistance, Lucretia again clarified the issue. "I think my brother again confuses opinion with the right of opinion" she said. "The ninety-nine hundredths can adopt such resolutions as they choose, in this spirit of love and freedom. But it forbids them to require of the one in the minority to adopt them under the penalty of disgrace." With this answer Stephen Foster expressed himself as satisfied, and after one or two further remarks the resolution was adopted.

When the account of the meeting was reported in *The Non-*

Resistant, the Society's official organ, Lucretia Mott was recorded as the only woman taking an appreciable part in the formal discussions of topics coming before the gathering. An occasional word here or there marked the extent of the participation credited in the Report to any woman except Lucretia Mott. This occurred in spite of the fact that the organization repudiated distinction of rank or inequality of sex. Of the nine members of the "Business Committee" four (Maria W. Chapman, Lydia Maria Child, Thankful Southwick, and Lucretia Mott) were women. Yet, in spite of the liberality of the Constitution, even such brilliant women as Mrs. Child and Mrs. Chapman seemed unwilling or unable to throw aside the shackles of the social usage of the time. But Lucretia Mott spoke frequently and at length.

At a late session of this same convention Lucretia Mott revealed herself as a pioneer in theories of education. The discussion of a resolution embodying a warning to nonresistants to exemplify in their own lives the mild principles of the society shifted to the question of the corporal punishment of children. In the argument on this question Lucretia Mott's views showed her to be a wise parent. She declared,

> The extreme cases which may be brought to demand corporal punishment are like the extreme cases brought to nullify so many arguments. The reason why such extreme cases occur is, I believe, because parents are not prepared. . . They overlook the fact that a child, like all human beings, has inalienable rights. It is the master that is not prepared for emancipation, and it is the parent that is not prepared to give up punishment.

The Non-Resistance Society bore its share of the attacks leveled against practically all reforms of the day, attacks even from reformers. Bitterly reactionary was Nathan Colver, who was living in Massachusetts in 1839. Though a nominally sincere member of the American Anti-Slavery Society, Colver could brook no action that advocated or even tolerated the idea of human rights for women. Angered by the breadth of the principles of the Non-Resistance Society, he raised his voice, in the meetings and in public, against the Society's theories and actions on the woman question. Yet, when the proposal was made that the Society should answer his attacks, Lucretia Mott expressed the hope that the Non-Resistant Society would take no formal action against Colver.

She advised further that theories should be adopted only after mature deliberation and with extreme caution:

Theories, she said, we are religiously bound to follow in action. . . . Let us examine, let us discuss — let us aid one another in comprehending every dictate of the law of peace and love, and then let us fervently pray for strength to act in accordance with our convictions.[26]

A few personal observations relative to Lucretia's presence in Boston at this time are recorded in Edmund Quincy's *Journal:*

Friday, 27th to Chardon St. again . . . The last thing. Lucretia Mott made us a beautiful & touching address after which we adjourned sine die & a most delightful with less difference of opinion & fewer disagreeables than we had any right to expect . . . after tea went with G. to Mrs. Chapman who had a gathering of friends to meet Lucretia . . . Had a very pleasant time indeed — it being somewhat different from the most of parties as you heard nowhere scandal or trifling but in every quarter high & interesting themes discussed.

Saturday 28th . . . called at Mrs. Chapman . . . Dined there by invitation so that I might see the last of Lucretia. She gave an account of her interview with Mary S. Parker, Phelps, etc. of the new organization. About 3 o'clock she departed for N.Y.[27]

As to any effect she may have made, Lucretia, writing Maria Chapman on her return to Philadelphia, retained her habitual modesty,

Tell dear Edmund Quincy that if any one was to be noted especially in our Non-Resistant Meeting for what they *said* that one I think should have been Adin Ballou — not L. Mott. As to my closing remarks in the Non-Resistance Mg. I would willingly furnish them could I call them to mind. I made the attempt soon after the meeting but succeeded so poorly that it was like "the manna of yesterday" & I gave it up. . . I should be glad for E. Wright to know that the turn he gave to my "explanation" in the Non-Resistance meeting is an admission of the right to be intolerant — was just the opposite of what was intended by me in the remarks made.[28]

In a letter from Newburyport, dated October 7, 1839, Henry C. Wright, who accepted the principles of the Non-Resistant Movement, summarized to Gerrit Smith the events of the 1839 Non-Resistance meeting as a session of "hearts knit together in love," as a time when "All our resolutions and Discussions looked to Human life," and when "we tried to do our duty and have committed the event to the hands of God." His single comment on those attending the meeting was: "We had Lucretia Mott with us who added much to the interest."[29]

Chapter Seven

A STEP AHEAD

Lucretia Mott was profoundly disturbed by divisions in the antislavery ranks, which appeared soon after the Society was organized. In Massachusetts, where the spearhead of the rift was forged, dissension arose among abolitionists who differed among themselves in their beliefs as to the best way of ending slavery. Garrison inspired a large group of followers who hoped that slavery could be abolished through unequivocal disapproval and appeals to reason and conscience; and their leader suffered no compromise on this method. On the other hand, a large body of Garrison's opponents thought that the solution to the problem lay primarily in the weapon of politics.

Other factors contributed to the dissension. Certain Northern ministers — led perhaps by genuine abhorrence of any action calculated to arouse wrath, or joined by a bond of sympathy to the Southern clergy, or being at heart not averse to slavery — protested any program designed to restrict the views or the utterances of preachers. New England pulpits, they felt, should be open to all the Southern clergy regardless of any sympathy with slavery which these Southerners might have. When the *Liberator* published a criticism of this latitude, resentment of the newspaper's policy flared high among a group of the Massachusetts clergy. To express the views of men who could not accept in its entirety the Garrisonian program, "Five Orthodox clergymen" issued a protest, the so-called "Clerical Appeal." Hand in hand with this sympathy for Southern ministers went generally a vigorous opposition to the right of women to appear on public platforms. Indeed, the successful speaking of the Grimké sisters had inspired the message of the Pastoral Letter of the Convention of 1837 — public speaking by women violated the sanctity of the home. Friction also had arisen between the central office of the Anti-Slavery Society and the Massachusetts Branch over the independence of the Branch in the allocation of its funds and the nature of its general attitudes on antislavery.

But chief among the causes of disturbance was the uncompromising tone of the *Liberator*. Slavery in the South and weak-

kneed opposition in the North to the system were denounced
equally by Garrison. He did not spare the alliance between Northern capital and Southern plantations; and no less bitter was his
feeling against an apologetic clergy. So uncompromising was the
Liberator that it had been banned from Southern post offices; the
state of Georgia alone had legalized an award of $5000 "to be paid
to any one causing the arrest and bring to trial and conviction, the
editor and publisher of the 'Liberator.' " In Boston Garrison had
to be protected from a mob bent on lynching him in the very
shades of the Boston State House. Many felt that the National
Anti-Slavery Society should publish an organ under its own control, and under all circumstances should free itself from "Garri-
sonism."

In no section of the country did antislavery receive more zealous and intelligent support than that brought to the cause by the
women of New England. The puritan conscience and New England ideals of liberty and education, undoubtedly inspired this
support, which resulted in an incomparably large number of energetic women's antislavery associations in the region. Abolitionists in both thought and action were the New England women as
they assumed the responsibility not only of securing funds for the
national body but of keeping alive the spirit of enthusiasm for
the cause. Spreading the doctrine of antislavery meant also an
acute awareness of the social, ethical, economic, and political issues involved in slavery. In an effort to stress the principles of
antislavery, many of these women let it be known that they approved the *Liberator*'s attack on slavery.

In her unhappiness over the state of friction in the Massachusetts Branch, Maria W. Chapman appealed to Lucretia Mott
for guidance, suggesting hopefully that Pennsylvania release to
Massachusetts the services of Charles C. Burleigh. Desirous,
though, as Lucretia was to pour oil on the troubled waters, she
felt that Pennsylvania could ill afford to heal the breach between
the Massachusetts Branch and the National Society at the price
of relinquishing Burleigh's imagination and foresight. She feared,
too, that his health would be endangered if he were drawn into
the controversy. "Moreover," she wrote, "he is needed here to prevent the 'flames extending to this part of the camp.' We shall look
for his return to us next week." [1]

As the lack of harmony between the Massachusetts Branch and
the National body persisted, the Branch decided to attempt to
build up a spirit of solidarity among the members of the Branch

itself. A logical beginning to achieve this end appeared to be an effort to secure to the Branch the wholehearted support of its women members. Therefore, when the Massachusetts Branch convened in 1838, an acknowledgment was made of the indebtedness of the Branch to the Women of Massachusetts. Further action was an effort to secure a continuation of the loyalty and support of the women. Possibly the group was just in the chastened mood described in the opening words of the Report of the Board of Managers:

The Lord reigns! If it were not so, the friends of humanity might despair. The Lord is omnipotent! But for this tyrants might exercise perpetual dominion. The Lord is sworn to execute judgment for all who are oppressed. Therefore, all shackles shall be broken and every captive set free, in this, in all lands.[2]

At this meeting a revolutionary amendment to the Constitution was passed, an amendment giving women the right to hold office and to vote on all issues.

Women having been given the status of membership by the Massachusetts Branch, the principle came up to the regional body, the New England Anti-Slavery Society, in its next meeting. At first it seemed that no opposition would be raised to the innovation; in fact, the proposition was accepted. But when a woman — the eloquent Abby Kelly of Lynn — was placed on a committee appointed to prepare an address to the clergy, liberality proved to exist in theory only. The Society was not prepared to carry the principle of equality for women too far into practice. At this juncture, devices of parliamentary practice came into action, devices destined to be used on many future occasions as technicalities to block favorable action on Woman's Rights. Twice a recount of the vote was called for; when the results showed no change, an effort was made to persuade Abby Kelly to decline the position that had been voted her. At first she was disposed to withdraw her name, even stating her willingness to resign from the committee. But, when it was borne upon her that her sex was the real reason for the opposition, she decided to stand by the vote.

Charles C. Burleigh, in the letter to Edward M. Davis describing the Mott home on the night of the burning of Pennsylvania Hall, asserted that Abby's presence on the committee was due to the fact that, at the time the question of the equality of women in the Society was originally voted on, some persons were absent "who don't like such movements and who would have contended

against the measure had they been present." When these persons
came to the meeting and discovered that the liberalizing measure
had passed, they said nothing, never dreaming that a woman
would dare to take advantage of the principle that had been established. Once confronted with the repellent fact that a woman was
prepared to accept bona fide presence on a committee, these ob-
jectors tried again and again to have the measure revoked.

Sparing no details of the maneuvers used in the endeavor to
discharge the committee, Burleigh made it plain that the object
of the shifting was to take from Abby Kelly the right of unequivocal membership in the organization.

This letter concludes with a tribute to Abby Kelly's eloquence
in defense of her position and with a further account of the attempts of the opposition to call for repeated voting on the question. When all votes showed the same count, an effort was made to
discharge the committee. This device too was doomed to failure
and Abby Kelly remained on the committee.

The next link in the chain of events that touched Lucretia
Mott, leading eventually to her participation in the Woman's
Rights Movement, was forged when the American Anti-Slavery
Society convened for the Sixth Anniversary Meeting on May 7,
1839, in the Broadway Tabernacle in New York. The question of
the admission of women as full members in the American Anti-
Slavery Society formed the crux of the discussions of this meeting
and became the main issue in the ensuing dissension which split
the Society into two branches.[3]

First of all, the program of the convention was balked by the
intrusion of parliamentary devices designed to block reform. At
the outset of the sessions, Nathaniel Colver, the persistent adversary
of woman's rights, proposed that the "roll call should be made
up according to former usage or men duly appointed" to "consti-
tute the roll." But Oliver Johnson, a consistant liberal, "moved
an amendment, substituting the word *persons* for men." This
amendment read: "Resolved that the roll of this meeting be made
by placing thereon the names of all persons, male & female, who
are delegates from any auxiliary society, or members of this society." In the multiplicity of motions, counter motions, and "calls
for order," that followed, headway seemed at a standstill, and at
the adjournment of the first session, no decisive action had been
taken.

At the next meeting, Garrison, determined that prejudice
against women should not be allowed to make a mockery of the

effort to secure freedom for the slave, succeeded in having a motion passed to the effect that no person was to be allowed "to speak
twice" on the subject until all others desiring to speak should have
spoken; and no person should speak longer than "ten minutes at
a time without the leave of the Society." Thus, filibustering was
for a time checked.

Among the delegates to this annual meeting of the Society was
Amos A. Phelps, often called "the logician" of the antislavery
movement. An honor graduate of Yale College, Phelps had maintained in the Yale Theological Seminary his high undergraduate
record. Entering the ministry, he became a tower of strength to
advocates of reform, a leader who never permitted his intellect to
compromise with convention and prejudice. From the pulpit of
the Pine Street Congregational Church in Boston he had attacked
slavery in his "Lectures on Slavery and Its Remedy." Basing his
arguments on the injustice of slavery, he made no attempt to
strengthen his appeal by the evasion of main issues or the use of
parliamentary tactics. When, therefore, the progress of events at
the 1839 Annual Meeting seemed lost in a hopeless maze of evasions, Phelps, concerned in furthering action on the main issue,
although unsympathetic on the question of Woman's Rights, attempted to end the deadlock by a motion providing that the term
"person" as used in the Constitution of the Society be understood
to include "men and women." But the motion was immediately
challenged.

Spirited discussion continued through four sessions of the Convention. At length an amendment was offered by the Boston lawyer, Ellis Gray Loring, stipulating that "the roll call of this meeting be made by placing thereon the name of all persons, male and
female, who are delegates from any auxiliary Society or members
of this Society." But Loring's amendment had to submit to a number of changed wordings which fortunately did not alter its basic
meaning before the vote was taken and the amendment passed.

When a division was called, the count revealed the fact that
the amendment had received 180 votes, against 140 votes in opposition. But the majority had not been overwhelming. Garrison,
Whittier, Charles C. Burleigh, Robert Purvis, Arnold Buffum
showed at this moment that their attacks on chattel slavery were
founded on the solid rock of human rights; other supporters were
Gerrit Smith, the social reformer from upstate New York, and the
Negro, David Ruggles. In addition to his success in healing ail-
ments by the "water cure" in Florence, Massachusetts, Ruggles

could be relied on to endorse liberal reforms whenever he had an opportunity.

But surprises were in store when the votes were finally registered. The men opposing the admission of women as full members of the National Anti-Slavery Society included some of the strongest, well-nigh radical, antagonists of Negro slavery. The "warm-hearted Beriah Green," beloved president of the democratic Oneida Institute in New York, had graciously permitted Lucretia Mott to speak at the organization meeting of the American Anti-Slavery Society. For Beriah Green it was one thing to allow a gentle-voiced woman to speak in public; but to concede to any woman the right of the principle of unqualified membership in the American Anti-Slavery Society was another, entirely different proposition. Beriah Green, therefore, voted against the measure. James Birney, the elder, had emancipated his slaves in Kentucky; but his son would not vote for the emancipation of women. Charles Torrey of New York was to die in a Baltimore jail while imprisoned for aiding fugitive slaves, but he too was among the reactionaries on the question of the rights of women.

Opposing freedom for women were certain well-known Negroes in New York — the eloquent Episcopal clergyman Peter Williams, the Edinburgh-trained physician James McCune Smith, and the spirited citizen William Downing. Most surprising of all, perhaps, was the attitude of Lewis Tappan, the brother of the Arthur Tappan who had paid Garrison's jail fine and had aided Prudence Crandall. Lewis Tappan's record was also characterized by sympathy for the oppressed. "Pray how does it happen," wrote one rhymster at the time,

> That thou, Lewis Tappan,
> The warm and true hearted of yore,
> Would woman exclude
> From where long she has stood
> And successfully plead for God's poor, Lewis T.
> And successfully plead for God's poor.[4]

But Lewis Tappan not only voted against the amendment, but led the minority to make a formal Protest against the decision on the ground that the step taken by the majority was inconsistent with the spirit and letter of the Constitution of the American Anti-Slavery Society.

In the six years that had passed since the foundation of the Anti-Slavery Society, friction on several points had developed to destroy harmony in the organization — differences of the views of individual members on the question of slavery itself, general policies, and the question of politics. In the division of 1839, the Protest of Lewis Tappan registered one view, but as Birney asserted, the woman question "had led to a split in the Anti-Slavery Society and to the organization of a new one." To this assertion Wendell Phillips replied that, "it was politics which had occasioned the split, and not the introduction of the woman question." [5]

When Lucretia Mott was asked in 1855 to give facts for the forthcoming history of woman's suffrage in America, she wrote,

Let me suggest then, that the opening chapters go further back than the S. S. Split in 1840 — Sarah and Angelina Grimké's labors in Mass. in 1835 and 6 aroused the Clergy; and the "Clerical Appeal" and "Pastoral Letters" were issued which J. G. Whittier and M. W. Chapman satirized in their Poems. The divisions in the A. S. Socy. began in N. Eng. in 37 and 8 — not only against Garrison as a no governt. man, but against women's public labors also. Some prominent abolitionists, who had before given countenance to the Grimké's, now either secretly or more openly acted against woman's co-operative action with men.[6]

And in the fateful year of 1839 she wrote to Maria W. Chapman:

I would not conceal from any my disapprobation of the proceedings of the new organization, from the beginning — the plans and maneuvers of the Ex. Com. in New York, etc., etc. — But if I spoke out my whole heart, it would be in pleading with my friends of the other side, not to be moved by these things, nor suffer themselves to be drawn from the ground of Non-Resistance. I judge you not as having acted improperly in your defense against the high-handed measures of your opponents, — indeed I rather regard you as laboring for the *whole* — not whatever security we may enjoy from a similar encroachments, we are in great measure indebted to your quick-sighted discovery and prompt exposure of. Still the local dissensions and the detail of divisions in your meetings and societies, I have not been willing should be told "in Gath;" and have therefore wished with L. M. Child, that "our dear and much respected friend Garrison would record them more sparingly in his paper." [7]

After the decision, the antislavery program in America was conducted by two organizations. But the new body, taking the name American and Foreign Anti-Slavery Society, expanded the program of the original body to a development of political action among abolitionists. This action was embraced as "the duty of exercising their political power in behalf of the slave." In fact the new organization adopted a "Liberty Ticket" nominating James G. Birney of New York for President of the United States and Thomas Early of Pennsylvania for Vice-President.

At the next annual meeting the National Society went into forthright action by placing on its Executive Committee Lydia Maria Child, Lucretia Mott, and Maria W. Chapman. But, Christopher Slocomb of Medway, Massachusetts, refused to be a delegate to the National body because he felt that the antislavery cause was weakened by the attempt to settle the issue by incorporating it with woman's rights.

The reawakening of the spirit of liberalism in the 1830's was indicated in England by an insistent cry for political reform and for reorganized social conditions, based upon broad, humanitarian principles. As England became increasingly sensitive to injustice, slavery was recognized as a shameful evil to be ended not only in England but throughout the world. The abolition of slavery, therefore, was the goal of the British and Foreign Anti-Slavery Society when it called a World Conference to be held in London, June 12 to June 17, 1840.

From January until June of the year chosen for the conference, news concerning the forthcoming meeting was kept alive in the *Anti-Slavery Reporter,* the weekly organ published "Under Sanction of the British and Foreign Anti-Slavery Society." The first announcement read:

Will you send your full proportion of delegates from the United States? They will receive a hearty and a kind welcome from an Englishman's heart. . . It will be a meeting of extraordinary interest. Not of politicians nor statesmen, warriors, nor literary giants, but of moralists, of philanthropists, of Christians, irrespective of names, sects, rank, or colour, the genuine, unassuming but tried friends of freedom.

But within two months the words of a "Circular" Letter specified that the committee wished to receive from antislavery societies the names of "the gentlemen" representing them. This was the sole reference to the sex of the delegates, for in the five successive issues of the *Reporter* the membership of the Conference was described as constituting "delegates who may be appointed by antislavery bodies both at home and abroad," or "Friends of liberty, both white and black," or "distinguished advocates of liberty," or "All who may . . . come under the general description of friends of the slaves." By these repeated reminders the anti-slavery bodies in America were urged to choose their "full proportion of delegates" and to send to England an immediate official notification of the names of the representatives who were promised "genuine and generous British hospitality."

The American Anti-Slavery Society, its hands untied by the 1839 decision which gave women voting privileges and by the general terms of the original invitation sent out by the British and Foreign Anti-Slavery Society, included among its five delegates to the London Meeting one woman — Lucretia Mott of Philadelphia. Among all the women in America active in the Anti-Slavery Society, Lucretia Mott was deemed the one woman best fitted to represent the National organization. Other women were sent as delegates from the branches — Lucretia herself being a delegate from the Philadelphia Female Anti-Slavery Society and also from the Pennsylvania Branch of the organization — but she was the sole woman representing the national body.

Other members of her delegation were William Lloyd Garrison, of Boston; Nathaniel Peabody Rogers, editor of the Concord, New Hampshire, *Herald of Freedom;* and a Negro, Charles Lennox Remond, representing the Maine Anti-Slavery Society.

The Society was not without warning as to what the effect of a woman delegate would be on the Convention. Writing on March 3, 1840, to a member of the Executive Committee of the American Anti-Slavery Society, the English reformer Joseph Sturge was explicit in his dire prophecy as to the reception any woman delegates would receive. "I am sure the kindest thing to them" he concluded in his letter, "as well as the best for our cause, would be for you to do all you can to discourage it." [8]

On the question of the selection of the delegates, Garrison, as the Business Committee reported, said "We will see whether the Convention will dare to reject the delegate of the American Anti-Slavery Society; and if they do, we will see whether the world will recognize such a Convention as its representative — whether it will stand as 'the World's Convention.' "

Immediately after this action of the Society Garrison wrote Lucretia Mott a letter that she must have liked. Dated April 28, 1840, it is a frank expression of his friendship for James and Lucretia Mott and an acknowledgment of "the many kindnesses" he had received from these friends "through a period of ten years." But the immediate significance of the letter comes toward the end. He wrote,

I have scarcely left any room to tell you how delighted I am to learn that you and James are soon to embark for England, in order to be at the World's Convention. My heart leaped at the intelligence; for I could not be reconciled to the thought that you were to remain behind. I am pleased beyond measure, and have only to regret that I shall not be able to go over in the same packet with you both; but duty required me to be at the anniversary of the Parent Society, which is pregnant with good or evil to our sacred cause.[9]

And just two days after Garrison's letter was written, the "beloved friends Lucretia and James Mott" were warmly recommended "To the Abolitionists of Great Britain" by the "Association of Friends for promoting the Abolition of Slavery and improving the condition of the Free People of Colour." To this document signed at "Cherry Street Meeting-house Philadelphia, 5 mo. 1st, 1840," by the "Clerks, Caleb Clothier and Anne Churchman," were affixed fifty other signatures.

When it became known that the American Anti-Slavery Society was including a woman among the delegates to the London Convention, the very novelty of this step taken by the Society produced a stir of censure and praise. As a rule, the detractors singled out Garrison as the target of attack, but Lucretia Mott did not escape admonition, unfriendly criticism, even rebuke. The editor of the *Emancipator* reminded her that she was ". . . a matron of mature years, sound judgment and cultivated mind . . . an accredited minister of the gospel" and as such she should treat with courteous regard the "views and feelings of those loyal subjects of a monarchical government, by whose courteous invitation the Convention is assembled."

Moreover, the writer declared that the sufferings of the slave cried out more pitiably for redress than the so-called wrongs of women and that should Mrs. Mott feel impelled to speak she should voice her opinions only after permission had been given her by the Convention.[10]

Less veiled is the language of the *Pittsburgh Christian Witness* which accused Lucretia of lacking respect for her sex and of consenting to be "The Tool of a Disorganizer for the purpose of accomplishing his ambitious designs." Conceding that Mrs. Mott had no superior in her virtues "for kindness, hospitality, benevolence and purity of life," and, although she was an utter moralist, the newspaper nevertheless called her a religious "latitudinarian," one whose zeal might cause her "to far forget the true dignity of womanhood in her intractable soul for what she terms principle."

Concluding, the article warned Mrs. Mott that if she tried to take her scat as a delegate in the World's Anti-Slavery Convention, her advisors would bear the guilt "of putting back the day of the slave's redemption, and sacrificing mercy and righteousness to an insane caprice." [11]

Garrison himself held no illusions as to the possibility of a woman's receiving a friendly reception at the English Convention. Confessing his uneasiness to George Bradburn, a member of the Massachusetts Legislature from Nantucket, he requested Bradburn to appeal to the English abolitionist George Thompson to have women recognized as equal beings in the Convention.[12] Then, in the words of his pilot's letter, written to the *Liberator* from the packet ship "Columbus," near Sandy Hook, May 22, 1840, Garrison shared his apprehensions with a larger audience. He asked,

With a young woman placed on the throne of Great Britain, will the philanthropists of that country presume to object to the female delegates of the United States, as members of the Convention on the ground of their sex? In what assembly however august or select, is that almost peerless woman, Lucretia Mott, not qualified to take a part?

He declared that should "one human being" be excluded, he might enter a protest though, referring to the members in the National Society who had organized a new body, he would "neither secede nor new organize."

Another pilot's letter, that of Nathaniel P. Rogers, also hinted of shoals ahead. Like Garrison, Rogers referred to the inconsistency of the English Anti-Slavery Society in its refusal to welcome women delegates to a convention in a country governed by a woman. He pointed out,

If Victoria can be high Admiral of England, the head of her navies and grand marshall of her forces by land, as well as head of the church, surely Lucretia Mott may bear testimony against human slavery in England in a peaceful quiet convention of Christians.[13]

Lucretia Mott, while grateful for the honor of being the one American woman chosen by the National Society, was not wholly engrossed with her immediate preparation for the trip. On the eve of sailing, she took the time to write a leisurely reply to a letter from Maria W. Chapman. After explaining her satisfaction in hearing from Mrs. Chapman and referring to Mrs. Chapman's pamphlet, *Right and Wrong in Massachusetts,* she goes on to make some comment on Richard Hildreth's *Despotism in America*: "Who would have thought so many new views and arguments," she wrote, "could be presented? What a nice little history, in the Introduction of the progress of Democracy in this country; When I finished it I felt as if I should like to begin and read it again."

Then she informed Mrs. Chapman of the failure of an attempt to induce the Pennsylvania Anti-Slavery Branch to take an active part in the friction between the Massachusetts Branch and the National Society, adding her regret that her own effort had not been strong enough to induce the Pennsylvania Branch to send a sympathetic reply to the Massachusetts Branch. Taking up the subject of the London Convention she expressed her disappointment that Lydia Maria Child was not going to London, adding that she herself would send Mrs. Child had she the means. "How sorry I am," she wrote, "that circumstances will prevent thy being there" and "Why can't Caroline or Anne W. represent your Socy? Who of the New Organization will be sent? No woman I conclude."

And just before mentioning her date of sailing she interposes a word indicating how close to her heart were the affairs of her church: "We should not be at the Anniversary Mg. in N.Y. if we were in the country for it occurs during the week of our Yearly Mg. which would keep us at home." A final note in this letter was a word on the state of Anti-Slavery as organized in America:

I am more & more convinced that new and old organization can no more walk together. Joshua Leavitt's editorials of late and Gerrit Smith's letter with the charges against his brethern surprised and grieved me much. I have even hoped that J. G. W. would have his eyes opened by such letters and denunciations but he certainly seems to be blinded & pours all his censures upon our party.[14]

In spite though of the rift in the American Anti-Slavery ranks, the Motts, "James Mott, Philadelphia and Lady," left New York for London on May 5, 1840, sailing on the packet ship "Roscoe."

Chapter Eight

"THE PROPER SPHERE
OF WOMEN"
GREAT BRITAIN—1840

Lucretia Mott has left a Diary describing her only visit to Europe. The almost day-by-day record in her delicately-lined, firm handwriting comprises a small, leather-bound book of 1,000 pages, bearing on its flyleaf the inscription: "Lucretia Mott, Philadelphia 1840/Memoranda during a Passage to & from/England and/Three Months Travel/in/Great Britain and Ireland." [1]

Among the thirty-two cabin passengers on the "Roscoe," commanded by Captain Huttleson, was the Motts' traveling party composed of the Philadelphians Sarah Pugh, Abby Kimber, Elizabeth Neall, Mary Grew, and Mary Grew's father, Henry Grew.[2] This group found congenial association in the abolitionists Isaac Winslow of Maine and his daughter Emily, George Bradburn of Nantucket, and Abby Southwick of Boston. Winslow was a signer of the Declaration of the American Anti-Slavery Society; and Miss Southwick was the courageous President of the Boston Female Anti-Slavery Society, who had refused to disband the meeting when a Boston mob invaded it searching for the English abolitionist, George Thompson.

Although sick in the heavy late-spring storms, Lucretia managed to move about from stem to stern of the small boat, while chatting with her fellow passengers. Apparently she kept her eyes open, for her Diary is alive with pictures of the storms at sea, the sociability of the passengers, the competence of the captain and crew, and the prevailing friendliness of all. A comforting fact for her was the sobriety of the passengers. But in 1840 sober, quiet seagoing travelers, as Lucretia described her shipmates, were not found invariably on the packet ships. Garrison, sailing on the "Columbus" a fortnight later, denounced most vigorously the drinking and the din of boisterous revelry throughout the ship. Not a moment's quiet, he observed, could be obtained.[3]

Lucretia was frequently down in the steerage trying to comfort the mothers, seasick themselves and worried in caring for their "children with measles." On the second Sunday at sea Henry Grew conducted religious services, referred to in the Diary as the "Meeting on 1st. day. Father Grew read & preached — some additional remarks well received." [4] The reference to "additional remarks" is clarified by an observation made by George Bradburn that Grew's sermon on the atonement was vague and lacking power of conviction whereas Mrs. Mott's words on "the importance of love and good works" awakened a thoughtful response among her hearers. In Bradburn's words, "the perception of disagreement or want of harmony between sentiments uttered by the two preachers may have had the good effect of setting some of the hearers to thinking. There are unthinking hearers as well as forgetful hearers of the words."

On May 27 the three-weeks' voyage came to an end, and an overnight stop in Liverpool inaugurated Lucretia's experiences in England. A three-mile ride from Liverpool by coach took her to the country home of the unorthodox Quaker, Isaac Crewdson. She was indifferent to Crewdson's recent secession from the body of conforming English Quakers; but the visit to his after-hours school for young factory workers gave her positive satisfaction. This social experiment she considered an example of "practical Christianity." With Sarah Pugh, Abby Kimber, and George Bradburn she had a "delightful visit" at Crewdson's "beautiful place." But, while she was enthusiastic over Crewdson's independence, over the social progress he achieved "in the instruction of the children employed in his Factory," she could not understand why these young Quakers were given lessons in the subjects of baptism and the Lord's Supper. She was also shocked by the ornate structure and the elaborate furnishings of the Meetinghouse, as seen in the wood carvings, upholstery, and carpets.

On their way from Liverpool to London the travelers spent nine or ten days in passing through some of the Midland towns of England: Chester, Manchester, Warwick, Oxford, and Windsor. In this bird's-eye view of a section of England, Lucretia admired the countryside, a region, it seemed to her, of pleasant meadows, vast moorlands, and winding streams that merged in a twinkling into little villages of thatched cottages huddled around low-towered churches. And from the doors of these simple cottages she often got glimpses of sturdy laborers, busy housewives, and rosy-cheeked children.

All this warmed her heart; but she was by no means blind to

what she considered the inequalities in British customs and traditions, to what seemed the manifestations of grave social differences. To her, Warwick and Kenilworth castles — structures that inspire in the average observer wonder, admiration, and awe — were not the sublime remains of the spiritual and artistic life of a past age. She thought these remains of the art and religion of a past age were "ruins indeed," "a catch penny." To her the boys' choirs in the English churches "bordered on the ridiculous." And, in her republican principles, she resented certain types of English charity. What particularly aroused her scorn was the "Hospital of the Twelve Brethren," a home for indigent tradesmen maintained on a bequest ample enough to permit the beneficiaries to dress, as Lucretia deplored, like gentlemen and to live an idle carefree existence. From her seat on the stagecoach lumbering through regions immortalized in song and story she marveled that the scarlet-coated drivers could entertain the passengers by reciting long passages of relevant English poetry, that they were so intelligent, so thoroughly steeped in the traditions, literary lore, and history of their country. "Fat, fine-looking John Bulls," she portrayed them, who "seldom left their seats" to give assistance to hostlers when horses were changed. But she was spellbound in pride to recall her Nantucket forebears by the sight of a "pleasant kitchen" "old furniture like Grandfather Folgers. Jack for roasting — large bellows, 3 cornered chairs, large andirons — pipe box, iron and brass candlesticks, etc."

At Stratford-on-Avon she was shown Shakespeare's birthplace, "much to the gratification of our company," she conceded; but irresponsive to the grandeur of England's great poetry, lacking interest in any poetry except that of the Graveyard School, she exulted that her husband stood on Shakespeare's grave. She was unable, however, to remain indifferent to the glory of the English universities: the stained glass in New College, the oak carvings in Trinity, the dignity of the Bodleian Library, and the grandeur of Christ Church.[5]

When the travelers arrived in London, Lucretia Mott learned that the credentials of the women delegates were not to be honored. According to Sarah Pugh, the representative to the Convention from the Philadelphia Female Anti-Slavery Society, information was received from the Executive Committee of the British and Foreign Anti-Slavery Society that the presentation of the claims of the women delegates would cause strife and dissension "injurious to the cause of emancipation." Pressure was even exerted on these delegates, as Lucretia wrote, to refrain from the attempt to achieve their right to be a part of the Convention. Two Englishmen, William Morgan and William Scales, confessed frankly that as an actual fact the term "World Convention" was meaningless, "mere Political license & that all power would rest with the London Com. of arrangt." Different men extenuated the decision of the Executive Committee in different reasons. The prejudice against women, displayed by Samuel Prescod, a Jamaican Negro, recalled the inconsistency of J. McCune Smith and Peter Williams at the 1839 meeting of the American Anti-Slavery Society. Prescod offered the gratuitous explanation that the recognition of women would lower the dignity of the assembly; but he was silenced by Lucretia Mott when she reminded him that the American Anti-Slavery Society had refused to listen to that "flimsy argument," when it was raised against the admission of Negroes to the organization.[6]

The reactionary Nathaniel Colver embittered the tension when he made the charge that women were "constitutionally unfit for public or business meetings." Confronting this persistent antagonist, Lucretia Mott made such a sharp retort to Colver that he stalked away from the group. In Sarah Pugh's report was the statement that after the committee denied the appeal presented by the women of Philadelphia no course was open to the visitors except to take the seats set apart for them. In Lucretia's words: "Were kindly admitted behind the bar politely conducted to our seats & introduced to many whom we had not met before."[7]

"Behind the bar" Lucretia Mott was surrounded by a not undistinguished circle of sympathizers; in this group were the American women delegates — Sarah Pugh, Abby Kimber, and Wendell Phillips' wife Anne, joined by a fourth American woman, Elizabeth Cady Stanton.[8] Mrs. Stanton, the bride of Henry B. Stanton, a leader in the newly organized American and Foreign Anti-Slavery Society, was not a delegate; but, self-consecrated from her early years to secure woman's rights, "she gladly took her seat with the rejected delegates." Forming a part of this little band were some well-known Englishwomen, including Lady Byron and Amelia Opie. Here also were Lucretia Mott's fellow delegates from the American Anti-Slavery Society, Garrison, Nathaniel P. Rogers, and Charles Lennox Remond. Garrison had arrived in London only to witness the confirmation of his ominous apprehensions. On the principle that the failure of the Convention to recognize the credentials similar to those he bore extended a like restriction on him, he then decided that he should sit with the rejected delegates.

The procedures of the assembly had barely started when Thomas Clarkson entered the hall, accompanied by his daughter-in-law and his little grandson. The appearance of the venerable Clarkson must have recalled to Lucretia Nine Partners School and the voice of her teacher Deborah Rogers who told the school children about Clarkson's *History of the Slave Trade*.

According to the official report of the Convention, as recorded in the *British and Foreign Anti-Slavery Reporter* the question of the recognition of the credentials of all delegates was opened on the floor of the Convention [9] by Wendell Phillips, the acknowledged orator of the American Anti-Slavery Society. But Phillips was more than a dynamic orator. Sharing Garrison's singleness of purpose and consecration to an ideal, he brought to nineteenth-century reform the force of wholesome logic. An honor graduate of Harvard University, he used his keen mind in the cause of justice, the mind that was like a finely-tempered sword in the hands of a master. Like a flash he penetrated the heart of issues, recognizing the principles behind deeds. With his temper consistently restrained, he presented arguments that became irrefutable, losing nothing by his commanding presence, his high social standing, his wealth. While wholly sincere in his adoption of the antislavery principles, he was more urbane, less impetuous than Garrison; but again like Garrison, his ideal of freedom embraced complete freedom for women as well as for Negro slaves.

As soon, therefore, as the aged Clarkson had withdrawn from the assembly, Wendell Phillips offered the motion "That a committee of five be appointed to prepare a correct list of the members of this convention with instructions to include in such list all persons bearing credentials from any Anti-Slavery body." Completely aware of the temper of the assembly, he followed this formal resolution by admitting his knowledge of the fact that a list of the delegates had already been prepared for the Convention by the Committee of Arrangements, a list he regretted that omitted the names of the women delegates from the Anti-Slavery Branch of Massachusetts. These women, he stated, had been chosen as representatives after their Branch had received the invitation from London, an invitation that declared itself to be "to the friends of the slave of every nation and of every clime."

But the main point urged by Phillips was directed against the authority given to the London Committee to settle the qualifications of membership in the World's Convention.

Following Phillips was young William Adam, a native of Scotland, listed in the *Catalogue of the Officers and Students of Harvard University for the Academical Year 1839–40* as "Rev. William Adam, Professor of Oriental Literature." In seconding Phillips' motion, Adam stated that he felt that his views on the issue were in entire concurrence with the opinion of Wendell Phillips; moreover he took the position that he also was excluded from the convention because he had credentials no different from those held by the excluded women delegates. To the surprise of the American delegates, George Bradburn, a reputedly consistent liberal, made no protest against the stand of the London Convention. Later he excused his action by declaring that the position he took was made "to bring out others." He added, however, that the Convention would lose its significance as a world's convention if any delegates were to be excluded. Several clergymen, among whom was Henry Grew, derided the very idea of admitting women, one divine even going so far as to declare that it would be better to dissolve the Convention than to give women the status of delegates.

Two Englishmen were conspicuous in taking a stand against their fellow countrymen on the London Committee: one was William Ashurst, an enthusiastic believer in America's democratic principles and an admirer of Garrison and Lucretia Mott; the other was Sir John Bowring — poet, linguist, scholar, liberal, and humanitarian.

By many, Sir John Bowring is distinguished chiefly as the scholarly editor of the *Westminster Review;* a great number — unaware, perhaps, of his authorship of the well-beloved hymn, "In the Cross of Christ I Glory" — pay unconscious tribute to him. After George Stacey, a member of the British Committee, attempted to justify the exclusion of the women, Sir John began to speak. Declaring that "the custom of excluding females is more honored in the breach than in the observance," he emphasized the fact that England's sovereign was a woman, "one who has been exercising her great and benignant influence in opposing slavery by sanctioning, no doubt, the presence of her illustrious consort at an anti-slavery meeting." "The delegation from America," he added, was to him "one of the most encouraging and the most delightful symptoms of the time."

The men favorable to the recognition of the women delegates confined their arguments to the points at issue. They cited the general terms of the invitation, the obligation of the women to represent the associations sending them, and the obligations of the Convention to honor the credentials borne by women. Moreover, these defenders of the principles involved emphasized also the subject of the Convention, the issue of world federation rather than the specific custom of one country, England, and the gravity of excluding delegates who had taken such a major part in the labors of the antislavery cause; and Phillips noted the fact that the delegates had not been selected by the Convention itself. Those speaking against the rights of women resorted generally to emotional appeals designed at one moment to make the subject appear ridiculous and to justify masculine sense of superiority and, at another time, to flatter women while consigning them to a state of childlike inferiority. And, like their prototypes who opposed the equal rights amendment considered by the New England Anti-Slavery Society, these reactionaries were mainly clergymen.

Finally, George Thompson took the floor. From this eloquent English abolitionist, a plea for the recognition of all delegates was naturally expected. But, in spite of his fearless antislavery crusade, in spite of the fact that women had protected him from mob violence in Boston, Thompson followed a vacillating course at the London Convention. At first he urged the importance of the question and the duty of the Convention to the constituents of the women delegates. He admitted that the idea of the equality of women was inherent in the resolution, but added that it was "contrary to custom, use and principle" although "a flimsy excuse for their exclusion." Then, Thompson, extolled by Garrison as the man who would "go for humanity irrespective of sex," moved the withdrawal of Wendell Phillips' proposition.

Consistency, reason, justice, and maturity of aspect took a holiday, while pleas of "English custom and principles," "the will of God," "the proper sphere of women," "the forcing of an abstract question," and "the numerical weakness of the defenders of the motion" were offered to support a prejudiced stand.

Having thus excluded the women delegates from the floor of the hall, the London Anti-Slavery Convention proceeded without further incident. But in the official list of male delegates, 493 in all, as printed in the *Anti-Slavery Reporter,* the name of one man, "James Mott, Esq. Eastern Pennsylvania," was starred. In explanation a footnote read: "Erroneously stated in a former number to be a member of the Society of Friends." In commenting on this footnote, Wendell Phillips said,

The Anti-Slavery Reporter had called James Mott "a member of the Society of Friends." The next number, which contained the official roll and report of our meeting, had this note affixed to his name: "Erroneously stated in a former number to be a member of the Society of Friends." They had found out in the interim that he was a "Hicksite" — and so this bantling of the British and Foreign Association became the organ of the Orthodox Quaker antipathy, and was made to settle that "Hicksites" were not Friends, though they were denied the right to decide who were members of their own body.

Lucretia Mott missed nothing of this procedure. In the set-off section of Free-Masons Hall she found herself in a position not entirely unlike the role accorded her in the American Anti-Slavery Convention of 1833. Again she was an observer at an assembly of men meeting to devise means to secure freedom for the slave while denying equality to women; and among the delegates to the London Convention she observed three signers of the Constitution of the American Anti-Slavery Society — Garrison, Isaac Winslow, and her husband James Mott.

But since 1833 some things had changed. The exclusion of women from the deliberation of an assembly receiving partial support from women had been accepted as a matter of course in 1833; but within a few years such exclusion had become a debatable question, a controversial issue leading to far-reaching but undreamed of consequences. From her seat in the gallery, Lucretia Mott heard the "woman question," which was not mentioned in 1833 at the organization meeting of the American Anti-Slavery Society, vigorously argued. She listened to attempts to placate women while denying them the status of maturity and equality; but she was cheered by the keen and fearless logic of Wendell Phillips, the high ground taken by Professor Adam, and the final efforts of the liberal members of the Convention to inject reason into the body by urging the registering of a Protest. This Protest, introduced by James Mott, specified that the Convention by excluding authorized delegates had permitted itself to be led solely by the London Committee and had been guilty of partiality in enforcing the rules of order.

The irony of this failure to secure a semblance of justice lay in the fact that the motion to have the Protest laid on the table was made by Nathaniel Colver. In 1839 Colver had tried in vain to breast the tide of liberalism as expressed in the Non-Resistant Movement; and in the same year he had fought, vainly it is true, the issue of admitting women into full membership in the ranks of the American Anti-Slavery Society. In London he was in a more congenial atmosphere. Doubtless he found the reactionary spirit of the Convention agreeable; and probably he felt that his part in the proceedings was settlement of an old score.

When the Protest was lost, Colver walked up to Lucretia Mott, saying, "Now, if the spirit moves you to speak on this subject, say on — you will be allowed to say what you wish." Silently she ignored his insult. But she was utterly fair to the Convention. "We discovered," she admitted, "before we left Philadelphia that the name of the Convention was changed and saw the letter from Josh Sturge — hence we recd. our credentials conditionally — & after being refused by the Com. we felt satisfied not to present them to the Meeting." [10]

The question was raised as to whether Lucretia Mott should not have registered an objection at this moment. She was accustomed to speaking in gatherings composed largely of men; she had addressed legislative assemblies in America; time and again she had defended in public her convictions. But, in spite of her outraged sense of justice, she realized that the trouble lay in the error made by the World Convention in placing authority in the hands of the London Committee. Authority, once given, had to be supported.

As a matter of fact she did endeavor to rouse English women to protest; but Sarah Pugh, in a letter to Richard Webb, July 2, 1840, attributed the failure of this effort to the fact that English women, having accepted for years a subordinate position, were powerless to take initiative in their own defense. Another side to the apparent unwillingness of English women to rally to Lucretia's support was offered by Anne Knight in a letter to Margaretta Forten of Philadelphia. Writing the Webbs on February 25, 1842, Lucretia quoted Mrs. Knight as having written to Margaretta that Lucretia would have received in England a more cordial, a warmer reception had it not been for her irreligion, that "she [Lucretia] rejects her Lord and turns with disgust from his 'hanging on a tree,' his being slain, his blood shed, that she recoils from what 'she calls so gross an idea' and desires not what the angels desire to look into — the scheme of redemption." Yet Mrs. Knight admitted that in spite of "this deep and hardened revolt," she herself "loved L. M. for her work's sake." [11]

Lucretia did not evade the criticism aroused by her silence. In a letter to Mrs. Chapman, written on the eve of the Motts' return to America, she brought up the subject:

Abby Kelly asks Wm. L. G. in a letter if, as they fear, L. Mott has sacrificed principle at the Altar of Peace — Now I don't know how far she will consider me as having done so — I have sometimes shrunk from a defence of our rights when others have gone forward and stood in the breech and I am very willing to crown such with laurels that I may not deserve. . . I was glad, however, that Wendell Phillips and Ann were not so easily put by and that he came forward and manfully plead for the right. I shall ever love Ann Phillips for her earnest appeals to her husband to stand firm in that hour of trial — and him for doing so.[12]

She continued,

Tell Abby Kelly if I am not bold myself I respect those most who are so — Tho' I fully believe if our English and Irish friends thought there were any in America whose foreheads were more as [sic] adamant than mine, thcy would be awe-struck — yes horrified! I never failed in our several tea-parties-soires, and to avail myself of every offer made for utterance for our cause and then I shrunk not from the whole truth as those who heard can testify.

And she explained this apparent self-commendation by adding, "Egotism must be excused for Woman's sake."

Responsibility for the rejection of the women has been laid to the New Organization of the Anti-Slavery Society, to the Quakers, and to the belief in the inequality of women.

There seems to be no evidence that the New Organization took any official action in the controversy at the London Convention by instructing its delegates to oppose the recognition of the women delegates. On the other hand, as noted in the Diary on July 11, Lucretia did write to John Morgan of the London Anti-Slavery office her "regrets," "that English Usage, American New Organization and sectarian proscription combined, have excluded herself and her friends from such participation in the labors of the Convention as they as American Abolitionists had a right to expect." It is difficult, therefore, to ignore the suspicion that the representatives of the American and Foreign Anti-Slavery Association to the London Convention should share, with Orthodox Quakers in America and England, the responsibility for the rejection of the women. One New Organizationist, however, Henry B. Stanton, was credited with voting for the acceptance of the "Protest." But he was the husband of Elizabeth Cady Stanton.

Were the Quakers responsible? Numbers of English Quakers in the London Convention were men given ordinarily to recognizing the equality of women in their Meeting, but they were bitterly opposed to the group of non-Orthodox Quakers — the branch of Lucretia Mott's affiliation. English Quakers might have remembered that Lucretia Mott's signature was appended to the letter sent in 1830 by the Philadelphia Yearly Meeting to English Friends. Lucretia observed that the visitors were told that the secret of the unfriendliness lay in the matter of religious faith, "that it was announced in London Yearly Mg. that we were coming, and that they were put on their guard." [13] In London the Motts stayed in an informal family boardinghouse, No. 6 Queen Street Place, Southwark Bridge, Cheapside, where several of the American delegates were stopping. Presumably, it did not take the host, Mark Moore, long to become impressed with the sagacity of Lucretia Mott. Like many other Englishmen, he may have heard of her eloquence. At any rate, he arranged for her a religious meeting in a Baptist assembly room, when, as she recorded the occurrence, "Some Friends, hearing of it, came forward and represented us in such a manner as to induce them to withdraw the grant."

On another occasion the Orthodox Quakers among the Americans were invited to tea at the home of the prominent English Quaker, Samuel Gurney. The explanation for the failure to extend the hospitality to the Motts was that the young people had to be "protected" against Hicksite principles.[14]

Her picture of yet another experience is an accusation of English Friends: "Tea at Crown and Anchor; the closing scene of abolitionists! . . . Here were about four hundred present, at three tables run the length of the room and the fourth across the 'top' in the center of which Wm. D. Crewdson sat as chairman. The speakers were, C. L. Remond, Campbell, Gov. of Sierra Leone, G. Thompson." A paper was sent up saying, "L. M. is confidently expected to make the next speech." "She was therefore called on — the President announced her, when J. Scoble who had a choice in her not thus exposing herself — stood and requested to first make some explanations of Campbell's speech as *that* was of *importance* — his request was drowned by cries of 'No! No! — Mrs. Mott' — so she had to inform them that she would endeavor to occupy but little time. . . . She was patiently heard — and no explanation was then begged by friend Scoble as the time was passed." [15]

The English William Howitt wrote to Lucretia Mott:

It is pitiable that you were excluded on the plea of being women; but it is disgusting that, under that plea, you were actually excluded as heretics. That is the real ground of your exclusion, and it ought to have been at once proclaimed and exposed by the liberal members of the Convention, but I believe they were not aware of the fact.[16]

Howitt's collaborator, Mary Howitt, paid gracious tribute to Lucretia. She wrote to her sister Anne,

The English Friends whose women go up and down preaching, and who have their meetings and discipline, have, nevertheless, refused to receive these women delegates from America. I wish thou could see and hear Lucretia Mott. She is a glorious, noble-minded woman and a plain Friend too. The English Friends will not receive her because she is a Hicksite. They also say they think women thus sent by an entire nation are out of their place.[17]

Yet it does not follow that the entire responsibility should be borne by the Friends. Strong prejudice was held, both in England and America, against women's taking part in public life. A step of progress here or a concession granted there was viewed as an impending change in the pattern of the social fabric. Certainly it was felt among a large group of men that any action leading to the emancipation of women should be opposed. Lucretia Mott was a magnetic public speaker. Perhaps the Convention was unwilling to risk the danger of radical utterances from Lucretia Mott, such as she might bring to the floor were she an accepted delegate. According to Wendell Phillips, even Thomas Clarkson had been virtually forced by the Committee to omit one-third of his prepared speech (the section relating to India).[18]

When Benjamin Robert Haydon, the English painter, refused to put Lucretia Mott's picture in the foreground of his painting of the delegates, he explained, "Lucretia Mott, the leader of the delegate women from America, sat. I found her out to have infidel notions, and resolved at once, narrow-minded or not, not to give her the prominent place I first intended. I will reserve that for a beautiful believer in the divinity of Christ." But within a week he observed: "Sketched Lady Byron and Lucretia Mott." [19]

But, despite the opposition, Lucretia Mott counted her trip a voyage of wondrous experiences. The Convention was a matter of a few days; but for three months she had opportunity to travel through Great Britain, to see the country and its institutions, to meet men and women of sympathetic feeling and broad understanding. Liking people, she enjoyed from the bottom of her heart the pleasures of English social life.

All reports concerning Lucretia Mott did not come to England from Orthodox Friends and members of New Organization. Her uncompromising independence and her eloquence were matters of public knowledge, and words describing her sincerity, simplicity, and modesty preceded her across the Atlantic. Many English men and women were eager to meet her. Elizabeth Pease, a member of a family of wealthy Quakers of Darlington, had been told by Maria W. Chapman of the indignity suffered by Lucretia at the hands of the Delaware mob. "She is," Mrs. Chapman had written to Elizabeth Pease, "a woman in a thousand and I hope you will become acquainted with her." [20]

Hospitality was shown the Motts by George Combe, the phrenologist, who had had a pleasant visit at the Motts' Philadelphia home in 1839. Learning that the Motts were in England, he eagerly renewed the friendship by introducing Lucretia to Lady Byron and welcoming the Motts to "Georgia Cottage," the Combe home in Edinburgh. In response to an invitation, Lucretia called on Harriet Martineau, making this reference to the visit: "Rode to Tynemouth on Railroad — walked a mile to seaside — found H. Martineau in comfortable lodgings seated at a window overlooking the sea — she received us cordially — entered into pleasant conversation and two or three hours passed almost before we were aware of it — James walked out to the shore and castle — her sister Greenhow called and sat awhile with us — a handsome and agreeable woman — many subjects were touched upon — the Furnesses, a favorite theme — the loss of so many friends a painful one." A day or two later Miss Martineau's letter of her own joy in the meeting is recorded also in the Diary. [21]

From Thomas Clarkson the visitors received a gracious call and an acknowledgment of the work in the antislavery cause performed by the "American ladies." Other entries in the Diary point to expressions of English hospitality, mainly from well-known English liberals. As Lucretia Mott went from one English home to another, to luncheons, teas, dinners, "soirees," she delighted in the "intellectual feasts" as she called them — the casual discussions that touched doctrines of religion, education, English and American social life, the sphere of woman, economic problems, prison life, the neglect of families, and even her own habit of knitting. For her there were no dull moments in these social gatherings, no incidents of significant unpleasantness in these weeks.

It was inevitable that she desired to see Thomas Carlyle, whose stormy advocacy of rugged independence had awakened admiration in America. Indeed, it was in America that Carlyle's *Sartor Resartus* was published before England was ready to accept the writing. Lucretia's call on Carlyle was not at first satisfactory. On the heart of the "Sage of Chelsea" the condition of the poverty-stricken working classes of England weighed more heavily than the sufferings of the faraway American slave: England's own social problem seemed the more immediate issue. Therefore, when Lucretia Mott, the American abolitionist, went to Chelsea she received a cool reception. But years before this visit Carlyle had written, in his "Essay on Burns," that sincerity makes an inevitable appeal to the human spirit, that words, "if they are earnest and sincere will find some response within us." [22] At any event, as he listened to her voice, such a "response" was awakened in him. And, as Lucretia concluded her account of the visit, "he was more free before we parted — gave us his autograph — Talked of Emerson, Furness, etc." [23]

After the Directors of the Glasgow Emancipation Society refused to include Lucretia Mott among the speakers at the Great Anti-Slavery meeting held in Glasgow following the sessions of the London Convention, the Glasgow Unitarian Congregation invited Lucretia to speak in their Chapel at a time of her own choosing. This invitation came through the courtesy of George Harris, minister of the Unitarian Chapel.

Concerning this speech, Lucretia writes in the Diary: "S. Pugh and self to Union Street conferred with Mrs. Harris about evening meeting — seemed anxious that all things should be right — questioned as to service — would we like to have prayers? Met at $\frac{1}{2}$ past 6 — house full — very attentive — abundant satisfaction expressed." [24]

On her way from Liverpool to London, Lucretia had made some general observations on Isaac Crewdson's after-hours school for factory workers. In her pleasure over this venture in what she described as "practical Christianity" she had barely recorded her disapproval of some features of Crewdson's experiment. But after the London Convention her observations were sharpened; one might even say that she began to look for inequalities. In fact after a visit to certain cotton factories, she conceded that the women and children seemed better than she expected to find them, that the homes appeared more comfortable than she had imagined them to be.

Lucretia Mott left Great Britain richer in friends, among whom was Elizabeth Cady Stanton. Because of the position of

Henry B. Stanton in the New Organization and the influence of friends antagonistic to the original American Anti-Slavery Society, his wife had felt aversion toward Lucretia Mott as "the strong-minded radical," "a very dangerous person," one to be shunned. Imagine Elizabeth's surprise at meeting the serene Lucretia as a table companion in Mark Moore's inn. Listening to a gentle-mannered woman holding her own in discussions among the men at the table, Mrs. Stanton was immediately won over. On her part Lucretia was pleased by the younger woman; and from this time on the name of Elizabeth Cady Stanton appeared again and again in the Diary. This attachment, which at the moment resulted in Elizabeth's sharing the emotions of the rejected delegates at the London Convention, developed into a lasting friendship between the two women. Years afterward Mrs. Stanton, in addressing by letter the Eighth Women's Rights Convention in Mozart Hall, New York, recalled the occasion of her meeting Lucretia Mott at the time of the 1840 London Convention:

They came to strike off the chains that bound the black man down, but to rivet them more firmly on those who fain would rise themselves; . . . This sacrifice of human rights by an allied Priest-hood, was offered up in the presence of such women as Lady Noel Byron, Mary Howitt, Anna Jamieson, and our own Lucretia Mott, the latter a delegate from one of the oldest and most efficient Anti-Slavery Societies in America. She, too, sat a silent spectator, though a public speaker, and a member of that sect of Christians who believe in women being moved by the spirit.[25]

Three delegates to the London Convention were James, Richard, and Thomas Webb of Dublin. An invitation to visit these liberals came to the Motts, and after the Convention this offer of Irish hospitality was accepted; at the same time the opportunity was afforded Lucretia to make an address at a Temperance Meeting in Dublin. This speech, as Richard Webb described it to Garrison, "a slice of peace, anti-slavery, moral reform, temperance and womans rights," was "listened to with great respect and attention." [26]

James and Lucretia Mott were immediately drawn to Richard Webb and his wife Hannah, and the visit in the Webbs' home was one of the Motts' happiest experiences in Britain. To Richard Webb is due a sketch of Lucretia Mott that appeared in the *Dublin Weekly Herald*. Describing her *"the lioness"* of the Convention, he added that she dwarfed "Clarkson, Buxton, O'Connel, Garrison, Thompson, . . . Birney."

When Lucretia learned of this tribute, her response, in a letter to Elizabeth Pease, was: "As to the lion part, we felt much more that we were created as 'sheep for the slaughter.' " She also commented ". . . abolitionists have praised each other too much." The days in London and Ireland with the Webbs were the beginning of a friendship maintained and expressed by an exchange of letters singly or jointly written by James and Lucretia Mott and their Irish friends, Richard and Hannah Webb.

While visiting the Webbs in Dublin, Lucretia sent to Maria W. Chapman an extremely long letter summarizing her own opinions of the procedure in the London Convention. "The World's Convention," she pictured as "no more than a conference of the British and Foreign A.–S. Society to be composed of such members as their Com. of Arrangement should choose to select," adding "that the name 'The World's Convention' was merely 'a poetical license' (alias a rhetorical flourish) — and that the 'Com' in their wisdom had seen meet to ordain and enact, that women should not compose part of that august body." "All arrangements of the said committee," she added, were to be "sanctioned and approved by the Conference." She explained the reticence of Englishwomen to protest their exclusion by the fact that English customs had kept women in a subordinate position, permitting them only the "drudgery" of publicizing the Conference and gathering funds to meet its expenses.

After recounting the failure to hold a public protest meeting of Englishwomen, she referred to the objections she had not failed to register with members of the New Organization.

These we improved & had many battles we came off as we think victorious. But a "World's Convention" has yet to be held. That the feelings of the British public would not have been so outraged as we were given to understand, our admission as abundantly evinced, in the readiness with which I have been heard in other places.

On August 26, the last day of their stay in England, "with full hearts," the Motts took leave of their friends and "rode down to the Patrick Henry, Captain Delano" and set sail for America. Among the twelve cabin passengers they found their abolitionist friend, young William Adam of Harvard. After an uneventful voyage of twenty-nine days the "Patrick Henry" reached port, and the Motts were once more on American soil.

Chapter Nine

ONE–THIRTY–SIX
NORTH NINTH STREET

Shortly after reaching Philadelphia James Mott published *Three Months in Great Britain,* a brief account of his travels revealing the author in his own stature as an individual, as a thoughtful man emerging from the shadow cast by his illustrious wife. James and Lucretia Mott saw eye to eye in the denunciation of social injustice and blind prejudice, in the refusal to be hidebound by the dogma of religious sects; but *Three Months in Great Britain* is a striking commentary on differences in character and temperament between the husband and wife. The book's objective comment and sustained gravity afford an immediate contrast to the incisive wit and personal flavor of Lucretia's Diary; but James Mott's enthusiastic response to the natural beauty of the mountains and lakes of Scotland is a far cry from Lucretia's final word on the environment of Stirling Castle — "girls tell me when to admire." [1]

In one of Lucretia's first letters to her new friends the Webbs, she said that "James' Book" was written hurriedly among the many duties that besieged the returned travelers, and that, although her husband had wanted her to assist him in his narrative, she had avoided the task because of her limited talent for "writing for publication."

In 1844 Lucretia Mott suffered deep sorrow in the death of her mother; a year or two later Thomas Coffin, her only brother, died. The mother's death laid a bitter burden upon her children, for, in spite of her seventy-three years, Anna Coffin had remained alert, sagacious, and competent; beyond question, she was the head of the family, and the family found it hard to imagine life without her. "I know too well the keenness of the separation between parent and child," Lucretia wrote her English friend Elizabeth Pease after the death of Mrs. Pease's father. "My dear Mother," the letter continued, "was taken from us, when I could ill bear such a shock to my nature. She was companionable in every way. Her grandchildn. as well as her childn. delighted in her society. She was vigorous in constitution of both body & mind, and promised a longer life than 73. But we had to yield her and resignation to the event has been a hard lesson. I therefore feel less able to preach it to others." [2]

This "resignation" was doubly hard because of the poor state of Lucretia's own health. A sufferer from chronic dyspepsia, she became seriously ill shortly after her return from England; for a time her life was despaired of. As word of her illness spread, grave concern for her health was felt throughout the country. In Philadelphia such a steady stream of inquiries poured into the Anti-Slavery office that Miller McKim resorted to posting on the door of his office bulletins on her condition. Weeks of uncertainty passed, but at length the bulletin read, "Lucretia Mott is better."

For some years Martha Wright had been certain that Lucretia's dyspepsia was the toll paid for the relentless strain of her sister's arduous public life. As early as 1834, Martha had found support for her theory in Amariah Brigham's *Observations on the Influence of Religion upon the Health and Physical Welfare of Mankind*. Brigham had protested a too active religious life, declaring his belief to be that excessive religious excitement and prolonged mental activity result in strain that eventually affects the brain. Predicting that insanity could eventually be the price paid by men and women who gave the body and mind no rest even while pursuing virtuous causes, Brigham admitted that it was the excess of strain and the abuse of men's mentality that led to nervous disaster. Sincere Christianity in itself, he insisted, was no cause of illness. Martha read Brigham's words avidly; she felt that this philosophy was plain common sense, that if adopted it might go far to alleviate her sister's physical suffering. In one of the Family Sheets written in the 1820's, Martha emphasized Brigham's theories in her own words:

I am convinced that Sister L's dyspepsia arises from too much mental exercise. I do believe if she let slavery take its chance, forswore mental feasts and quarterly meetings, — let woman's rights, tight lacing and the study of Anatomy alone — and took a cherry-time journey to Aurora, without credentials from the meeting, that her health would be as good as ever, without the necessity of discarding coffee.[3]

Lucretia accepted, though not too seriously, Brigham's theory as endorsed by Martha. In a letter to Edward M. Davis, the husband of her daughter Maria, she confessed that she had been advised by her physician to take more pleasure and relaxation, exchanging antislavery efforts for a little harmless dissipation. But, as she told Edward, her reply to Dr. Noble's advice was that she would change her program if the doctor's wife would consent to take his patient's place in social reform. To this suggestion Dr. Noble vouchsafed no reply.

At the crisis of Lucretia's illness, in 1844, Martha came down from Auburn to Philadelphia to assist in the nursing. "Sister L's slow recovery," she wrote her husband, "throws an additional gloom over everything." But, according to Martha, Lucretia was not too ill to ask for a report of "all the political news" that had transpired "since her illness," not too ill to keep her husband "awake half the night talking to him" and to demand, in general, "an attentive audience when she sits up in bed at 2 o'clock her nap of 4 or 5 hours over." [4]

But as soon as she became convalescent, Lucretia resumed her social interests and became once more the active inspiration of the family life; though it is likely that even when confined to her room, she maintained her influence in the household.

Life in the Mott home was almost twofold: members of the family and close friends lived in an association of informal, personal relationship; while those connected with the Motts in reform movements only were more or less restrained. But the distinction was barely perceptible, for reformers moved about the home almost as freely as the family itself.

For a number of years just before the middle of the nineteenth century the Motts lived in a spacious house in North Ninth Street, just a square or two beyond Market Street, then called High Street. "One-thirty-six North Ninth Street," as James Mott's home was usually identified in *McElroy's Philadelphia Directory,* was a large dwelling located next to one-thirty-eight, where the Motts' daughter, Maria Mott Davis, and her family lived. In this pleasant neighborhood resided a congenial group of Philadelphia's conservative, well-to-do families. A connecting door on the second floor joined 136 North Ninth Street with 138, thus unifying the comforts of both homes. "If Edmund Quincy will come," wrote Lucretia, extending an invitation through Maria W. Chapman, "please say to him that we have plenty of room & shall be right glad to have him stop at our house. Edward M. Davis & family are passing a few weeks at Germantown — but their house is next door to us, with a communication from the chambers so that Adin Ballou or any other whom Edward has invited to his house can come directly to 138 where a hearty welcome awaits them." [5]

The house, a typical red-brick, Philadelphia dwelling, boasted of no distinction in style, but was always an abode of gracious hospitality. The heart of the visitor could but respond to Lucretia Mott's serenity and her unfailing capacity for friendship. The entire family enjoyed bringing their friends together and conveyed the feeling that they were honored by the presence of their guests. Even the transient visitor became immediately at home as he enjoyed a sense of his own worthiness, a feeling that he was an indispensable link in the chain. Edmund Quincy often referred to the Motts' home as "the household of faith." [6]

Lucretia furnished no pattern for the caricatures which often portrayed the feminists of her day. Indeed, very few of the leaders of the Woman's Rights Movement of the nineteenth century were remotely like the burlesques of womanhood sketched in some of the mid-century cartoons. She particularly was no zealous escapist from natural ties, no advocate of a "sphere for women" existing in shadowy unreality. While her strong arguments for rights for women were uttered unreservedly, she accepted the prose of actual living. Religion was her bulwark, family ties close to her heart; yet she was wise enough to know that neither religious freedom nor the sanctity of the home could be assured if injustice remained unchallenged. Prejudice, therefore, that threatened sex, race, or creed was a menace to the security of life itself. She also held the firm conviction that an expertly regulated household not only assured the well-being of the family but was a joy in itself. In the account of her experiences in England, she had noted particularly "a conversation on housekeeping" with Lady Byron.[7]

The maintaining of a home in the mid-nineteenth century was no sinecure, as it imposed on the housewife a relentless ritual of laborious duties, a burden of scheduled and unscheduled hand-performed tasks. Though "protected" in the vaunted "sanctuary of the home," and often relieved from the actual performance of housework, the wives and mothers of comfortably situated families took their homes seriously, and they had to be busy persons. Lucretia Mott, though provided adequately with hired assistance in her home, could rarely fold her hands in idleness. But it is doubtful if any of her contemporaries in public life, any leader of the reformers of the age approached her as a gracious hostess or even compared with her as a meticulous housekeeper. "Gathered & shelled $\frac{1}{2}$ bushel peas today & a peck yesterday — so many men consume much, also cauliflowers, southern potatoes." A chance remark

made by her in one of the family letters gives this evidence; and
more follows:

Large wash dried today — partly ironed — sorry for the soiled coun-
terpane on guests' bed — all clean now . . . up early, move out parlor
furniture, ready for the man to take away the carpets & shake them
. . . she is good help — always pleast. & ambitious to accomplish —
Kitty is regular as clock-work. . . We had 40 to sit down & some
childn. at a side table. The farm supplied nearly all the provisions.[8]

Amid this ceaseless round of cares, she remained serene. "She
is proof," Richard Webb asserted, "that it is possible for woman
to widen her sphere without deserting it, or neglecting the duties
which appropriately devolve upon her at home." [9]

In the 1840's Lucretia's immediate family, with the exception
of the sister Martha Coffin Wright, lived in Philadelphia, almost
within a stone's throw of one another. They were Lucretia; her
sister Eliza Yarnall; her married daughters, Anna Mott Hopper,
Maria Mott Davis, and Eliza Mott Cavender; and the two unmar-
ried children, Thomas and Martha; and, of course, the in-laws,
and the nieces and nephews and grandchildren. This group was
kept intact by endless visiting from home to home and by weekly
family gatherings, graphically pictured in Martha's words:
". . . the next family meeting is to be here. They go thro with
the Alphabet — beginning with the Browns' and ending with
Yarnall — they are being pleasant — bringing together weekly
those who did not meet very often & keeping up the family interest." Yet, when in 1844 it was proposed by Edward Davis that
the family follow the custom of so many Philadelphians by pur-
chasing a large farm outside the city for a summer retreat, Lucretia eyed the proposition with disfavor. It was her fear, she
protested, that the family "might become clannish" in caring for
none but themselves; and "that the being so constantly together
wd. produce satiety." But Martha Wright's main objection to
the proposal was that in the last analysis it would mean too much
work for "Sister L. who for five years has been too much burdened
in that way, having a family of 12 to think for tho she had not to
work with her hands."

This family circle was widened by the presence of relatives
coming to Philadelphia from Nantucket, New York, and Ohio, as
well as the friends who dropped in casually. "A continual stream
of callers from 10 in the morning," wrote Martha, "till near 11 at

night, during Yearly Mg. week, or the wk. previous. Among them were several English acquaintances and Dr. Channing." [10]

The continuity of the "stream of callers" can be readily understood for at the Motts one could meet wide-awake, challenging people. Associates in reform movements came from all places, not only to rub shoulders with celebrities, but often to meet less well-known people, and even wayfarers. Robert and Hattie Purvis, Sarah Douglas, Charles C. Burleigh, and Cyrus M. Burleigh were of the intimate circle, as well as Abby Kimber, Mary Grew, and Sarah Pugh.

On more than one occasion Sojourner Truth found a comfortable way station at the Motts' fireside. "My name was Isabella," this remarkable ex-slave once explained,

. . . but when I left the house of bondage, I left everything behind. I wa'n't goin' to keep nothin' of Egypt on me, an' so I went to the Lord an' asked him to give me a new name. And the Lord gave me Sojourner because I was to travel up an' down the land, showin' the people their sins an' bein' a sign unto them. Afterward I told the Lord I wanted another name 'cause everybody else had two names; and the Lord gave me Truth, because I was to declare the truth to the people.[11]

"Up and down the Land," although principally in the North, she traveled before and after the Emancipation. Her pleading for poverty-stricken Negroes — barely existing in squalid, restricted sections of Northern cities — reached the halls of Congress and even the White House. A bond of understanding linked the cultured Lucretia Mott and the unlettered Sojourner Truth as both women shared an unshaken faith in God's righteousness. In the spring of 1853, Sojourner Truth brought an inspiring message to the Philadelphia Female Anti-Slavery Society.[12] Among the twenty "Autographs of Distinguished Persons" whom Sojourner designated as her friends, was the name of Lucretia Mott.[13]

Other visitors were the Hutchinsons, a family that gave informal concerts of antislavery songs, songs often improvised for the occasions. Daniel Neall introduced Lucretia to the Hutchinsons by saying, "This is Mrs. Lucretia Mott and her daughters . . . I thought you should know one another. Mrs. Mott's a great abolitionist, but she's a fine cook too." [14] After entertaining the Hutchinsons in the 1840's, Lucretia suggested that the young singers should go to England where, she thought, they would stir up antislavery sentiment through their spirited music.

Miller McKim, having decided that his path of service to humanity lay in broad activity in social reform rather than in the confines of a sectarian pulpit, now made his headquarters in Philadelphia. In the Mott household he and his wife Sarah ("one of the finest Quaker girls of Chester Co." as Lucretia described Sarah Allibone at the time of her marriage to Miller McKim) [15] could often be found. As the years rolled on, the friendship between Sarah McKim and Lucretia Mott cemented the relationship between Miller and Lucretia, which had originated years before in the discussion of theological doubt and faith. Lucretia and Sarah McKim spent much time together. A member of the family relates that, on one occasion, Lucretia, while sitting with Mrs. McKim, observed a feather floating above her head. "Without a pause in her conversation, as the story has come down through the family, Lucretia captured the piece of down, took scissors, needle and thread from a reticule at her waist, unstitched a seam of the cushion on which she was seated, tucked in the feather and repaired it before Grandma McKim's fascinated eyes." [16]

This inborn sense of thrift developed in Lucretia Mott an aversion to wastefulness that asserted itself in a number of amusing incidents. One family legend concerned her passion for conserving writing paper. To indulge this whim she wrote on backs of envelopes, the margins of programs, unfilled pages from the letters of others; in fact, any scrap of paper that she could reach, served for her family correspondence. No persuasion could effect a change in this habit. One valorous member of the family, attempting to thwart Lucretia in her passion for saving writing paper by making her a gift of stationery, succeeded only in meeting this response: "This paper is too pretty for the little I have to say. Aunt Martha has given me an added lecture on the cheapness of note paper. One wd. suppose you had all learned by this time that the old lady choseth to do as best suited her, while there is so much extravagance in almost everything we use for instance. . . . Assurg. her at the same time that I never wrote on old envelopes to any nice people." [17]

Yet, on the occasions of marriages among her relatives, Lucretia did not consider it too expensive to engage a silversmith to design for the newly married couple a set of flat silver duplicating her own pattern. Moreover, to each of her grandchildren she presented a silver pitcher handmade to her order.

Her generous and unfailing responses to the appeals for as-

sistance became so well known that it is said that every blind beg-
gar of Philadelphia could find his way unguided to 136 North
Ninth Street. One inspired member of the family suggested that
two chairs be placed just within the doorway of the Mott home
and be dubbed "Beggars' chairs." [18]

When Edmund Quincy had called the Mott home "the house
of faith," he had in mind no anchorite's cell, for he pictured the
abode as "very handsomely furnished" with "everything as comfortable as can be." [19] The attractiveness, however, did not stem
from the quality of the furnishings. It is true that the high-
ceilinged rooms, conforming to the Philadelphia taste of the
nineteenth century, were spacious; bright-colored carpets, taken
up, beaten, and put down yearly, covered the floors; Victorian
chairs and sofas framed in solid walnut or mahogany offered ease
and sociability in spite of the slippery horsehair coverings; and
on the walls were family portraits and likenesses of one or two
close friends. The general atmosphere bespoke good judgment and
competence, but the magnetism of the home was Lucretia Mott
herself.

It seemed that there was always room for one more at the long
table in the dining room, that there was always space for more in
the parlors. Each guest regardless of station, creed, race, color, or
relationship to others in the gathering, felt at home. Conversation
at the Motts was apt to be spirited, challenging, even partisan, for,
in the mid-nineteenth century, friends, even families, were divided sharply over the towering social issues of the day. But, by
some magic, as differences in feeling and convictions were buried
in objective discussion, personal thrust rarely appeared, and the
atmosphere in this home was kept friendly. Not hesitant in this
circle to advance his own controversial views was Henry C. Wright,
a nonconformist whose *Errors of the Bible* had banned him from
orthodox circles but had assured him a hearty welcome in the parlors of Lucretia Mott's home.

Writing his "Letter from Philadelphia" for *The Non-Resistant*,
of February 1841, Wright described "A Social Meeting at Lucretia
Mott's." Here were Charles Burleigh, almost a member of the
family; Daniel Neall, victim of the tar-and-feather attack in Delaware; Thomas McClintock, a vigorous Philadelphia radical; and
others. In the course of the evening the subject of despotism arose
with a resultant crossfire of opinion as to what despotism really
was, how it manifested itself, what its limits were, where it usually
appeared, who were its victims, who were acknowledged despots.

The dispute, carried too in a conversational tone, waxed and waned as sparks of wit and wisdom were enkindled. The conclusion of this discussion, as Mr. Wright reported, was that despotism was:

. . . *not the abuse* of power — not to beat, starve or cruelly treat a man after he is subjected to human will — but to subject a man to *human* will, in church or state, and punish him if he refuse, this is despotism. He that claims a right to subject man to *human* will is a despot. God's will is our only law.

Lucretia herself pictures one of the dining-room conversations,

We had quite a talk here the other day, whether Jefferson was not quite as worthy of political reverence as Washington. Miller took part in it. I've not room or details. Cath. Beecher, Miller, S. Pugh, & Abby, Mary E. [Lucretia's cousin, Mary Earle], & a Virginia abolitionist at the far end of our table were our teachers. Lydia Gillingm. & Annag., who with Ed. & Maria & Geo. Lord made a long table — Patty & baby & nurse Mary Ann in Brooklyn. Our subject was the attempt to prove Shakespeare's Plays not all written by him — & how sorry they wd. be to believe that we had not one Shakespeare. I asked why not more joyful, cd. it be shown that there were ten — that it came of superstitious idolatry to make one fellow being an object of worship.

Continuing this letter to Martha, she tells how the group was startled by this spark:

Was it not a reflectn. on the great Creator, that only one Messiah had come to man — more worthy of him that one for every age had appeared — or whenever a necessity as Foxton — My pet says — Cathe. bore the heresy better than I expected. Miller stayed behind as they went to the parlor to laugh & ask me — or rather congratulate me, on delivering myself of my Messiah hobby that's not just his language but the quintessence — as mother used to say.[20]

Martha described another incident:

Early on that Day Sister L. called on Wm. Lloyd Garrison the great man, the lion in the Emancipation cause and invited him to tea here the next day — innumerable jackals were also invited, yesterday was spent in preparation — there were about 50, counting our own family. For awhile it was interesting till the Garrison and a few of his particular jackals left to attend a Committee for an hour or two, leaving a pet lion from the Western Quarter who makes his home here master of the field — the conversation then took a metaphysical turn on the subject of heaven and its opposite.

But Martha found it impossible for her to continue the letter in the running dialogue between Lucretia and her mother: "Sister L. is reading slave laws on one side, Mother on the other making sundry questions etc."

Although Martha's love for her sister was almost idolatrous, her own ironic humor led her to sallies of wit on Lucretia's hospitality. Lucretia's "dinner parties" seemed to Martha "pleasant," but she felt that she would "expire" to have to go thro with [them], that the incorrect marking of a pillowcase was not "matter of the consequence," and that "it is nice to care as little about such trifles," as she always meant to care. Indeed, she protested that if she "lived in the city and had the wealth of Girard," she would prefer entertaining "in a succession of small parties." At one time, Martha deplored the fact that the family had been unable to see anything of "Sister L." because she "has a house full of Yearly Meeting company which prevents our seeing her." [21]

Garrison declared that he was never in Philadelphia without going to the Motts where he was sure of a "home-like reception, affectionate and delightful." He, too, was almost a member of the family. Samuel J. May made frequent visits. "We have a friend staying with us — a Unitarian — one of heaven's own, Sam'l. J. May of Syracuse, N.Y. You probably know him as conspicuous in the early A.S. movements — as well as in the Non-Resistant Convention. He is an advocate for women too — it is fitting therefore that this should be his stopping place." [22]

And among other visitors were Maria W. Chapman and her sisters; Theodore Parker, the eloquent Unitarian minister of Haines Street Church, Boston; Frederick Douglass, who had cast off the shackles of slavery to become one of America's foremost orators; and Arnold Buffum.

Early in 1836, John Quincy Adams recorded in his *Diary* that in company with Benjamin Lundy he had visited the Mott home to attend "a large tea and evening party of men and women — all of the Society of Friends." The conversation upon "slavery, the abolition of slavery, and other topics" was so informal that Mr. Adams and Mr. Lundy remained "until between ten and eleven o'clock." Lucretia he described as "a native of the island of Nantucket, sensible and lively, and an abolitionist of the most intrepid school." [23]

Emerson wrote his friend Elizabeth Hoar that he liked Lucretia Mott very well. But, the Sage of Concord added, Lucretia was "not quite enough an abstractionist for me and her will is more illuminated than her mind. She too is a cousin of Mary Rotch . . . I shall go to the Cherry Street meeting and hear Lucretia speak if I can. She blames Mary Rotch for not letting her light shine, not the vice of Americans generally. Me too she taxed with living out of the world, and I was not much flattered that her interest in me respected my rejection of an ordinance sometime, somewhere."

Later, in a letter to his wife Lydian, Emerson said that Lucretia Mott was the best person he had seen "across the miles of the endless squares" of Philadelphia. He had called on her, taken dinner with the Motts and heard her speak at the Quaker meeting. "She is," he told his wife, "the handsomest of women and a tutelar and beneficient genius of her church here; so lovely, so liberal, so refining. I do not wonder that they are too proud of her and too much in awe of her to spare her, though they suspect her faith." In another letter he referred to Lucretia's courage in speaking at the Quaker meeting when the Friends had obviously been warned against listening to her.

To the Transcendentalist Margaret Fuller, Emerson wrote that he had had "several very satisfactory interviews with Lucretia Mott & with Mary Cox." And in another letter he says "Lucretia Mott I have seen much and she is beautiful to me." [24]

New workers in the reform movements were always cordially welcomed by Lucretia Mott. To spur interest in Anti-Slavery and Woman's Rights, women of Western New York had engaged an alert young Oberlin College woman, Sally Holley, to make a campaign of public addresses.[25] "I am pleased that your state has the above services of Sally Holley," wrote Lucretia Mott on July 5, 1852, to Mrs. Adeline Roberts of New York in answer to Mrs. Roberts' request that Lucretia come to New York to make a speech. "I have great hopes of these new Recruits," she continued, "who have youth on their side, while some of us older warriors may begin to retire from the field and give place to them. We hope to have the stirring labor of Sally Holley in this state before many months. My husband was out of the city, & I waited his return to confer with him before answering the letter which accounts for the two days' delay." [26]

After Miss Holley visited the Motts in Philadelphia she wrote Stephen and Abby Foster a frank impression of her evening at 136 North Ninth Street. The house, she called, "a palace of a home" where she was met at the door by William Lloyd Garrison "with all his winning urbanity." Lucretia Mott, she said, "expressed herself as 'happy' to see the guest," but James Mott to Sally Holley "seemed more like some statue than flesh and blood and all that passed or what was said seemed to fall on his heart as impassive as moonbeams on ice." In the course of the evening's "table talk," the subject turned to the conventional custom of calling women "by their husband's given names." Then it was that Lucretia startled Sally Holley and perhaps the entire room by observing that "People would sooner call my husband Mr. Lucretia Mott than me Mrs. James Mott." These words were from the lips of the Mrs. Mott who had refused to make a speaking engagement with Adeline Roberts without conferring with her husband. Sally Holley concludes this episode by saying that Lucretia's astonishing remark evoked only "silence and dignity" from the "honored spouse." [27]

Lucretia's happiness in having her friends around her knew no bounds; and there was never on her part any evidence of consciousness that she gave anything to others. Note the warmth of her invitation that she wrote to Maria W. Chapman in 1847:

Do come and make us a visit. Tis true we have no Eliza Lee Follen here, unless indeed she comes too but we will make our home as attractive as possible. We shall have Garrison and Douglass and Buffum and we hope some others of the worthies. I write particularly now to remind thy sister Caroline that her promise of coming is yet unfulfilled. We shall expect her the last of this or beginning of next week, and indulge the hope that her sisters will not let her leave alone. Anne Warren and thyself are entirely too great strangers hereaway. The acquaintance formed with Deborah is worth preserving — and I love those dear younger ones, enough to wish to greet them under our roofs. We shall open E. M. Davis house and can accommodate abolitionists a score. Will thou drop us a line if my delay has not made it too late, saying when we may look for you at 136 9th Street? . . . Love unbounded to E. L. Follen. She must come while we feel so well acquainted with her, and seal an intimacy that promises us so much pleasure. How glad I am, that we saw her & her sister & their lovely Charles in their own house. I can now think of her there in that pleasant corner of your parlor when we enjoyed so many tete-a-tetes, which are so pleasant to recur to. . . With love unfeigned to your household thy sisters — and any quantity to thyself. I am, thine ever Lucretia Mott.

And a postcript to this letter follows:

We had hoped for Wm. L. Garrison's company & aid at our meeting, but he may do much more by going to England & Scotland than

by remaining at home or coming here, so we try to resign him cheer-
fully. We think he will remove some of the Sectarian prejudice, that
was arrayed against him in 1840. The disposition to receive & hear
Fredk. Douglass at the British & Forcign Meeting seemed a little evidence of repentance at their past mis-doings. . . Why can't Wendell P.
come — ask him from us — we wd. greet him most cordially and his
Anne too, if her health will admit of her accompy. him. My best
bed shall be made for them, if on return of Mail you say they will
come. Please answer as soon as it is ascertained who will favor us.[28]

Distinguished foreigners visiting Philadelphia were apt to be
piloted, sooner or later, to 136 North Ninth Street. In a letter
written on February 25, 1842, Lucretia said:

Another lion has just arrived in the city — Charles Dickens. Our
childn. had a strong desire to see him. I too have enjoyed the benevolent character of his writing, tho I have read very little in them. I did
not expect to seek an interview nor to invite him here, as he was not
quite one of our sort — but just now there was left at the door his &
his wife's cards, with a kind & sweet letter from our dear friend
E. J. Reid–London introducing them & expressing a strong desire that
we would make their acquaintance. There is not a woman in London
whose draft I would more gladly honor.

Yet Lucretia Mott made no pretense of sharing the enthusiasm
that Americans were showing for Dickens:

I regret that in Boston & New York they have been so extravagant
in their reception of him.

However, her desire to have "a word or two with Dickens"
prompted her to call on him when he reached Philadelphia,

. . . but he was promised that we could have but a few minutes interview. We tried to engage a visit from him, but his stay in this city was
only 3 or 4 days & was engaged all the time. 5 or 600 gentlemen
called on him the morng. we were there. Jas. Mott talked to him about
his travels in the south and hoped he would not be deceived by the
outside appearance — but try to get a peep behind the scenes. I too
said a word or two on the same subject.[29]

Among the Englishmen who had given the Motts hearty reception in Great Britain was Lord Morpeth, Seventh Earl of Carlisle. Lord Morpeth was the brother of Kate Stanley, the Duchess
of Sutherland. For Lucretia Mott, Lady Stanley cherished such a
warm affection that after the birth of her second daughter she

wrote her sister, "We settled to call it Rachel Lucretia after 'Mrs. Mott.' " [30]

During the fall and winter of 1841–42 Lord Morpeth traveled in the eastern part of the United States, later publishing a diary of his travels in the country. Lucretia wrote to the Webbs on February 25, 1842,

I have not told you what a nice visit we had from Lord Morpeth. . . We felt some hesitancy about calling on "his lordship," thinking he would not remember us, but in a letter from Dr. Channing to his son who is passing the winter here, he expressed a hope that we would see him, so we went to his lodgings, card in hand reducing him to a common man, on our Republican principles.

While Lord Morpeth was in Philadelphia he enjoyed the opportunity of meeting "an intelligent few abolitionists," as Lucretia described the group invited by the Motts to meet the English traveler.

But the new friends could not take the place of the old ones whom the rift in the Anti-Slavery Society had alienated from the Motts. "You wish to hear all we can tell you of J. G. Whittier . . . Truly he is almost lost to us," she wrote. "Months & months pass without our hearing from him. New Organizn. claims him, and not without far too much reason. Maria Chapman wrote me that he was in a few moments at the Boston Fair." Additional news of Whittier and the New Organization follows:

Now I would prefer to write something pleasant about him. He seemed to enjoy going from place to place with Joseph Sturge, and we were glad of their calling on us. I can't help loving Whittier & J. Sturge so, even tho' they have wronged us, in the course they have pursued. So long as they retain any sympathy for the suffering bondsman, I shall feel a tender regard for them, even tho' in other respects they go halting. This is my feeling toward each component part of that London Convention with the very slight exception of N. Clover & one or two others. Even Jesus, "the son of the Blessed," treated hypocrites with severity. You will see in the Liberator, that Colver was ready to make excuse for the Mg. houses being refused — "a work of Grace was going on."

But Colver remained the persistent thorn in her flesh: "You will see H. B. Stanton's name among the 3rd party speakers in Boston. How sorry I am that he has thus sold himself! They might have had Colver, if we could have him — and Whittier — and T. G. Weld." But, the inevitable fairness persists, "Our New Organ. abolitionists are not idle. Let us give them credit for all the good they do." [31]

Lucretia Mott's joy in her family and friends did not permit her to withdraw from the less fortunate people of Philadelphia. Although her early efforts to start a Fragment Society were frustrated, in the 1840's she and certain other Philadelphia women founded the "Association for the Relief and Employment of Poor Women." During her presidency, this organization developed a method of bringing together a self-help group of worthy industrious women. In pleasant rooms, often in Lucretia Mott's own home, women could do their household sewing or at a small profit for themselves, could hire their talents to others. In one year, according to the Secretary's Report, 256 garments were made, $23\frac{1}{2}$ lbs. of carpet rags sewed, and 25 bed coverings quilted. Lucretia Mott was president of the association for years, giving guidance and advice, and rendering in an indirect way financial aid to the needy. [32]

Growing into popularity in the 1840's were the "Rosine Associations," organizations named after Rosa Giovanni who in her native Italy had established clubs for the relief and reclamation of so-called "fallen women." As plans were being drawn for founding a Rosine group in Philadelphia, Lucretia Mott, "ever true to the principle of equal rights," as a report reads, asked if the benefits of the association were to be extended to all women without the distinction of color. When her question met with silence she declined membership in the new organization. But the Philadelphia Branch of the Rosine Society dropped the color bar. [33]

In the 1840's James Mott had retired from business with a competency ample enough to keep his family financially secure. The three older daughters were married and settled in homes of their own; and the younger children, Martha and Thomas, were virtually grown up. At this time Lucretia could go and come at will in answering the direct call of the Inner Voice or in uttering her own beliefs in response to the demands from without that were crowding upon her. This was her opportunity, her duty, as it seemed to her, to take a place among the radicals of the day, even to accept leadership among the reformers. As pleasant, therefore, as the Philadelphia life was, Lucretia Mott could not long permit herself the luxury of devoting herself wholly to her family and friends and to the needy around her.

Chapter Ten

"IN THE WAY CALLED HERESY"

The news of the refusal of the World's Convention to honor Lucretia Mott's credentials served but to heighten, in the eyes of many Americans, the stature of a woman already a leader among free thinkers and social reformers. As the mid-century approached, therefore, Lucretia had little leisure, scant opportunity to devote herself wholly to her family and friends. For a short period the state of her health enforced quiet and rest; but not long after the return from Great Britain, she was beset by a steady and insistent program of public speaking. Then it was that she found herself answering the call of the Inner Voice to declare her own convictions, to protest dogmatic thought and action. Published reports of her words appeared, reports, however, that were more or less faithful to her utterances. From the widened audience, her frank independence did not always receive a sympathetic response; and her words, often garbled or reported out of context, furnished the basis for increasingly insistent charges of heresy. Naturally these charges reached her ears.

In a postscript to her husband's letter to Richard Webb dispatched from Newcastle-on-Tyne just before the Motts left England, Lucretia had asked, "Will you let us hear from you sometimes or are we too radical, too altogether heretical? If it be bigotry or heresy to believe the sublime truths of the Gospel as we have learned them in the school of Christ, 'I glory in such heresy.'"

For unequivocal statements of "such heresy," one may turn to these letters written by Lucretia Mott soon after her return from Europe and also to the public addresses she delivered in this period.

First, there are the letters to the Webbs [1] "As to Theology." Thus, Lucretia speaks from her heart in a letter addressed to Richard Webb on April 2, 1841, "I am sick of disputes on that subject; though I cannot say just as my husband has — that he 'don't care a fig about it' — for I want those I love, should see their way out of the darkness and error with which they are surrounded." When Miller McKim sought her counsel in 1834, she had advised him to observe "the general tenor of the invaluable writings, the spirit of the whole" rather than to perplex his mind "with inferences from isolated passages here and there." Now she felt that the time had come for a direct statement as to her faith, for something further than a discussion of what she had formerly designated as the attitude of an intelligent person toward "the Scriptures." "I think," she wrote, "that so much harm is done by teaching the doctrine of human depravity & a dependence on a vicarious atonement, that I feel constrained to call on all everywhere to yield such a mistaken and paralyzing dogma." "As to the mere opinion of 'Trinity' of 'Unity' or any such purely speculative indulgence, affecting not the life or practice, 'the long-headed reasoning man,' and 'the warm, enthusiastic, poetic minded man' may each follow his convictions harmlessly."

This led to a discussion of Unitarianism. Her own views, however, on this subject may be inferred from the general tenor of her words rather than from specific comments on the underlying principles of Unitarian faith and practice. At this time, she said,

Richard is greatly mistaken in saying our Friends are "declaredly Unitarian" Why they would be horror struck at the idea of it, but we perceive that some are searching Elias Hicks' writings & remembering his sayings in proof that he was as much opposed to Unitarian as to any other sect. They are nevertheless, Unitarian in sentiment, whether they know it or not, and so was Wm. Penn & some other of our early Friends. But they as well as some of our modern Friends throw a veil of mysticism and obscure expressions around them reserving to themselves an understanding of "Christ-the-Light" which many of their readers fail to perceive. This practice strikes me as not quite honest and yet, when questions are put, to see how we may be caught in our words, we have high authority for parrying a little at least so far as to say, "I will also ask you."

But the charge of Unitarianism had evoked further comment from her, as it led to continued discussion of her own religious stand. Referring to George Combe's recently published work on phrenology, *The Constitution of Man Considered in Relation to External Objects,* she maintained that Combe erred in representing Quakers as Unitarians and in stating also that the Hicksites rather than the Orthodox Quakers were the dissenters in the Separation of 1827. To her the cardinal issue in the manifest significance of Quakerism, in Quaker "stability & usefulness as a society," as she phrased it, depended not so much on what was thought about the principles of the Society as on the "strict adherence" by Quakers to the "cardinal doctrine of the sufficiency of the 'Light within' and righteousness without." More significant than adherence to dogma, she believed, was the inner power given man to realize an upright Christian life. In her words, "Our veneration is trained to pay homage to ancient usage, rather than to truth, which is older than all. Else why church censure on marriages that are not of us? on Parents conniving? on our members being present at such etc." Repeating the same criticism that she had brought to her grandfather before the Separation, she now said, "Oh how our Discipline needs revising & stripping of its objectionable features: I know not how far yours may differ from ours, but know we have far too many disownable offences."

But if, she wrote on April 4, 1850,

. . . while we refuse the pecuniary aid to the Ministry we countenance nearly all the machinery which supports him — Sabbath & Bible worship — belief in human depravity — a distinction of morals for the natural & spiritual man — a superstitious reverence for Jesus crying blessed Lord & Savior instead of doing the works wh. he said — mak'g a kind of righteousness & atonement of him, if not exactly after the Calvinistic pattern; if this is our course, it will satisfy a wily & grasping priesthood, and our invective against the hired minister will amount to very little. . . Thou asks how far Quakers in general agree with H. C. Wright's views of the Bible — the authority for war — slavery, etc.

(In *Errors of the Bible*, Henry C. Wright had not hesitated to present his reasons for rejecting the Bible as an infallible spiritual guide, to repudiate a vicarious atonement, and to disavow his belief in the immaculate conception.) Her answer to this query about Wright was,

Why dost thou not know that save the comparatively few abolitionists & comeouters, Friends regard him as one of the World's people, if indeed they knew that there is such a man, and never read his numerous letters & essays. They have never been in the Orthodox "Friend," nor defiled the pages of the Simon pure "Friends Intelligencer" (Hicksite) — and the reading of most of our monks & nuns is confined to such accredited Periodicals. You have little idea how ignorant both classes of Quakers are of our reformatory journals. H. C. W. goes almost "beyond the beyonds" for anybody.

As to the writings of Quakers of an earlier day, her opinion was that "Old Quaker writings," contained, in spite of their verbose style, "a vein of liberal thought running thro' them, threads of wisdom and liberality not found in the writings of her contemporaries." But "Transcendental writers & Unit'n free-thinkers," she added, turned more readily to "these old Quaker writings" than "the descendants of these 'sons of the morn'g,' " the Quakers of her day who, she believed, were more concerned with the rites of Quakerism than with "great principles & testimonies of truth." In the Philadelphia Yearly Meeting, held just before she wrote this letter, she had noted ample evidence of this emphasis upon outward forms and ceremonies while there was seemingly little progress in efforts to reach a goal of breadth and sincerity in religion. "In the free scope for the exercise of 'concerns,' " she protested, ". . . we were well nigh preached to death. Meeting going was advocated threadbare. Gravestones denounced in full measure. Music very wicked! The slave had to sigh, 'if not whistle' for a hearing." Her final verdict at this time on the Philadelphia Yearly Meeting was: "The game is not worth the candle."

Lack of conformity to set customs did not disturb her because it was her belief that the drab hat and the dull colors, the pronounced simplicity of the styles adopted by Quakers, were meaningless once the inner sincerity was lost or whenever controversy reared its head over essential beliefs and doctrines. To her, lines of dress became important only as an expression of inner faith and humility of spirit. Moreover, she felt that even though the unaffected piety of the early Quakers had vanished she would prefer that the young should be brought up to independence of empty forms rather than that the elders should repudiate and discard what had originally been an expression of their sincere beliefs.

At this time she herself had ceased attending the afternoon meetings for worship, going instead to make friendly calls on unemployed Irish weavers or Negroes who also needed sympathy. In these matters she had preferred to make her own judgments, feeling that in visiting distressed workingmen she was living up to Christian principles of worship as faithfully and with as much piety as in attending Quaker meetings.

But her strongest resentment was evoked by the matter of authoritative power in the Society, and nothing disturbed her more acutely than the restraining force exerted by the governing boards over the other Quakers. Shortly before she wrote to Richard Webb in 1842, Isaac T. Hopper, James S. Gibbons, and Charles Marriot, members of the Executive Committee of the American Anti-Slavery Society, were disowned by the New York Monthly Meeting, an action to be "endorsed" by the Quarterly and the Yearly Meetings of the state of New York. James S. Gibbons was the husband of Isaac Hopper's daughter Abby, and

Charles Marriot was a highly esteemed businessman. But all three men, Quakers in good standing, were members of the Executive Committee of the American Anti-Slavery Society.

Inasmuch as the *Anti-Slavery Standard* was the official organ of the American Anti-Slavery Society, it may not be unreasonable to believe that the members of the Executive Committee of the Society may have shared responsibility for the sentiments expressed in the Society's authorized publication. But, at the time the charges were raised by the New York Meeting against Hopper, Gibbons, and Marriot, there was no proof that they by word or deed, individually or with others, had made any overt attacks on slavery; nor was it even suggested that they had given any aid to runaway slaves.[2] Among reformers, this procedure of the New York Meetings had evoked unequivocal censure. Not unexpected, therefore, was Lucretia Mott's outspoken denunciation of what she termed the highhanded procedure of the official Quaker bodies of New York.

Moreover, in this same year she was to feel the weight of Quaker authority exerted against her own liberty. As a member of the New England Non-Resistance Society, she attended regularly the annual meetings of the organization. In 1842 she wrote Richard Webb that an effort had been made by the authority of her Meeting to discipline her for her connection with the Non-Resistance Society. "I wish you could see," began her statement to him on this point,

. . . a correspondence growing out of my going to Boston last autumn, to attend the Non-Resistance anniversary and attendg. New York Mg. on my way home. The Elders & others there have been quite desirous to make me an offender for joining with those not in membership with us & accepting offices in these Societies. But our Friends here know full well that such a position is neither contrary to our Discipline, to Scripture, to reason, nor sense. I was permitted to answer for myself & I found proof enough in the practice of Friends from the days of Wm. Penn to the present — of such "mixtures" they failed of bringing action against me.

In this resentment against the dictatorial powers given to the elders over the large body of Quakers, her words were,

They would say, "this ought ye to have done, and not leave the other undone." But in this as in some other sects, we have taken the liberty to judge for ourselves. The Select order among us has come in for a share of opposition. After nearly 30 years experience and observation of the results of this establishment, we have come to the conclusion that nearly all the divisions among us have had their origin in these meetings — Clothing a few of our equal brethren, with power to judge the Ministry, selecting here & there one to ordain for the Ministry, and placing these in elevated positions, it is no difficult matter for them to regard themselves "the heads of the tribe" and to act accordingly. . . . The assumed authority of Men's Mgs. & the admitted subordination of women's is another cause of complaints — indeed an entire radical change in our Discipline would be the result of another movement or division with us.

"Moreover," she continued,

. . . there may be something for us to do in bearing a faithful protest against intolerance as well as in sympathizing with those who have become discouraged and disaffected so far as to meditate a withdrawal from the Society. . . . I have not been able to see that another division will afford more than a temporary remedy for the evils under which we are laboring; while our present Discipline remains as it is giving power to a few over the ministry we may expect such results to follow. A radical change is called for. . . . Many among us would feel little inclined to associate under restrictions, which they have felt all too binding. Entire come-outerism is to be feared in its shattering tendency with our young people. What then is the right step to pursue?
    I have frequently noticed that persons who were once useful in our society, withdrawg. from it, become rather contracted & selfish — shut themselves out from society at large, and grow older, following their natural inclination for association connected themselves with sects far behind the intelligence & light of their parents. This has been remarkably the case with the families of those who were cruelly severed from our society 20 years ago in New England — called New-light — a case has lately occurred in this region. These remarks may not apply to all . . . Wm. L. Garrison never was attached to any sect. Sarah Pugh, from the time of the Separation among us, never felt her interests enlisted with either side. I have no fear of her talents rusting from want of use. The effect, however, of dissent on young people in their eschew'g our order, & absent'g themselves from our Mgs., is, that they may in time be caught up, by some proselyting spirits, and made bigots of, in a school far behind our Quaker monastery.

    But in her protest against the domination of the Quaker Ministers and Elders, she did not advocate another religious Separation. To her, the division of 1827 was such a painful ordeal that she felt "that the advantages predominate — I mean of religious Associations. It requires constant watching care that we yield no principle, but only concede minor points for the sake of unity."

This discussion of her "irreligion" she concluded by explaining that she did not claim the right of practical indulgence in actions definitely proscribed by the Discipline, that she did not claim the right of practicing all her own convictions, but that in the absence of direct proscription of action she had the right to think for herself. Her own attitude, she protested, never included an "attempt to draw or define, the precise relation to the Father — nor is a trinity acknowledged in our galleries." "We rather urge," she continued, "obedience to manifested duty, as the means of acceptance with the Searcher of hearts. This is the old-fashioned Quaker doctrine 'neither is there Salvation in other.' "

Unaffected by egoism, she was quick to recognize what she regarded as essential truth in the thoughts of others. On May 9, 1841, the Unitarian minister, Theodore Parker, preached in Haines Street Church, Boston, a sermon from the text, "Heaven and Earth shall pass away; but my words shall not pass away." There was grave need, declared Parker, that men should distinguish between the "transient" and the "permanent," that is, between what he designated as religious forms, creeds, and human interpretations of Scripture and what he called the inner reality, the general law, the eternal truth of the infinite God. He proclaimed his inability to accept as divine inspiration every word in the Scriptures. While recognizing the word of Jesus as "real Christianity," as "pure religion," he considered the history of Christianity as quite another thing. He proclaimed a reverent belief in "the eternal truth of God," but rejected as essentials to Christianity every expression of that eternal truth which man had voiced and sectarian creeds had imposed on men throughout the ages. Jesus, he recognized, not as the infinite but as "the organ through which the infinite spoke." Protesting the conventional acceptance of religious dogma, Parker declared that "authority is taken for truth, and not truth for authority." This maxim was often used by Lucretia Mott; whether or not before Parker's words is uncertain.

As Lucretia informed the Webbs, Parker's sermon "created a great stir in New England & led some of the old Unitarians to tremble for their reputations as Christians." In her words, "a major controversy" arose. On all sides the minister met sharp dissent, and he was barred from exchanging pulpits with some other ministers in Boston. But Lucretia Mott believed that Parker was "full of faith in the real groundwork of religion in all ages, on which the truths of Scripture are based: not on miracles or inexplicable creeds."

Further, she added,

We shall not make much progress as Christians until we care to read & examine the Jewish Scriptures as we would any other of the ancient records. By what authority do we set so high a value on every text that may be drawn from this volume? Certainly not by any command therein found. On the contrary, again and again is there an appeal to the inner sense. Why even of yourselves judge ye not what is right?

"Parker's remarks on the Bible," she continued, were very much to her liking, for in her opinion "genuine respect for the Bible would not be lessened by a less-idolized regard for the literal text of the Scriptures." She described herself as "a constant reader of the Bible," reading the book with enlightened appreciation but with no formalized veneration, no adoption of "a peculiar and solemn style of pronunciation — all the ed terminations full etc.," as she described it. It was the "Good and the True" that should be venerated "while we respect not prejudice and Superstition." She said,

I have never given my faith a name. The distinctions among Christian professors are found, on an analysis, to be but hair-breadth, and it is puzzling to bear in mind the distinctive points in their creeds. We give a more orthodox hue to ours by retaining some expressions which do not convey our real sentiments. I do not wonder that Richard asks what we mean by our professions. If he should hear some of our preachers, he would understand us better. The hearers are often told that they are not called to rest their hopes of selection on the "sacrifice without the gates of Jerusalem." The divinity of Christ is held — not by miraculous power — so much as his spiritual creation. "The son of God with power according to the spirit of holiness." [3]

Lucretia Mott was as outspoken to her American as to her Irish friends. At the time of the London Convention, Elizabeth Cady Stanton, the young bride, had carried her religious doubts to Lucretia. Writing in 1841 to Mrs. Stanton, Lucretia assured her, as she had tried to explain in London, that she was not disturbed by charges of heresy and infidelity as long as she could keep before her eyes, as ideals of practical righteousness, an enlarged liberty of opinion, unrestricted religious belief, and a sympathetic tolerance that allowed each man to select his own theories and forms of religion. [4]

For his forthright utterances against slavery, and for the aid he gave runaway slaves, Joseph Dugdale of Green Plain, Ohio, had suffered disownment by his Meeting; but his proscription had gained for him the sympathetic understanding of Lucretia Mott. "When once compromise of principle is made for peace sake and to please men," she assured Sarah Dugdale in a letter written in October 1845, "we may expect darkness and opposition to follow. . . What will be the ultimate result of all these high-handed measures, we cannot foresee. If all can preserve the temper and spirit toward our persecutors, that Joseph & Ruth manifest, there will be little fear." [5]

During the decade, 1840–1850, Lucretia delivered many public addresses. Early in October 1841, she preached in the Quaker Meetinghouse on Rose Street in New York. After a slight hesitation, a seeming lack of ease, ascribed by one reporter to the criticism which had been leveled at Lucretia on account of her anti-slavery utterances, she spoke with great feeling of the fact that the Quakers of her day seemed indifferent to the significance of the Inner Voice. Modern Friends, she felt, departed from the "ancient testimonies" when they engaged in trade with slaveholders, when they took active participation in politics supporting the "agents and actors" in a war, when they violated the sacredness of the right of an individual to arrive at his own religious beliefs. Sectarianism especially, she denounced, as the binding force of creeds and "the tendency to disparage all good works not done within the enclosure of one's own particular sect." Because the tone of this speech was so "mild, gentle, calm and affectionate," as a member of her audience wrote, the full force of this castigation of the Quakers was not realized until hours after the gathering had dispersed.[6]

When Lucretia addressed the 1842 Baltimore Yearly Meeting, she "drew crowds of people of various sects" to hear her. "Be still and know that I am God" was her text; but her audience, "composed of various denominations and many of the first men in the city," was implored to denounce the evils of the day. In Baltimore, as in New York, the mildness of her manner challenged the convictions of her hearers; in fact, she was described as "the gentle missionary of humanity."

An incident of this Baltimore visit was said to be the "Conversion to Anti-Slavery of a Dr. Snodgrass," described as a "son of a slaveholder." According to the account in the *Liberator,* Dr. Snodgrass had gone to the meeting with the intention of inciting violence; but he succumbed so completely to Lucretia's magnetism that he remained quiet under her words and "went back to his office an altered man." [7]

Shortly after this Baltimore Yearly Meeting, Lucretia Mott

delivered a speech in the Unitarian church in Washington that startled the large "audience composed of members of Congress, officers and judges and literary men." Many people had standing room only in the church, and others had to be turned away. As in her other speeches she protested the intolerance of orthodox religion and the wrongs of society, particularly, the wrongs of war and human slavery. Again, her manner was described as "calm, deliberate, yet forcible and eloquent."

When the graceful, frail-appearing Lucretia Mott was about to begin this address, a woman in the audience arose from her seat and for an instant stood with extended hands as though transfixed.[8] One reporter told of a member of Congress who "twitched" in his seat when the speaker dwelt on the subject of slavery, and Emerson wrote that he heard that the sensation that attended the speech was like "the rumble of an earthquake" and "that no man would have said as much & come away alive. I like her very well, yet she is not quite enough an abstractionist for me, and her will is more illuminated than her mind." [9] It was the belief of the correspondent of the *Pittsburgh Gazette* that there was not in the United States another woman who could approach Lucretia Mott in eloquence and exalted intellectual attainments. This same observer expressed his intention of trying to have the address published in spite of Lucretia Mott's unorthodox views on "the cardinal points of the doctrines of the churches of the day."

In the next year, Thoreau wrote of having heard Lucretia Mott speak at the Hester Street Meetinghouse in New York. "After a long silence," he said, "Mrs. Mott rose, took off her bonnet and began to utter very deliberately what the spirit suggested. Her self possession was something to see, if all else failed, but it did not. Her subject was 'The Abuse of the Bible,' and thence she straightway digressed to slavery and the degradation of women. It was a good speech," concluded Thoreau, "transcendentalism in its mildest form." [10]

When the "Semi-Annual or Autumnal Convention" of the Unitarians was held in Philadelphia from Tuesday, October 20, through Thursday, October 22, 1846, Lucretia and her sister Martha attended the gathering. At the first meeting, the assembly chose, in the form of three Resolutions, the program of the sessions: a tribute to the spirit of William Penn, the responsibility of Christians for the moral tone of American life, and the need for spreading the Gospel throughout the world.[11] The morning of the third and last day of the sessions, soon after the introduction of the Third Resolution, Lucretia Mott was invited on motion of the Reverend Mr. Furness to take a seat in the Convention. Responding to this invitation Lucretia addressed the assembly. In the report of this speech, it was noted that she urged greater simplicity in the utterances of ministers, freedom from "ambiguous and deceiving phraseology," and independence of thought and action. Courage especially, she declared, was the cardinal need of ministers, courage to reject belief in a vicarious atonement and the divinity of Christ; then she emphasized the need of especial strength to support these so-called heresies.

Writing to her husband, Martha Wright told of how Dr. Furness approached the pew where Lucretia and Martha were sitting, talked quietly with Lucretia for a few minutes, and then proposed to the Convention that Lucretia Mott be invited to take a seat among the scheduled speakers. The suggestion made by Dr. Furness being "heartily responded to," continued Martha, Lucretia "went further forward . . . and when the right time came she made an elegant speech." Martha was overjoyed that she herself was present at this gathering, declaring that Lucretia exhorted her hearers "to dare to utter their sentiments boldly & without clothing them in unintelligible language adopted by Sectarians [and] spoke of the sensualist Solomon and of woman's bondage." [12]

But one member of the audience reported that after making a formal protest to the presiding officer of the Convention, he had received the assurance that "By the help of the Lord" it would "never happen again." And a writer to the *Anti-Slavery Standard* declared that although Dr. Furness had said that the invitation to Mrs. Mott was given after a "unanimous" vote was recorded, the fact of the matter was that "All did not vote." [13]

Lucretia herself asked the Webbs: "Have you noticed what a step the Unitarian convention took in this city, in graciously permitting a woman to speak? And such a woman! That made a stir in our Zion, and increased the opposition to that woman too! " [14]

Philadelphia's medical schools attracted to the city young men from all parts of the country, particularly from the South. Indeed, an unproved charge, made at the burning of Pennsylvania Hall, was that the mob was fanned into violence by Southern students among the crowd. Lucretia Mott may have been inspired to reach Southern students when she expressed a desire to preach to the young men studying medicine in Philadelphia. On the other hand, as she said, she may have simply wished to bring a message of spiritual import to young scientists. Her proposal met with such warm response that a meeting was arranged for February 1849. "Some 20 or 30 rose to go out while the subject of slavery was pressed upon their attention," as Lucretia informed Joseph and Ruth Dugdale. "Part of this number," she continued, "halted at the door and remained to the close. Many went away for want of room — and a quieter, more attentive audience I have not often had." [15]

After referring to the conventional method of beginning religious services with a hymn or prayer, she implored her young hearers to deprecate any need of "measured lines or the music of voice" to awaken "melody in the heart." The individual must make his own responses to religion without the atmosphere of a program of music, without the mediation of a constituted leader. She believed that the mature man or woman needs no intermediary for direction to the throne of grace. She took this opportunity to criticize "a belief in human depravity and a vicarious atonement, imputed sin and imputed righteousness," and slavery was described as indefensible unrighteousness.

But the core of her address was her summary. Here she stated that she was "a worshiper after the way called heresy — a believer after the manner which many may deem infidel." Nevertheless, she said that her faith was:

. . . firm in the blessed, the eternal doctrines preached by Jesus, and by every child of God from the creation of the world; especially the great truth that God is the teacher of his people himself; the doctrine which Jesus most emphatically taught, that the kingdom of God is within man — that *there* is his sacred and divine temple.

This religious doctrine, she added,

. . . is simple, because it appeals to self-evident conviction. It is divested of mystery and mysticism, for it is not necessarily connected, with anything miraculous or extraordinary. . . Christianity has been lamentably marred in its glory and beauty, by the gloomy dogmas of the schools. Many, however, are now enquiring for themselves, are acknowledging the heavenly light within them. They begin to understand the divine mission of Jesus; how it is what his coming was and ever is to bless mankind, by turning everyone from his iniquities; that, in him, in the great truths which he preached, all nations shall be blessed.[16]

In the summer of 1847, Lucretia Mott delivered a sermon in the Unitarian church on Nantucket. A week later, she held a religious meeting at Worcester. The Worcester sermon, entitled the "Reforms of the Age," aroused lively comment, and diverse opinions. On this occasion she declared that reformers themselves must have greater faith if they would reach the heart of man, and that ecclesiastical assumptions should be opposed whether they resided in the Church of Rome or in a Quaker Meeting; again she deplored as "impious" the doctrines of total depravity and Vicarious Atonement. Her advocacy of unconventional religious reform was protested as wholly "gratuitous." She was soundly denounced for her comparison of orthodox Christian leaders to the Scribes and Pharisees; and for all of these utterances she was called an "infidel" and "heretic."

From New England the Motts traveled to Syracuse, New York, where Lucretia found a warm welcome in the Unitarian church pastored by her old friend and co-worker in the antislavery cause, Samuel J. May. In this Syracuse sermon she reiterated the doctrine preached in Worcester with the effect of having her speech called "the boldest, the most nervous and pointed" of her addresses of the time.

Early in 1838 a group of twenty-four liberals issued a call for an Anti-Sabbath Convention to be held in Boston. The signers of the Call, among whom were Garrison, Charles Burleigh, Maria W. Chapman, Henry C. Wright, and James and Lucretia Mott, stated that the sole issue was the attribution of exclusive holiness to the seventh day and the attempt by "penal enactments" to force the observance of any one day as the Sabbath. Lucretia Mott was a member of the "Business Committee," that is, the Convention's Executive Committee.[17]

After taking an active part in the general discussion, she extolled, in a scheduled address, the idea of "Consecrating" all of one's time "to God and to goodness." The part of this address, however, that became the target for the sharpest darts from the conventional thinkers of the day embraced her words on the unmediated acceptance of scriptural authority. Taking as her point of departure the language of Jesus in regard to his baptism by John, she questioned her hearers as to whether they believed that "the example of the ancients, whether Prophets or Apostles, or the 'beloved son of God' himself" was "sufficient for the entire regulation of one's action at the present day." Instead of blind conformity to the letter of the Bible and to unquestioned acceptance of established religious practices, she stressed the significance of man's power of reason to choose a recognition of the spirit of the present age. She declared, "We must be willing to stand out in our heresy" "to act out our convictions," and not seem to "harmonize with the dicta of prescribed authority." Creeds and forms, she felt, should be less binding than the dictates of justice, peace, and mutual love. The world's need was for independence, for men to separate themselves from the advice of preachers — to arrive at their own views of life, to do their own thinking, to obey the truth that would make them free. The keynote of this address was the emphasis she placed on the innate power of man to achieve a noble life. As she expressed it, "The kingdom of God is right even at the door."

A veritable fusillade was leveled at the Anti-Sabbath Convention, the name itself of the gathering being anathema even before reports of proceedings were available. Not a little of the censure fell on Lucretia Mott. She was described in the *Boston Recorder* as "another prominent spouter on the platform," a person "of graceful mien, with a pleasing benignant aspect," showing "by almost every sentence which she uttered that her soul was rankling against the kingdom of God and his Christ." She was likened to the queen tagged by John Knox as having "a proud mynd, a crafty witt an indurant hairt against God and his truths."

On the other hand, the *Boston Christian World* placed her at the head of all the women of her age, a woman ranking with Fox and Woolman. Her repudiation by the Quakers was claimed in the *Christian World* as "proof of the low spiritual and moral conditions" of the Society of Friends.

A not insignificant contribution to the body of nineteenth-century sectarian literature was the *Autobiography* of the excommunicated Irish-Spanish priest, Joseph Blanco White. Blanco White's account of his religious experiences, revealing his unorthodox views on the Scriptures and "his doubts on the Trinity and Atonement," led to his renouncing Catholicism for Anglicism, then finally to his accepting Unitarianism. This confession touched a sympathetic chord in Lucretia Mott's heart and mind. Writing to Richard Webb in 1847, two years after the appearance of his autobiography, she confessed that she regarded the work as the best "radical or heretical work that has appeared in this our age because the religious sentiment continues as alive & while his mind is undergoing all the phases from gross superstition to arch heresy." She regretted, however, the fact that more light was not thrown on "the period of his 'Unbelief'" and that more of his correspondence with American radicals was not included in the text. On the whole, however, she felt that the work was "admirably done." It was said that she left "sixty or seventy carefully written notes" on Blanco White's *Life*.[18]

The fact that criticism of Lucretia Mott was rarely overt before the middle of the century is no refutation of its existence. Chief among her antagonists was George F. White, described by Lucretia as "the notable 'Hicksite.' " George F. White, however, usually confined his attacks to generalities, provoking one member at least of Cherry Street Meeting to complain "If he would call Lucretia's name, he would be more honest."

Her failure "to assume the kneeling posture in prayer and also the standing posture while others pray," her frequent attendance at the conventions of the Unitarians, a word spoken here, a phrase there in gatherings of the liberals of the day combined to set tongues wagging in censure. Although denounced, she was not officially molested, for, in Emerson's words, "Friends think so much of her." Surprisingly, in the face of the knowledge of her heterodoxy she continued to hold offices in the Meetings of the Philadelphia Friends. Particularly indicative of the regard in which she was held by the majority of liberal Quakers was the fact that although denounced as a heretic, she was kept on the Education Committee of the Society and thus assisted in the making of plans for the "rightly guarded school education" for Quaker children.[19]

Cherishing membership in her Meeting, Lucretia Mott tried to evade direct questions as to her beliefs on points of doctrine. First with her always, however, was her emphasis upon the spiritual basis of her faith. In spite of her admiration for Henry Buckle, she declared that this scholar erred in placing greater faith in the intellect than in the spiritual and moral powers of man. The progress in human society, she felt, was due to the development of man's spiritual nature, to the "better understanding of God dwelling with man, the Holy Spirit being with us, and to man's regard for his fellow being." To Buckle's statement, that no new religious law had evolved since Jesus of Nazareth, Lucretia Mott maintained that no new law in the truth was needed, Jesus himself having declared that he preached no new doctrine. What was needed, said Lucretia, was "a better carrying out of the law, a better life, a better recognition of the Divine and of the great duties of life springing from the right worship of the Divine and the eternal." [20]

When occasion demanded a forthright avowal of faith she was

not one to quibble. One need go no further than her words in the address to the Unitarians in 1846 and in the sermon to the medical students in 1848. In these addresses she left no doubt as to her convictions on the doctrines of human depravity, vicarious atonement, the divinity of Jesus, and orthodox authority. But, while not accepting orthodox religious principles, she emphasized that her religion was positive: "My faith is firm in the blessed, the eternal doctrines preached by Jesus, and by every child of God from the creation of the world." Indirect attacks rarely moved her to explanation or defense. Meanwhile, no formal action was taken against her by her Meeting; but opposition, within the circle of Quakerism and without, was unconcealed; and she was aware of it. However, she stood her ground. She held her convictions as she raised her voice, "that gentle voice," in Cherry Street Meeting, and beyond Philadelphia in her Society and in the gathering of reformers, against blind adherence to dogma and creeds, against the thoughtless acceptance of principles of belief and faith. In no uncertain terms she continued to preach "practical righteousness." And to many it was Lucretia Mott's practical righteousness in words and in deeds that spun the web of her influence. To her, the "inward spiritual grace" led inevitably to the "outward visible sign." She could not separate the two. She did not hesitate to say that the divine light within man was the power of God, the Divinity that inspires to justice and truth.

Chapter Eleven

THE LAUNCHING OF
WOMAN'S RIGHTS

"Absolute justice and truth," as Lucretia Mott had reminded Miller McKim shortly after the beginning of their friendship, led to equal rights for women. This "lugging in the woman question," therefore, was for her no accident. For years she had followed the opinions of writers on the status of women. She knew what had been said and thought on the inequalities suffered by women; especially was she aware of the measures proposed to remedy the injustice. Mary Wollstonecraft's *Vindication of the Rights of Woman with Strictures on Political and Moral Subjects* included a plea for the right of women to take part in "the deliberations of government." Here was the core of the problem, the basic principle of freedom, which women of later generations were wise enough to accept and urge in the struggle for Woman's Rights. Lucretia said that she "was greatly astonished that such a work should be condemned and out of print." [1]

The inadequate and inferior education meted out to women in all parts of the world had drawn the fire of Mary Wollstonecraft. Two incidents are indicative of the American side of the problem. On October 28, 1636, "by a vote of the General Court of the Colony of Massachusetts Bay," "Harvard College" was founded for "the education of the English & Indian youth of this Country in knowledge: and godliness." Although in this vote of the General Court no enlightenment as to the sex of the "English & Indian youth" is found, the meaning is clear that Harvard was for American males. For the higher education of American women, nothing at this time was done.

The second event occurred in 1834. In this year the first *Annual Report of the Oberlin Collegiate Institute* appeared, containing these significant words: "They attend recitations with young men in all departments." Complete liberality at Oberlin, however, was not attained at a single bound. In the beginning it was thought prudent and logical to provide "instruction in the useful branches taught in the best Female Seminaries," courses that, it was presumed, most of the women students would choose. But as a history of Oberlin College reads, "when the first college classes were begun in the autumn of 1834, members of the female Department participated in some of them, and thus, for the first time, college students shared their class instruction with women.[2]

At Oberlin concern was felt for the effect of the experiment "upon the manners of the young gentlemen and especially the modesty of young ladies and in general upon whatever pertains to purity, propriety and progress in all desirable improvement." But after the initial experiment in coeducation, the decision was reached that, far from being harmed from this association in the classrooms, the students had emerged unscathed, that the association had produced happy results "in the cultivation of both mind and manners."

The old ghost of women's inferiority, however, was not laid at a single stroke. The authorities of Oberlin, aware that it was not deemed modest for women to appear on a public platform, took the precaution, in the first years of its hazardous experiment, to appoint male substitutes to read the commencement addresses written by the young women. Against Oberlin's adherence to this practice of the times a voice of protest had been raised by one of the women students shortly after the opening of the college. This radical was none other than Lucy Stone, an early graduate of Oberlin, one of the notable women of the nineteenth century. As an undergraduate she became president of the Woman's Debating Society; but she was not happy about some of the restrictions on women students. "We shall leave this college," she charged at the inauguration of the Woman's Debating Society, "with the reputation of a thorough collegiate course, yet not one of us received any rhetorical or elocutionary training." "Not one of us," she continued, "could state a question or argue it in successful debate." [3]

Significant things were happening elsewhere; in 1837, four years after the opening of Oberlin, a brave New England woman took a step that led to a far-reaching climax in American education for women. It was Mary Lyon, a frail-appearing schoolteacher without funds, who sought to establish a "higher seminary for women," an institution also in which the Christian virtues were to be stressed. Mary Lyon seemed ambitious to build bricks without straw, but she never wavered, never lost her hopes or her faith; and finally, in the establishment of Mt. Holyoke Seminary, she realized her dream. The venture seemed revolutionary; and far-seeing as Mary Lyon was, she hardly envisioned her budding school as the spearhead in a crusade destined to overcome belief in the mental inferiority of women. In the idea recognized by Oberlin and in the establishment of Mt. Holyoke Seminary, progress at last seemed started toward a recognition of woman's need for an education comparable to that considered necessary for men. Yet two hundred years had to pass after the founding of Harvard College before the first step was taken toward the higher education of American women.

Women endured other grievances besides inequalities in education. Women could not sue or be sued except in the name of their husbands; nor could they execute legal documents. This condition was suffered by both American and English women, to say nothing of women in other countries. Lydia Maria Child was competent as editor of the *Anti-Slavery Standard;* but when she set about drawing up her own will, she needed her husband's signature to make the testament legal.[4] And Jane Welsh Carlyle, another brilliant woman, met rebuff when she took upon herself a mission of appeal against excessive income taxes. Approaching the tax collector she met this response, "Mr. Carlyle's signature is needed to verify Chapman and Hall's statement, for we can do nothing with your oath." [5] The irony of this lay in the fact that Mrs. Carlyle knew only too well that had her husband attempted to protest the taxes, his unpredictable temper would have defeated the desired aim.

Lucretia Mott believed that her views on women's rights were the result of her Nantucket heritage. "I grew up so thoroughly imbued with women's rights," she emphasized again and again, "that it was the most important question of my life from a very early day." Youthful experiences heightened by mature considerations led her to resent strongly the subordinate position of women. Indeed it was a rare sermon or other speech delivered by Lucretia that did not include an allusion to women's rights. For years she had advocated the doctrine of complete equality for women; yet it was the visit to Great Britain that drew her up sharply to the need for action. Of course the decisive factor was the reactionary position of the London Convention; but while traveling about the the country she saw much to make her aware of the prejudice. As she learned of the inadequate wages grudgingly paid to women for laborious work, as she saw repeatedly the deliberate efforts to keep women in a servile state through inferior education and training, the resentment provoked by the Convention did not wane. Gracious British hospitality had warmed her heart; she could rejoice in her new British friends; but she could not forget the wrongs suffered by English women.

In her speech on August 9 at the Unitarian Chapel in Birmingham she reminded her listeners of the limited education doled out to English girls, the education that prevented them from "occupying their proper places in society." And, despite the respect she maintained for competent housekeeping, despite her mastery of cooking, sewing, knitting, and mending, she maintained a sense of relative values that enabled her to put first things first. She knew that the custom of restricting the training of girls to "a little reading, a little writing and a little sewing," of keeping them in a so-called "protected state," circumscribed their interests, achievement, and imagination. Part of the responsibility for the injustice, however, she shifted from the shoulders of men. "Women," she acknowledged, "should train themselves to take a dignified place in the world, to be rational companions, to share the responsibilities of life."

In one of Richard Webb's letters to Lucretia Mott, he included a line introducing a friend, Charles S. Cochrain, of Dublin, on the eve of Cochrain's first visit to America. Mentioning Cochrain's liberality on the woman question, he quoted some of the visitor's words on the subject. What irked Lucretia in Cochrain's "liberality," was his admitting a willingness to "allow" women certain rights. As she responded:

I move that the word "be allowed to," be omitted. Our freedom has so long been "by sufferance and at will of a superior," that we cannot expect a ready recognition of independent judgment — the servitude of woman is by so many of her kind kept and guarded as a sacred thing, that we need not look for mental fetters to be soon broken. I wish we could send him some of our papers & periodicals without subjecting him to postage.[6]

In May 1845 while attending the Ohio Yearly Meeting, Lucretia was granted permission to hold a special audience with the women. Such was the magic of her words, so convincing were her arguments, that one of her listeners years later wrote that this lecture was not only "the first public Suffrage speech by a woman, for a woman in that region of the country," but that many Ohio women treasured that speech as the inspiration of their conversion to the Woman's Rights Movement.[7]

A few years after speaking these far-reaching words, Lucretia Mott attended the Fourteenth Annual Meeting of the American

Anti-Slavery Society, convened in May 1848 in the Broadway Tabernacle, New York. At the opening session of this gathering, she
made an address on "The Law of Progress," a speech that was
destined to be placed among her first full-length, completely reported addresses.

Beginning, she designated "the law of progress the advancement from knowledge to knowledge, from obedience to obedience
as a principle that was worthy of the contemplation of the wisest
of men." As she continued, she pointed out the growth in the organized efforts directed toward universal peace, temperance, religion, and antislavery. Calling religion "the subject of priestcraft,"
she implored her hearers to advance beyond the progress of the
Reformation, which was marked by its attacks on popery, religious hierarchies, and priests of designated parishes. Present-day
reformers, she added, were advocating, and rightly so, complete
individuality of belief as one looked independently to God for
guidance. In her optimism she claimed the advent of a new day,
a day of such religious progress that pulpits were no longer "the
little high, narrow isolated boxes," but broad platforms wide
enough to admit even women preachers. "Progress toward a great
peace reformation," she said, "was marked by evidences that
civilized nations were beginning to believe that even defensive
war was to be shunned." And the temperance leaders, she felt, were
preaching " 'total abstinence' from all intoxicating liquors."

The climax of her words was reached in her discussion of the
development of the Anti-Slavery Society from 1833, with its declaration of the abstract principles of human freedom, to heartening
evidences in 1848 of a growing belief in the need of concrete steps
to blot out every existence of slavery. In her words these evidences
of progress were illustrated "by the response in the hearts of those
who have not been blinded by their sectarian prejudices, by the
fact that both the pulpit and the press are enlisted to some extent
in behalf of the suffering and the dumb," and by the attitude of
legislative assemblies.

In the ringing appeal of her conclusion, she advocated the immediate abolition of slavery instead of the protests raised in meetings and the inactivity of waiting for the "natural end" of the
wrong.

This speech was characterized by compactness of form in its
closely knit arrangement of ideas on religion, war, temperance, and
slavery. But its appeal is to the heart also. One disinterested observer described it as "a strain of eloquence and truth, which was

really delightful." And the New York *Herald,* despite its evident delight in criticizing reformers, contented itself with the sole observation that Lucretia Mott sat at the reporter's table, her "knitting on the table beside her." [8]

When Lucretia Mott presented this summary of events indicating a "law of progress," she could point to no steps toward organized action for human rights for women in America. Possibly she felt that the time was at hand to promote action for the establishment of such a needed movement. At any rate, after traveling in the spring of 1848 from New York City to the western part of the state for religious meetings and for a visit with her sister Martha in Waterloo, she had reached the decision to take action to bring about a change in the position of women. The time was at hand to carry out a suggestion made by Mrs. Stanton in 1841. "Remember," Lucretia reminded Mrs. Stanton several years after, "the first Convention originated with thee. When we were walking the streets of Boston together in 1841, . . . thou asked if we could not have a Convention for Woman's Rights. Then when Jas. & self were attendg. the Yearly Mg. at Waterloo in 47 or 8 was it? thou again proposed the Convention which was afterward held at Seneca Falls." [9]

Lucretia Mott and Elizabeth Cady Stanton had been drawn together at their first meeting. With broad vision, both women realized the need for action on the problem of woman's rights, and both had faith in the justice of the cause. When the moment, therefore, for action arrived, these women, instead of being ambitious for leadership, kept their eyes steadily on the goal. Unselfishly, each disclaimed the honor of initiating a movement destined to reach undreamed-of stature in the years to come.

Moreover, in all probability Elizabeth Cady Stanton believed that Lucretia Mott was, at the time, the only woman in America capable of evoking response to the movement. Lucretia's public speeches in the Meetings of the Society of Friends had gained for her an experience destined to serve her in good stead as she raised her voice to advocate reforms close to her heart. She was at ease on the platform with the ability to think on her feet. She had the reputation of being a convincing and pleasing speaker, a reputation due originally to her sermons but enhanced later by her addresses in the antislavery societies, the Non-Resistance organizations, the Free-Produce meetings, and the Anti-Sabbath movement. Then too, in carrying her message of reform she had traveled widely in the Middle West and in lower Canada.

In 1848, Elizabeth Cady Stanton, destined to become a power as a public speaker, was comparatively unknown outside her state; Susan B. Anthony, the future leader of the Woman's Rights Movement, was teaching school in upstate New York, while engaged also in the cause of antislavery; and the other leaders prominent in the crusade for complete justice for women were yet to appear. But no issue was ever closer to the heart of Elizabeth Cady Stanton than the question of Woman's Rights; and at the moment she was aglow with the importance of making the right start. She could not afford a false step; the launching must be sure. Her affection for Lucretia Mott is unquestioned; but she could not have been blind to the fact that Lucretia's name was a drawing card. Lucretia needed no urging to inscribe Woman's Rights on her banner. But never relinquishing her belief in the interrelationship of social wrongs, she asked, "Are you going to have any reform or other Meeting during the sittings of the Convention?"

From its start, the Woman's Rights Movement had its opponents as well as its promoters. All churches did not open their doors to pioneers; and despite the enthusiasm of Lucretia Mott and Elizabeth Cady Stanton, the cold reality was faced that there was no certainty that proceedings could be conducted in all assembly rooms without noisy and hostile interruptions. It was hardly an accident, perhaps, that the choice of a meeting place fell upon the Wesleyan Chapel in Seneca Falls, New York — a church founded in 1843 almost exclusively by separatists from the Methodist Episcopal Church on the issue of slavery. This church, representing the protest against one form of oppression, might well be hospitable to a group suffering from another sort of oppression.

The story of the preparations for the Seneca Falls meeting has been often told: how Lucretia Mott, her sister Martha Wright, and Elizabeth Cady Stanton, aided by Mary Ann McClintock and Jane Hunt, both Quakers of Waterloo, labored to draw up a program.[10] Their task was to write a "Declaration of Sentiments" and, like their predecessors in the inauguration meeting of the American Anti-Slavery Society, these five leaders of Rights for Women chose the Declaration of Independence as the model. It is said that, sitting around a sturdy mahogany table now honorably housed in the Smithsonian Institution at Washington, they studied the Declaration of Independence word for word, building up their own "Statement of Grievances" by repeating and adapting and paraphrasing the language of the original document to fit the purpose at hand.

After the Declaration was written, the pioneers, in spite of Lucretia's protest, prepared the following notice for the town's newspaper, the *Seneca County Courier:*

Woman's Rights Convention

A Convention to discuss the social civil and religious condition and rights of women will be held in the Wesleyan Chapel, at Seneca Falls, New York, on Wednesday and Thursday, the 19th and 20th of July current; commencing at 10 o'clock A.M. During the first day the meeting will be exclusively for women, who are earnestly invited to attend. The public generally are invited to be present on the second day, when Lucretia Mott, of Philadelphia, and other ladies and gentlemen, will address the convention.[11]

Lucretia was not sanguine as to the success of the undertaking but, unwilling to throw cold water on the effort, she wrote Mrs. Stanton on July 16 that although she feared that the season of harvesting was an unpropitious time for calling a convention, yet it was a beginning which might lead to eventual success. Then, always the devoted wife, she added, "I requested her" [Mary Ann McClintock] "to tell them how poorly my husband was, and that it was not likely I should be able to go to Seneca Falls before the morning of the Convention. I hope however that he will be able to be present the 2nd day." [12]

As the moment approached for the opening of the meeting, the leaders of the movement were thrown almost into a panic by the problem of choosing a presiding officer for the sessions. In 1848 women were unaccustomed to wielding the gavel, and so great was the concern of the leaders for the success of their venture that they did not wish to draw criticism at the start by departing too far from accepted conventions.

Even the experienced public speaker Lucretia Mott would not assume the risk of bringing ridicule upon the gathering by attempting to fill a role accorded up to that time to men alone. Later, she was to recall the opening meeting of the Philadelphia Female Anti-Slavery Society in these words:

When . . . we came together to form the Female Anti-Slavery Society, which I am rejoiced to say is still extant, still flourishing, there was not a woman capable of taking the chair and organizing that meeting in due order; and we had to call on James McCrummel, a colored man, to give us aid in the work. You know that at that time, even to the present day, Negroes, idiots and women were in legal documents classed together; so that we were very glad to get one of our own class [laughter] to come and aid in forming that Society.¹³

This she said in 1853. It requires, therefore, little imagination to understand that in 1848 the very thought of presiding in the public meeting appalled even the leaders of the Convention. Of course, there is the possibility that these farseeing women may have rejected the dubious honor of the chairmanship for the opportunities of free discussion open to them from the floor. But tradition is that they felt unprepared to undertake the established routine of conducting a formal assembly.

It was by no mere chance that James Mott was called to the chair. Tall, handsome, erect, he made an imposing presiding officer, inspiring confidence and respect by his commanding presence, restraint, and fairness. James Mott was more than "Lucretia Mott's husband"; he was in his own right an independent thinker. He had made the decision to leave the Orthodox Quakers before his wife felt that she could take the step of Separation; he was active in the organization of the National Anti-Slavery Society in 1833; his name was included in the Call to men of Pennsylvania for the formation of the Pennsylvania Anti-Slavery Association, and for years was its president. As a Friend he was highly respected for his piety and judgment; and significantly he believed firmly in women's taking a position of equality with men. As early as 1820 he had confided to his parents his inability to understand why the Society of Friends failed to accord to men and women the same power in the "meetings for discipline."

When the gavel sounded, Elizabeth Cady Stanton stated the object of the meeting, reading with dramatic intonations, pauses, and gestures the "grievances" enumerated in the "Declaration." Then Lucretia Mott made the opening speech urging in a few words the necessity of inaugurating a progressive movement aimed to raise woman from her degraded position. She pictured the economic, social, and political wrongs which were imposed upon women; and placing emphasis upon the essential issues, she stressed specifically the need of equal opportunities for both sexes. Moreover, she entertained the group with "a witty original sketch" written by her sister Martha, who could always inspire a competent pen.

Discussion on the proposals in the "Declaration of Sentiments" was spirited and unabated. No official count of the number of times the "Declaration" was read seems available, but the Minutes record that the document was not only read at each of the six sessions of the Convention, but was reread and discussed "paragraph by paragraph," and after much consideration some changes were suggested and adopted. The propriety of obtaining the signatures of men to the "Declaration" evoked animated discussion; but a vote in favor of the men was finally recorded.

After this, the Resolutions, eleven in number, were placed before the assembly. These measures were directed toward concerted effort to secure better educational opportunities for women, particularly in the professions of law and medicine, to demolish the barriers opposing the advancement of women in industrial occupations, to nullify laws restricting women's property rights and the guardianship of their children, and to obtain the right of political representation through unrestricted suffrage. All the Resolutions, except the one demanding the vote, passed unanimously.

This Resolution, advanced by Elizabeth Cady Stanton, had been opposed originally by Lucretia Mott. It has been stated that Lucretia feared that the demand for the ballot would be ridiculed, and thus the cause would be retarded. One answer to her apparent timidity could lie in her Quaker religion, in her belief in the certainty of the attainment of utter justice once the hearts of men were converted to truth and righteousness. She may have failed to understand the underlying principles of suffrage; but she exerted no opposition to Mrs. Stanton's proposal.

On the issue of suffrage Mrs. Stanton was adamant. She was convinced that on this principle the future of the cause was doomed to failure or success. On this issue she was warmly supported by Frederick Douglass. The former slave knew that the achievement of the right of suffrage was the first step toward complete freedom. Not limiting this right to men, he poured forth his challenging eloquence in defense of Mrs. Stanton's Resolution covering suffrage for women. And through his assistance the suffrage became a part of the program for women's rights in America.

But it must not be forgotten that it was Mrs. Stanton who insisted from the first that the ballot was the goal to keep in sight.

On the other hand, Lucretia Mott was a forceful figure at the first Seneca Falls Convention. Not being in the chair she was free to speak when she saw the need of limiting the discussion to relevant topics, of focusing argument, of pointing to flaws in opposition; she established courage in a timid and unsure group; withal she did not permit the meeting to get out of hand. And during the two days of the conference she spoke more frequently and at greater length than any other woman. Finally, it was Lucretia Mott who arose to present the last Resolution: "Resolved, that the speedy success of our cause depends upon the zealous and untiring efforts of both men and women, for the overthrow of the monopoly of the pulpit and for the securing to women an equal participation with men in the various trades, professions and commerce."

Including the four signers of the Call some of the future leaders in the Woman's Rights Movement were present. Among these pioneers were Amy Post and Mary H Hallowell of New York and Catherine A. F. Stebbins of Ohio. There were men too taking an active part in the sessions. Besides James Mott and Frederick Douglass were Richard P. Hunt, an active liberal in New York State, Thomas McClintock, a leader in the Free-Produce Movement, and William S. Nell, orator and associate of Douglass in publishing the *North Star*. One hundred signatures were appended to the Resolution, with Lucretia Mott's name leading. In the final words of the Official Report: "The meeting was closed (at the end of the sessions) by one of Lucretia Mott's beautiful and spiritual appeals. She commanded the earnest attention of that large audience for nearly an hour." [14]

Just two weeks after this Convention of Seneca Falls a follow-up meeting was held in the Unitarian church in Rochester, New York. This fortnight proving to be time enough for the women to overcome their reluctance to presiding, Mary H. Hallowell was elected president of the organization. Such an expression of independence did not meet with unanimous approval. Elizabeth McClintock, Mary Ann's sister, declined to accept the secretaryship for the reason, as she was reported, "of being unprepared to have a woman the presiding officer." Moreover, as the *Report of the Proceedings* reads, "To our great surprise, two or three other women — glorious reformers well deserving the name — coming from a distance to attend the meetings, at first refused to take their seats upon the platform or otherwise cooperate with the convention for the same cause." Lucretia Mott may have been one of these "glorious reformers." The innovation, however, was accepted by the majority of the women, and the sessions moved along to make history.

At this Rochester meeting, convening on August 2, 1848, Lucretia Mott assumed the responsibility of answering two time-honored arguments advanced by the opponents of equal rights for women. One argument was in the guise of praise, a specious plea for the protection of woman in the hallowed precincts of the home where she would be shielded from the rough winds of public life; the other contention lay in a recourse to the authority of St. Paul, who had handed down to women the admonition to recognize the duty of obeying their husbands. Annoyed by the words that echoed the banalities of the London Convention, Lucretia Mott "replied in a speech of great sarcasm and eloquence." With utmost composure she listened to the nineteenth-century disciples of St. Paul, and then responded: "Many of the opposers of Woman's Rights who bid us to obey the bachelor St. Paul, themselves reject his counsel — he advised them not to marry." [15]

The question of the inferiority of women implying their need for guardianship and protection, called forth a more extended answer. "Does one man have fewer rights than another because his intellect is inferior," Lucretia Mott asked. "If not why should a woman?"

Long ages of repression, she admitted, could have stunted the development of woman's intellect; but this injustice was no reason for one's concluding that woman was innately inferior to man. This point she stressed again and again, protesting that a condition induced by injustice should not be urged as a reason for excusing or continuing the original injustice. But she would make no false claims to attain rights for women. As she warned Elizabeth Cady Stanton, "Thou wilt have hard work to prove the equality of women with men, facts are so against such an assumption, in the present stage of woman's development. We need not however *admit* inferiority even tho' we may not be able to prove equality." [16]

She was too levelheaded to be swerved from her course by misguided though well-intentioned efforts of liberal men. One supporter of the cause of Woman's Rights, the Negro William S. Nell, was so sympathetic that he attempted to eulogize women, claiming that they were superior to men in their intellectual and spiritual power. At these words, Lucretia immediately arose, acknowledging her gratitude for Mr. Nell's motive and eloquence in "styling woman the better half of creation and man a tyrant." But she added that man had become so accustomed "to speak of woman in the language of flattering compliments that he indulges in such expressions unawares . . . man was not a tyrant by nature but had been made tyrannical by the power which had by general consent, been conferred upon him."

Her wish, as she stated it in concluding her reply to Nell, was that women might achieve rights equal to those enjoyed by men.

She had no desire for women to be rated superior. And far from
assuming their superiority, she admitted that women were tyrannical when allowed to be irresponsible for their actions.

In answer to the complaint that the voices of the speakers could
not be heard, she waived the right of women to offer the excuse of
natural weakness of voice. She would not resort to an argument
based on special pleading for women. It was her belief that women
entering public life on the issue of their "Natural rights," should
ask for no concessions on account of physcal handicaps of sex. "It
is," she declared at this assembly, "the duty of the speaker to make
herself heard. The secretary, therefore should speak louder. I
believe that with sufficient practice women can and will make
themselves heard in a public assembly." [17]

Thus, at these conventions in Seneca Falls and in Rochester,
Lucretia Mott stressed duties as well as rights. It was not enough,
she thought, to plead for the rights of women while forgetting the
duties of women, particularly the duty of elevating the lowly and
aiding the weak. But in her final speech at the Convention she
alluded to the improvement in the special offerings to women in
the journals of the day, and to the fact that "the sick mentality of
the 'ladies' Department" was giving way "to more substantial
food." Her very last words carried a hope of encouragement.

Following these two meetings in New York in the summer of
1848, other workers became a part of the national campaign for
human rights for American women. Susan B. Anthony, Caroline W. Severance, Lucy Stone, Frances Gage, and others took up
the challenge. But it was the united force of the pioneers of 1848
that assured the auspicious start of a campaign which was to endure until victory was achieved in another generation. The hand-
ful gathered at Seneca Falls and at Rochester were responsible for
taking the initiative, particularly, "the promoters and movers,"
Lucretia Mott, Elizabeth Cady Stanton, Martha Coffin Wright,
Mary Ann McClintock, and Jane Hunt. And regardless too of Lucretia Mott's modesty, of her consecration to many other reforms,
she was, as reported by the secretary "the moving spirit of the
meetings." [18]

Chapter Twelve

THE PATH FROM SENECA FALLS

Although Elizabeth Cady Stanton was the direct inspiration of the Seneca Falls Convention, popular acclaim hailed Lucretia Mott as its most prominent member, "the leader of the movement." While Lucretia herself acknowledged that she had needed no urging to inscribe Woman's Rights on her banner, she took no satisfaction in the tribute to her leadership. The price of publicity she had found to be garbled reports of her speeches, misinterpretation of her views, and adverse criticism. Less than three weeks after the First Seneca Falls Convention, the meeting was discussed as a

Woman's Rights Convention — This is the age of revolutions. . . . The flag of independence has been hoisted for the second time on this side of the Atlantic; and a solemn league and convenant has just been entered into by a Convention of women at Seneca Falls to throw off the despotism under which they are groaning and provide new guards for their future security. Little did we expect this new element to be thrown into the cauldron of agitation, which is now bubbling around us with such fury. We have had one Baltimore Convention — one Philadelphia Convention — one Utica Convention — and we shall also have, in a few days, the Buffalo Convention. But we never dreamed that Lucretia Mott had convened a fifth convention, which if it be ratified by those whom it purposes to represent will exercise an influence that will not only control our own Presidential elections, but the whole governmental system through the world. . .

Now though we have the most perfect confidence in the courage and daring of Miss [sic] Lucretia Mott, and several others of our lady acquaintances, we confess it would go to our hearts to see them putting on the panoply of war, and mixing in scenes like those at which, it is said, the fair sex in Paris lately took a prominent part. . .

The convention of Seneca Falls has appealed to the Country. Miss Lucretia Mott has propounded the principles of the party. Ratification meetings will no doubt shortly be held; and if it be the general impression that this lady is a more eligible candidate for the Presidential chair than McLean or Cass, Van Buren or old "Rough and Ready," then let the false laws be abolished forthwith from this great republic. We are much mistaken if Lucretia would not make a better President than some of those who have lately tenanted the White House.[1]

In 1848 the spirit of antagonism between the North and the South was kept alive in Congress by repeated attacks on the anti-slavery movement. When, therefore, the regular fall meeting of the Eastern Pennsylvania Anti-Slavery Association was held in December 1848, there was much talk in the group on the value of addressing Congress and state legislatures through petitions. Discussion also arose on the need for sending assistance to Negroes colonized in Canada, on Free Produce, and on the Free-Soil Movement.

In summarizing the events of the sessions, the *Anti-Slavery Standard* of December 28, 1848, indicated that Lucretia Mott, beyond an endeavor to keep the topics within the limits of anti-slavery, took little part in the discussions. Only one speech of any length was credited to her, a speech of warning to the Society against confusing "temperance, peace, theological and judicial reforms" with antislavery. She said that, while, individually, members could embrace interest in all reforms, the Society itself should limit its program to the discussion of antislavery, the fundamental aim of the Anti-Slavery Society. This speech and her final plea for "higher principles," which she called the willingness to share the sufferings of the needy, constituted practically all that she had to say in the lively sessions of the three-day meeting.[2]

Soon after this meeting, the New York *Weekly Herald* published an editorial under the title, "Movements of the Ultras-Petticoat Politicians, Proposed Dissolution of the Union." In this leader the newspaper stated that the Southern protest was led by "Mr. Calhoun, Mr. Foote, Mr. Metcalf and others"; "the other faction" was indicated as being led by "Lucretia Mott and her associates with the prominent Free-Soilers and Abolitionists." Lucretia was described as,

. . . this lady [who] may have running in her veins some of the blood of her Roman namesake, though, from the unseemly, unfeminine and indelicate exhibition she has been lately making of herself before the world on the subject of slavery, the rights of women, and other old maidenish crochets and idiosyncrasies peculiar to that interesting class of the human race, we have grave doubts of the consanguinity.

After extolling "the Christian dignity and position of womankind and the divinely established order of things," the newspaper continued:

What a pity it is that Lucretia and her body guard had not another Brutus to avenge the wrongs they are now suffering from the horrible indignities and restrictions of male monsters, proud Tarquins, and Southern slaveholders! Miss Lucretia is a great woman, and has raised a great dust wherever she has pursued her peregrinations throughout the country. . . The Roman Lucretia, by the wrongs she endured, and the tragical and suicidal death she suffered, kindled the flames of rebellion, changed the form of government in her day, and founded a republic. Our Yankee Lucretia is no doubt, ambitious to follow the example of her great prototype; and impelled by the overbearing insolence of the Southern Tarquins can no longer restrain herself from ringing the tocsin of revolution, dissolving the bungling constitution of our forefathers. Lucretia the first raised a republic. Lucretia the second is bent on ruining one. In these days of political violent eruptions, we would seriously recommend the friends of the constitution to keep their eye on Lucy, and see that she has no suicidal dagger concealed under her clothes; for if she should take it into her hands to complete the parallel, there is no knowing but she might get a Brutus, or a brute of some sort or other, to avenge her wrongs and involve us in all the horrors of anarchy and insurrection.[3]

In word after word, extended through three columns, the *Herald* continued a torrent of virulence, which was a far cry from the newspaper's brief reference to Lucretia Mott's very lengthy speech on the "Law of Progress" delivered just a few months before. In singling out Lucretia, the newspaper's attack may have been sharpened by two things — the advice given by Lucretia that the program of the Pennsylvania Anti-Slavery Association should be confined to antislavery, and the events at Seneca Falls. In either case tribute is paid to the leadership of Lucretia Mott.

No specific reply to these attacks seems recorded, but Lucretia may have had them in mind when she wrote Mrs. Stanton on November 27, 1849:

I have become somewhat callous to or by the repeated stripes that have been inflicted upon me, as representative of a larger demand for women. . . We have to learn to endure hardness as good soldiers in all their great reformatory movements.[4]

When the Woman's Rights Convention met at Syracuse in the fall of 1852, Lucretia Mott, over her protest, was unanimously elected president. In the course of the proceedings she took active part in the discussions, frequently leaving the chair in order to stress her views. Early in the first session, she introduced a Resolution embodying the principle she had stressed in Anti-Slavery meetings. This embraced her belief that a degraded condition and imposed inferiority resulted in satisfaction with the imposed injustice.

After some delay the Resolution, aimed to counteract the opposition of women satisfied with their position, was unanimously adopted.

At this meeting the assembly was forced to listen to a repetition of the claim for the "natural rights" of women, contention on this occasion being advanced by J. B. Bingham, a schoolteacher of New York. Bingham's argument was that women could be "only true, lovely and happy" in the home, that "women ought to be keeping at home," and that the real object of the present convention was merely to glorify the leaders by placing them in the public eye. In reality Bingham, as Lucy Stone afterward described him in a letter to the *Liberator,* was mild and inoffensive; but Gerrit Smith proposed turning this objection over to Lucretia Mott that "the power of a woman" might be felt.

This "power" in Lucretia's words repudiated the necessity of reserving the sheltered role for women because of a belief in her incapacity to face the rude encounters of the world. Citing the strong women glorified in Biblical narrative, Lucretia boldly brought St. Paul to her defense, arguing that St. Paul's giving women directions for preaching, of his going so far as to advise women not "to pin their faith on 'ministers' sleeves,' " proved that he recognized the fact that women were preachers. But she noted there was no wisdom in adhering too closely to the philosophy of a bygone age, or in believing that "all the advice given by the Apostles to women of their day was applicable to an age avowedly more intelligent." The Scriptures, as she had declared again and again, were to be read intelligently in order to enable one to discriminate between literal translation and subjective interpretation.

Drawing on her experiences in the Anti-Slavery Society, she recalled how a program against slavery had been hindered in that organization by discussions on irrelevant topics. She said that man had inherent rights to himself and his earnings, that none had a right to imbrute him, that it was essentially sinful, and that slaveholders were "man-stealers." The wrongs of slavery, she insisted, were self-evident; but the time of the Anti-Slavery Conventions had been virtually absorbed by needless arguments. It was her hope that the program of the Woman's Rights Movement would be confined to the issue of the inherent rights of women and not cluttered by talks on morality, religion, and theology. A lesson should be taken, she said, from the mistakes made by the Anti-Slavery Society. In his account of this Convention, Samuel J.

May noted that Lucretia Mott's "wisdom, purity and singleness of heart gave her a skill and aptness in the discharge of her duties, far greater than she could have acquired by the study of 'Jefferson's Manual.'" [5]

In the aftermath of criticism of the Convention, Lucretia Mott received no quarter. Styling the Convention "The Last Act of the Drama," the *Liberator* reported, as from the New York *Herald* that

> The farce at Syracuse has been played out. . . In point of ability, the majority of the women are flimsy, flippant, and superficial. If Lucretia Mott, Mrs. Oakes Smith, Mrs. Pauline Davis, Lucy Stone and Mrs. Rose, particularly the latter, are exceptions they but confirm the rule . . . we find that the same men and the same women, including Lloyd Garrison, Rev. W. H. Channing, Rev. Mr. May, Gerrit Smith, the Joneses, Lucy Stone, Horace Greeley and Lucretia Mott, that have been actively engaged in those agitations are equally busy in this. *What a pass are we brought to at last.*[6]

Another newspaper, however, described Lucretia Mott as "the master-mind of the Convention . . . a woman whose towering intellect and benevolent heart, combined with every other virtue that can make life more pure and holy, have rendered her an object of admiration and reverence throughout the Christian world, wherever there is a spark of Godlike benevolence to sympathize with human progress or admiration of that which is good." The newspaper added that, although "ostracized in a measure by the Conservatism of the religious society to which she belongs, and though occupying in some instances what fair minds may perhaps regard as rather extreme ground the influence of Mrs. Mott in the promotion of truth and right far outweighs that of a thousand whose religion consists only in going to meetings."[7]

It was at the Convention of 1852 that Susan B. Anthony entered formally into the ranks of the Woman's Rights Movement. Protesting that her picture with that of Lucy Stone should be placed on a "Suffrage Calendar" honoring Elizabeth Cady Stanton's eightieth birthday, Miss Anthony wrote,

> . . . only Lucretia Mott's picture should go there with Mrs. Stanton's for those two women were the first to call a convention and to make the public demand in such a manner as to startle the nation from Maine to Louisiana. It is those two women, therefore, whose names and whose pictures should stand side by side at this time of celebrating Mrs. Stanton's 80th birthday. So I insisted that my picture should be

dropped out as I was not converted to Suffrage until two years after and did not attend a woman's rights convention until four years after 1848.[8]

After 1852 scattered references to Susan B. Anthony appeared in Lucretia's letters: "Our faithful Susan B. Anthony," "I honor S.B.A.'s . . . devotion," "Susan B. Anthony deserves a medal, I know and I hope there are those who will appreciate her and bestow one upon her."

The friendship between Susan and Lucretia was cemented by Martha Wright, who, accepting the need of suffrage as the cardinal principle in the Woman's Rights program, was bound to Miss Anthony.

Obviously designed to break up the meetings of the reformers was the strategy used to make it impossible for the committees of the Woman's Rights Movement to secure assembly halls for scheduled gatherings. Hiding behind subterfuge or facing the pioneers in unabashed hostility, the managers of public and private halls shut their doors in the face of committees seeking the use of the buildings; and just as unsympathetic were the officers of many churches. One friendly exception was the Broadway Tabernacle in New York. Within the precincts of this hostage, erected in the 1830's on Broadway between Anthony Street and Catherine Lane reformers in many causes — Anti-Slavery, Temperance, World Peace — had been made to feel at home.[9] And when, after a decade or more, a movement was inaugurated to secure human rights for women, this too found sanctuary in the Broadway Tabernacle.

In September 1853 Lucretia Mott went to New York to attend the Woman's Rights meeting and the "Whole World's Temperance Convention." This meeting of the Temperance organization was called by a radical minority after the "Leading Delegates" of the original planning committees of the Convention had rejected the membership of women in the body. In the evening of the second day of the Convention, after Lucy Stone, Arnold Buffum, William Lloyd Garrison, Mrs. G. H. H. Nichols, and others had spoken, the chairman introduced Lucretia Mott as "one whose simplicity and uprightness of character make all compliments from me, from any one, an impertinence."

The Minutes of the Convention report that the theme developed by almost all the speakers was the necessity of legal force to prohibit intemperance, the enactment of a national "Maine Law" to convert the country to sobriety. But Lucretia Mott felt that the speakers in not considering temperance in its relation to man's spiritual and moral nature, had viewed the subject too superficially. Political action, she declared, would follow as soon as the moral significance of temperance was held in esteem.

This was the keynote of her address. And in pointing to the harmonious tie binding "all these great reformatory movements" to the progress already made in the cause, she urged the effort "to stir up the pure mind in themselves, in the cause of truth — to hold up the light higher and higher, and cause it to shine brighter and brighter before more sustained action." [10]

From these sessions, Lucretia went to the Fifth Annual Meeting of the Woman's Rights Movement, called for September 5 and 6, 1853, in the Broadway Tabernacle. No apprehensions were felt by the women; and during the first session of the gathering it was found possible to follow the program in its prearranged order. But the tide was at its ebb. During the five years that had passed since the group was launched at Seneca Falls, opposition to the movement had grown apace. "I have all the rights I want," was the response of many American women to the movement. And a redoubtable response it was; for, if a goodly number of women did not desire these newfangled "Rights," opposition to the crusaders was thereby supported, even sanctified. Thus, a sense of righteousness justified every maneuver aimed to checkmate the steps of reform. But much water had streamed over the dam in the five-year interval between Seneca Falls Woman's Rights Convention of 1848 and this fifth annual meeting in 1853. In 1848 Lucretia Mott, with the other leaders at Seneca Falls, would not assume the risk of a woman's taking the chair; in 1853 she was President of the Convention. In her opening address she declared that the present and indeed the *only* issue before the Woman's Rights Association was the establishing of the principles of the "coequality of woman with man, her right to practice those acts of life for which she is fitted by nature." She felt that if these principles were maintained, details of their application could easily be worked out. Conceding that it was her belief that the world was not wholly unfriendly to woman, she warned the Convention to follow the order of business and attend to the addresses of the speakers. Save for some mutterings the morning hours were undisturbed.

But scarcely had the evening sessions started before a horde of men and boys stormed the orderly assembly by a din of ear-splitting "hisses, stamping and screaming from the gallery." The ensuing bedlam drowned the voices of the scheduled speakers, among whom was Francesca Anneke, a member of the Polish group traveling in America with Kossuth. In the face of discordant laughter and insulting cries, the eloquent Wendell Phillips tried in vain to secure a semblance of attention to the words of the foreigner, a respect for womanhood, even a sense of national pride. "We are," he appealed, "the citizens of a great country [laughter and cries of 'hey, hey'] that has extended to Kossuth a welcome from Maine to Georgia; and this New York audience is now looking upon one who stood by his side on the battle fields of Hungary [a yell and a cry of 'turn him out'], one who has faced the cannon of Francis Joseph of Austria for the rights of the people, and this is the welcome you give her to the shores of republican America."

"Go back to Boston," hooted the crowd from the gallery, "dry up," "take a drink." Thwarted, Wendell Phillips gave up, and, in the absence of any police protection, other speakers, women as well as men, made no attempt to be heard.[11]

In the face of the uproar it was the diminutive Lucretia Mott who maintained decorum. But this moment of peace in the face of the clamor was but a lull before the storm; reticence and dignity were no match for prejudice and mass hysteria. Adjournment was inevitable for, the secretary of the meeting reported, "some portion of the speakers' words were lost and other portions incorrectly heard." [12]

At this discouraging moment the skies were not completely beclouded for members of the organization living in the Middle West suggested a meeting away from the scene of hostility, pledging a cordial welcome in Cleveland, Ohio. With gratitude the invitation was accepted; but, when the leaders of the Association assembled a few weeks later on the stage of the Melodeon, a concert hall in Cleveland, they faced an audience taut with apprehension. Although no visible menace disturbed the proceedings, the atmosphere was charged with memories of the New York riot. What had occurred in New York could be repeated in Cleveland. On the platform were William Lloyd Garrison, Wendell Phillips, Lucy Stone, and Abby Kelly Foster of Massachusetts; Ernestine Rose, the native Polish woman who had offered the woman's cause in America her gifts of beauty and eloquence; Martha Wright, the secretary of the Association; Amy Post, the Reverend Antoinette Brown, and Susan B. Anthony of New York; Charles C. Burleigh of Connecticut, the loyal advocate of many reforms. And the Motts from Pennsylvania were present. There was a welcoming committee of several men and women from Ohio, Michigan, and Indiana.

Again, Lucretia Mott, wearing her "slate colored silk robe," stood out among the many women gathered in Cleveland. Around her on the stage of the Melodeon were plainly garbed Quakers; present also were defiant leaders of dress reform, "bold" and "immodest" in their "full bloomer costume"; and the fashion plates of the day were not absent, the women whom no program of "rights for women" could lure from the magic of the ruffles and puffs, pleatings and loops, fringes and passementeries of early Victorian fashions. Several men on the platform wore shawls. In her style of dress, Lucretia Mott was a distinctive and distinguished figure.

As she began to speak, her low-pitched tones reaching the utmost limits of the hall were listened to closely. Significant among her remarks was her criticism of the charge of "infidelity" leveled at men and women who dared to reject conventional opinions on moral and social problems. "By what right," she asked, "does

. . . Orthodoxy give the insidious name of Infidel, affix the stigma of infidelity, to those who dissent from its cherished opinions? What right have the advocates of moral reform, the Woman's Rights Movement, the Abolitionists, the Temperance advocates, or others, to call in question any man's religious opinions? It is the assumption of bigots. I do not want now to speak insidiously, and say sectarian bigots, but I mean the same kind of bigotry which Jesus rebuked so sharply when he called certain men "blind leaders of the blind" . . . I want that we should consider these things upon this platform.

Here in Cleveland she again paid tribute to the intelligence and character of the women of Nantucket, again refuting the argument advanced as to woman's need for protection against the rough winds of public life.[13]

It was natural that Mrs. Stanton should seek advice from Lucretia Mott on the subject of writing a history of the Woman's Rights Movement, the monumental work destined to appear as the *History of Woman Suffrage* by Elizabeth Cady Stanton, Susan B. Anthony, Matilda Joselyn Gage, and Ida Husted Harper. In answering this letter, Lucretia urged Mrs. Stanton to meet her at Auburn or at Mrs. Stanton's home where the two women could collaborate in the "very valuable work" which should not be hurried. The opening chapters, Lucretia suggested, should go further back than the date of 1848, because significant events pointing to the Convention at Seneca Falls were "Sarah & Angelin Grimké's labors in 1834 & 6," "The Clerical Appeal," "the Pastoral Letters," "the divisions in the A.S. Socy. . . . in N. Eng. in 36 & 7," and "the first Convention of Woman in New Y. 1837." To her, Sarah Grimké's *Letters on the Equality of the Sexes and the Condition of Woman* was a work on the woman question second in its importance only to Mary Wollstonecraft's writing. She recalled the description of the Nantucket women which she had presented to the Cleveland Convention of 1853; she recollected the London Convention, saying that "Garrison refused to take his seat in the London Convention, because the women delegates were rejected." She also provided Mrs. Stanton with an account of the achievements made by women in law, medicine, and public speaking.[14]

Following her theory of "practical righteousness," Lucretia Mott extended her crusade for Woman's Rights beyond attendance at conventions.

In 1848 Elizabeth McClintock had renounced the secretaryship of the Rochester Convention because the presiding officer of that gathering was a woman. Barely a year was to pass before this young woman was to exhibit so much confidence in the abilities of women that she began to dream of a career for herself among the wholesale merchants of Philadelphia.

Keeping a store was no new project for women. Lucretia Mott's mother had augmented her family's income by the proceeds from a "shop of goods" in the Coffin home in Nantucket; and many other enterprising American women had made small sums of money from their shops. But Elizabeth McClintock desired to enter the world of business on an equal footing with Philadelphia's wholesale merchants. No little "thread and needle" shop did she have in mind, as she visualized the possibility of engaging in "big business." With one or two of her friends in western New York, therefore, she went to Elizabeth Cady Stanton for advice. Mrs. Stanton felt that Elizabeth's desire was "hardihood," and she wrote that "these woman's rights conventions have spoiled our lovely maidens." But she laid the problem in the lap of Lucretia, hoping that employment for the young woman might be secured in the establishment of Lucretia's son-in-law, Edward M. Davis.

"There must be," the practical Lucretia advised,

. . . a beginning to everything. The reasons urged for declining your, or the suit of Eliz. and Anna have some weight. The subject has been discussed among numbers of Merchants in Market St. The fact of a serious application flew like wild fire. Morris L. Hallowell, who is in the same business as Edward said he thought he should be willing to receive them with some conditions however, which would not be so easy of compliance.

Then, suggesting that the ambitious young women would do well to start at the bottom of the ladder by applying for employment as clerks in a retail store, she extolled the virtues of Philadelphia as a city offering opportunities in business to interested young women. "Women," she said,

. . . have always been employed in our stores; and some have done quite a large wholesale and retail business. Sarah Tyndale has lately retired from the China business with a handsome fortune. Hers was said to be the largest and most handsome Porcelain store in the country.[15]

"Other women I would name hereaway," the letter continued,

. . . who have retired from business with a competence. I hope that Elizabeth and Anna will pursue their prospect — come on here and they can better judge by personal observation, and inquiry, than others here can decide for them. As far as we can aid them, our services are at their command.

The letter ends in a hospitable invitation to Mrs. Stanton herself to come to Philadelphia to make the Motts the "visit so long talked of and half promised."

In the meanwhile she continued to encourage Elizabeth McClintock to enter the Philadelphia business world by seeking employment at the bottom of the ladder in one of the large stores of the city. Otherwise the innovation threatened failure. The idea was a hopeful sign, "a determination to act as well as call conventions to talk." And she was far from throwing cold water on the suggestion; she herself was encouraged because the idea had elicited "discussion up and down Market Street."

But the response of the Philadelphia merchants left Martha Wright in no conciliatory mood. "I am sorry you had not the opportunity of proving to those wise gentlemen," thus she wrote Elizabeth McClintock,[16]

. . . that women with that "quick perception," that they are so ready to give them credit for do not require the years of "training" that men do, from their account, to enable them to perform the arduous duties they speak of; and even admitting that they do, it is absurd to talk about "spending years of womanhood to acquire what their girlhood might have learned" as if every woman had not already served an apprenticeship in her home, and was not perfect in the obtuse science of "sweeping" "running" (etc. etc.) and even in the severe labor of opening a box. I have seen some women that could quite eclipse certain men I could name. . . .

In the stagnation that occurs periodically in those wholesale establishments it is not surprising that your application should have raised "a tempest in a teapot" and set Market Street in a ferment: No doubt they gladly grasped at something exciting. Men are so desperately idle when business flags a little, having no resources of knitting and sewing to fill up odd moments, that they have become inveterate gossips sometimes, to a degree quite painful for women to witness.

Especially was Lucretia Mott sensitive to the inequalities of salaries doled out to women teachers. When, therefore, a group of Americans under the guidance of Horace Mann met in Philadelphia in October 1849 to start an extensive inquiry into the condition of the common schools, the movement, later perpetuated as the National Education Association, was heartily endorsed by Lucretia Mott. In this step to improve American elementary education, she and others saw an opportunity to do justice to the great band of elementary teachers in the country, most of whom were women. Among the topics discussed at this 1849 gathering were "the organization of schools into districts, school attendance, text books, methods of instruction, and the salaries of teachers, especially the compensation paid to female teachers." On this last question there was much discussion; and a resolution for the equalization of the salaries of women and men was presented to the assembled group by scholarly William Duncan, an ordained minister, later to become Professor of Classics in the University of Louisiana. Duncan's resolution was defeated by those using the old but popular argument of woman's inferiority. Foremost in the opposition was Bishop Alonzo Potter. In the development of public education in Pennsylvania, Bishop Potter has been credited with contributing advanced and solid ideas to the subject of school architecture, but in 1849 he was not interested in the effort to raise the salaries of women teachers. As Lucretia Mott wrote: "Never did I long so to say a word for women as in that Convention — and I resolved to do so, following Horace Mann's last speech — but Bishop Potter was so quick with the concluding prayer that I could not." [17]

Perhaps Lucretia admitted a grain of truth in the allusion in the Philadelphia *Ledger* to the apathy of Philadelphia women concerning their "Rights." Certainly she was frank to inform Mrs. Stanton in 1851 of the difficulties she was encountering *"to awaken sufficient interest to hold a Woman's Rights Meeting* in this city." "As to Penna.," she admitted,

. . . with the exception of a few radical Quakers & Hicksites, whose names are cast out as evil, there is too much darkness on the subject, to bear such a glare as a National Convention. We must labor more in a smaller way. We want forerunners to come "crying in the wilderness." It is far more difficult than we found it out West. Still there are numbers here who feel a deep interest in the cause. Few however are accustomed to public speaking . . . We have been looking around for a suitable place to hold a Meeting or Convention in. There will be difficulty in obtaining one for that object — or such an one as we should like.[18]

Notwithstanding her lack of faith in the women of Philadelphia, she urged Mrs. Stanton to call a meeting there, promising to do all she could to make the gathering a success.

A few years later, however, Horace Mann wrote that the spirit of the Philadelphia women on their rights was "very intense" in spite of a "counter spirit" in the city; Lucretia Mott, he thought, was "too ambitious because she claimed for women all the highest things in all departments." [19]

Toward the end of the year 1849, the elder Richard Henry Dana of Boston delivered a speech in Philadelphia, placing an "Address on Woman" just before his discussion of Desdemona in his lecture series on Shakespeare. Believing that women were physically, mentally, and morally weaker than men, Dana, with eloquent arguments, advised a sharply differentiated life for women. Moreover, he criticized severely the newer demands for women, designed, he argued, to draw them from the shelter of the hearth into the harsh atmosphere of public life.

In the words of one critic:

Mr. Dana is not at all of the modern school, who affect to make woman what she is not, never had been, and never can be, man and woman both, or perhaps we should rather say, simply man, for the unsexing philosophy ignores the woman altogether.

Mr. Dana is old-fashioned enough to believe in essential differences of sex, mental and moral marked as the physical; which result in corresponding diverse, yet united, healthy development. He thinks with Shakespeare that Lady Macbeth called with propriety upon the spirits to "unsex her"; a proceeding which would be quite a wasting of words with some of the modern holders of women's rights. Of those rights, as Shakespeare understood them, as Milton understood them, as nature indicates them, as the Bible teaches them, no more resolute, chivalric defender can be found than Mr. Dana.[20]

Richard Henry Dana was one of America's most eloquent public speakers; and in this address he suffered no loss of words to arouse in Philadelphia strongly adverse sentiments against woman's rights. In his words the new movement was "a threat" to the city's conventional patterns. To offset his speech some liberal Philadelphians approached Lucretia Mott with the request that she answer Dana. That she was considered an opponent worthy to take up the gage thrown down by one of America's greatest lecturers is recognition of the high quality of her public speaking. Though averse to controversy, Lucretia consented to speak, the result being the "Discourse on Women" delivered in the Assembly Building in Philadelphia on December 17, 1849.[21]

Making an historical approach to the subject, Lucretia conceded the lowered status of women throughout the ages, but pointed out illustrations of woman's natural ability, wisdom, and power — facts confirmed, as she argued, by Biblical narratives and modern events. Her answer to the charge of woman's inferiority was that the condition of women was due to a systematically imposed program of repression: unequal educational opportunities, different standards of wages, restricted openings in employment, and denial of political rights.

Then she repeated the argument she had brought again and again to her explanation of the degradation of the slave: that the consequence of oppression upon its victim is a state of mental degradation which enforces the enslaved to hug his chains in satisfaction with this oppression.

In her attack on the prejudice directed against the legal rights of married women, she said, "On no good ground can the legal existence of the wife be suspended during marriage, and her property surrendered to her husband." Conceding that "public sentiment among more intelligent people may protect a married woman from the ultimate depths of utter degradation in losing control of her property," she reminded her audience that women of all ranks could suffer as long as the law remained on the statute books. No woman, she felt, could be safe until the law was repealed.

In the light of Lucretia Mott's religious views, her words on the ballot are impressive. "Far be it from me to encourage women to vote," she said, "or to take an active part in politics in the present state of our government." Nevertheless, she conceded,

Her right to the elective franchise, however, is the same, and should be yielded to her, whether she exercises that right or not. Would that men, too, would have no participation in a government recognizing the life-taking principle — retaliation and the sword. It is unworthy of a Christian nation. But when, in the diffusion of light and intelligence, a convention shall be called to make regulations for self-government on Christian principles, I can see no good reason why women should not participate in such an assemblage, taking part equally with man.

As in her other addresses, Lucretia Mott lost no force in this discourse through her optimism and her concessions of points of right and strength in the arguments of her opponents. But she insisted that the "new generation of women" fortified by increased educational opportunities would be prepared to meet the difficult challenges of life. In concluding the "Discourse" she urged that woman should cease to ask for her rights as "favors," but should claim as a "right the removal of all hindrances to her elevation in the scale of being."

The *Discourse on Woman* was printed for private distribution; but as late as 1869 a second printing was issued because of a demand for the speech from England.

During the early years of the efforts made to bring complete citizenship to women, many speeches were made, and much was written to defend the cause of woman's rights and challenge the opposition. Repeated time and again were discussions of the political, civil, and ethical principles at issue, pictures of the inequalities suffered by women, and plans for the redress of the wrongs. Following the English pioneer, Mary Wollstonecraft, American women had not been silent. As early as 1837, in a series of open letters entitled *Equality of the Sexes,* Sarah Grimké pointed out that the inferior status of women could be traced to faulty interpretations of the Scriptures.[22] By Catharine Beecher, a teacher and member of the brilliant Beecher family, an enlightened education for women as well as for men was proposed for the solution of the problem.[23] Then Margaret Fuller, the Transcendentalist, published in the *Dial* for July 1843, "The Great Lawsuit — Man versus Men; Woman versus Women." [24] In 1848 this work, a leisurely approach to the woman question, appeared as a book, *Woman in the Nineteenth Century.* In its logic and richness of illustration, this work is a supreme achievement among the discussions on the woman question.

At the Woman's Rights Convention, held in Worcester in 1850, Wendell Phillips made a memorable address on this subject; [25] and shortly afterward "Reflections" on this Convention by Mrs. Harriet Taylor of London appeared as a report in the *Westminster Review*. Later this report was enlarged and published under the title *Enfranchisement of Women*.[26] And not to be forgotten is that in 1869 John Stuart Mill presented an analysis of the subject to Parliament.[27]

Margaret Fuller's *Woman in the Nineteenth Century* remains unexcelled; but, barring Wendell Phillips' address, no speech of the moment made a profounder impression than Lucretia Mott's *Discourse on Woman*. Preceding Wendell Phillips by two years, Lucretia Mott touched every cardinal aspect of the question presented by her successor; while she even went beyond him as she included in her address discussion of education, unrestricted fields of employment and fairness of remuneration for labor, equality before the law, particularly, in regard to the right of married women to hold property and to be guardians of their children, the right to the ballot, and the opportunity to engage in all professions including the profession of the Christian ministry.

In regard to Mrs. Mill's essay, Lucretia, in 1851, wrote Mrs. Stanton:

It is from the pen of a woman too, in great part, which adds to the interest of the article — for no man can write on woman's wrongs, as an *intelligent* sufferer of our own sex can. A Mr. Taylor of London called on me a day or two ago, a son of the author of the article — she was a widow, and lately married J. S. Mill, one of the conductors of that *Review,* as you know. He assisted her in writing it — altho' he says *she* wrote it. She sent me a copy printed in pamphlet form. Her son gave me a few for distribution. I can only spare one for thee, which I herewith send. I have seen extracts from it in the Tribune, I think, but have not before read the whole article. It is beautifully written. I wish it could be reprinted and extensively circulated. I have sent one to Garrison, asking its publication entire, in the Liberator.[28]

To later generations much of this earlier reasoning appears as efforts to justify the obvious. But in the middle of the nineteenth century it was necessary to convince an indifferent, if not hostile world, a world of many women as well as a world of men, that the movement was more than the organized ambitions of a group of unnatural females. Speeches had to be made; and the leaders in the movement, exerting their intellect, wit, and persuasion, appealed in turn to the emotions, the interests, the reason of their hearers. Thus they hoped to gain the attention of hearers not infrequently assembled from pure curiosity.

During these early years Lucretia Mott was undoubtedly the foremost figure in the Woman's Rights Movement in America. With no ambition for prominence she never thrust herself forward, but accepted the role accorded her. On the other hand, she needed no argument to enter the crusade for human rights, "Natural Rights in contradistinction to conventional usages," for women. Attending the early meetings of the Woman's Rights Movement she filled important offices, and she lifted her voice in the discussion of issues. Her speeches, ranging in style from informal talks to long addresses on the subject of woman's rights, were heard in the sessions of the conventions and in sermons delivered on her travels. Again and again one notes that she reiterated these points: freedom from the restraints of Orthodoxy, equal opportunities in education, in employment, and in remuneration for labor; equality before the law, particularly in regard to the rights of married women with regard to property, children, and suffrage.

At the conventions she insisted upon discussions being kept to the essential topics, and she maintained the necessity of women's speaking clearly. In her plan for absolute fairness she advocated a friendly hearing for the protests and arguments of opposers to the cause, maintaining that strength was derived from adverse criticism. She was not swayed by flattery, especially by that designed to lure the reformers from their goals. Frequently she was denounced because of her unorthodox religious views. Evincing no effort to shun the blurring of issues the opposers of justice for women welcomed reactionists in other fields, the sure target being the advocate of freedom in religion, freedom of conscience, freedom for the slave. Few of Lucretia Mott's hearers persisted in their attacks on her; but for years she was not only the armor of defense for the adherents of the Woman's Rights Movement but the storm center of attacks against the Cause.

The temper of her mind inspired her to lay her strongest emphasis upon the need of stressing the "principles at stake," what she termed the coequality of woman with man and the right of woman to practice what she termed "those arts of life for which she is fitted by nature." To her the great issue was principles not measures. Her desire was to promote intelligent thinking; her belief was that the essential steps to victory in a righteous cause lay in the ability of the leaders to remain in the path of logic. But it was logic as the handmaid of religion.

When it was suggested at one time that Washington be selected as the place of a meeting because of its importance as the seat of government, Lucretia Mott, strong in her faith in the power of righteousness, objected to a belief in the importance of political support to the program of the Convention. "You may rest assured," she protested,

. . . that the political men of the country, the partisans of politics, will be ready enough to take up our movement, when by making these moral appeals we have been instrumental in calling forth such a sentiment, that there shall be a demand for our rights from the people. Then without our appealing to the powers that be directly, the powers that be will come to us and be ready to yield what has been so long denied us.

In its gentle force spiritual integrity was the essential gift she brought to the Woman's Rights Movement. As she again and again emphasized: "Our weapons are spiritual weapons; on them we confidently rely for success. To prejudice we oppose love; to moral corruption spiritual purity; to the spirit of slavery the spirit of repentance."

Set in the crypt of the Capitol of the United States is a statuary group of Lucretia Mott, Elizabeth Cady Stanton, and Susan B. Anthony, the work of the sculptor, Mrs. Adelaide Johnson. In placing Lucretia Mott as the central figure and yet slightly to the front of Mrs. Stanton and Miss Anthony, the artist has achieved a faithful and happy interpretation of historical fact. And just as happy, it would seem, is the clarity of the portrayal of Lucretia Mott's character, for the marble seems to portray her strength and wisdom, her gentleness and serenity.

Chapter Thirteen

ANTISLAVERY

Although women had the right of unrestricted membership in the American Anti-Slavery Society, their part in the national organization was largely limited to holding "Fairs" as means of raising funds for the Society. This method of increasing finances and at the same time of spreading antislavery doctrine developed so rapidly that a National Fair, held annually in Boston, soon became a part of the program of the Anti-Slavery Society.

Cyrus M. Burleigh of Plainfield, Connecticut, a brother of Charles Burleigh, and, like him, an uninhibited reporter, has left in his diary [1] a lively sketch of a visit he once made to an Antislavery Fair held in Boston in 1844. In the picturesque array of articles offered for sale Cyrus Burleigh noted "a table cover . . . from the hand of Harriet Martineau," "caps and aprons and baby clothes." "The book table . . . supplied with a most beautiful array of books & pictures, writing material & paper," [a] "rude musical instrument," "a curious inkstand," "a little cottage made in Swiss fashion," "Yankee work boxes," and a medley of other wares donated for the sale.

Presiding over these offerings for the "glorious cause" was Maria W. Chapman, looking, as Cyrus Burleigh wrote, "like a born queen of the race." But Mrs. Chapman, giving no thought to her beauty and distinction, believed that spreading the doctrines of freedom was as important as making money for the cause. She, therefore, started an annual, the *Liberty Bell*. Wider in its range of content than the *National Anti-Slavery Standard* and the *Liberator,* and cast in a format different from these two newspapers and the minor sectional publications of protest, the *Liberty Bell* was a pocket-sized magazine presenting varied offerings of prose and verse. In content the articles ranged from stark discussions of the injustice of human bondage to compositions in which literary qualities were not sacrificed to theme or to conscience.

During the years of its existence many noted men and women contributed to the publication. Outspoken and direct appeals for liberty were written by William Lloyd Garrison, Wendell Phillips, Edmund Quincy, Frederick Douglass, Samuel J. May, and

Parker Pillsbury. In the *Liberty Bell,* however, other voices were heard; new notes were sounded in appeals for human freedom; and the contributions included prose and verse in French, Spanish, and German. One issue of the periodical contained a letter from Lady Byron entitled "To the Anti-Slavery Advocate"; other British contributors were Richard D. Webb of Ireland, and Lord Morpeth, Thomas Clarkson, Joseph Sturge, and William Howitt of England. Mary Howitt translated a fantasy from the German of Uhland entitled "The Blind King." Sonnets by Theodore Parker, William Lloyd Garrison, Maria W. Chapman, James Russell Lowell, Thomas Wentworth Higginson, George T. Burleigh, and William W. Story appeared in the columns; and other forms of verse were written by Eliza Lee Follen, Emerson, and Longfellow. In one number was an account of the London Convention by Nathaniel P. Rogers, who stressed particularly the repulsion of Lucretia Mott "by the thick-soled heels of 'British Usage.' "

In the fifteen years of its existence, only four illustrations found space in the magazines, one of these being the frontispiece of Volume V, a mezzotint of the portrait of Lucretia Mott, painted in 1841 by J. Kyle.

Mrs. Chapman was aware of Lucretia Mott's aversion to writing; but, reluctant to omit from the column of the *Bell* one of the most significant reformers of the day, she asked Lucretia in 1842 for a line or two. In reply Lucretia protested her inability to write anything "worthy of the Liberty Bell"; but in her desire, as she said, to influence "the more gifted to contribute of their abundance," she sent on to Mrs. Chapman some lines dedicated to Dr. Channing by Benjamin Rush Plumly, described by Lucretia as "a good abolitionist." These lines, she thought, ought to find place either in the *Liberator* or the *Liberty Bell.*

Unwilling to accept the substitute, Mrs. Chapman sought help from Lucretia Mott's son-in-law, Edward M. Davis. "If Lucretia would but write a word," Mrs. Chapman pleaded, "it would be a great thing. I dare not venture to tease her." And a letter to Miller McKim, dated Oct. 7, 1843, contains these words: "I do not ask Lucretia to write this year, though I wish she would do so, for having asked her every year from the beginning with entreaty, I fear she is so determined against it, as to render it a mere teasing on my part." [2]

Influenced, perhaps, by the menace of slavery, or perhaps, by her personal regard for Mrs. Chapman, Lucretia finally wrote a paper entitled "Diversities," which was published in the *Liberty*

Bell in 1844. "In the prosecution of the divine work of giving de-
liverance to the captive," the essay begins,

. . . the interest of those engaged is variously brought to bear on the
several departments in the field of labors. . . Each reformer, "the religious sectarian," "the statesman and politician," "the vigilant pro-
tector of the fugitive from bondage," "the reformer who advocated
abstinence from slave-grown products," should exert his power to the
overthrow of the outrageous system.

In direct words, antislavery was presented as an effort to destroy an unjust institution. Addressed to the antislavery reformers,
to those convinced of the injustice of slavery, "Diversities" limits
its discussion largely to the ways open to the advocate of anti-
slavery. Convinced of the unrighteousness of slavery, Lucretia
made little effort in this writing to do aught than dwell on what
could be accomplished through the independent, uncompromising
action of those convinced of the justice of the antislavery effort.
The writing lacks the magnetism of her spoken word, the charm-
ing informality of her letters. Unadorned by imagery and unsupported by emotional appeal, the essay is the word of one reformer
to another. Reviewing the *Liberty Bell* for 1845, Nathaniel P.
Rogers of the *Herald of Freedom* said that it was as difficult to
speak of Mrs. Mott's discussion of reform movements as to speak of
her since she "and all her contributions, are too evenly and unex-
ceptionally balanced and complete to allow comment." But two
years later, Lucretia wrote another paper for the journal, a sort of
footnote to "Diversities." This second writing made clear her firm
opposition to the attempt to end slavery by the purchase of slaves.
In her opinion the method was a fallacious gesture that benefited
the slaveholder, by putting money into his hands and thus enabling him to buy more slaves. Slavery was in this way, she maintained, spread by Abolitionists. She pointed out that the sum
obtained from the purchase of slaves by Abolitionists went eventually into the coffers of the slaveholder, giving an "indirect support" to slavery and "thus keeping up the inducement, either to
kidnap the poor creatures on the coast of Africa or to 'breed' and
raise them for sale in the Southern slave states." [3]
Like Mrs. Chapman and many other thoughtful American
women, Lucretia Mott viewed her part in the Anti-Slavery Society
as transcending the effort to pour funds into the coffers of the Society. She did not oppose the work of the Philadelphia Fair, of
which her daughter Anna was the most efficient chairman; more-

over, she showed positive interest in the general work of the Philadelphia Female Anti-Slavery Society. But, in accepting the importance of raising funds for the antislavery program, she showed
also that her interest in the cause transcended these efforts. On one
occasion when the Philadelphia Female Anti-Slavery Society de-
bated at some length a motion to appoint a committee to take the
responsibility of stimulating the lagging interest of the members
in antislavery, the motion was rescinded largely because Lucretia
Mott said that a greater interest in antislavery would be secured
if each member were held responsible for bringing to the attention of the society "instructive and interesting Anti-Slavery items
of news." She herself continued to note important happenings,
reporting among other items: the enactment of a law passed by the
Pennsylvania Legislature to prevent the kidnaping of runaway
slaves; the repeal of a law permitting for six months the bondage
of slaves brought into the state by their masters; and the action of
the Swedish government in abolishing slavery in St. Bartholomew.
She influenced the Society to send a petition to the Legislature in
support of a proposal "to procure to all its citizens, otherwise duly
qualified, the right of suffrage without regard to complexion."
Through such efforts she aimed to keep the Philadelphia group
of women in the path of logical thought and action on the subject of slavery.

But her antislavery program was not limited to Philadelphia.
In the winter of 1841 she visited the state legislatures of Delaware,
Pennsylvania, and New Jersey. In each assembly she was granted
"a patient and respectful audience." [4] Less successful was she in
her effort to bring a message to Congress, although the aged statesman, John Quincy Adams, was requested to secure the permission
for her. Concerning the incident Mr. Adams recorded in his *Diary*,
under date of January 3, 1843, that he had been requested by "Mr.
Kurtz and Mr. Bancroft . . . members of the Society of Friends"
to use his influence to obtain the use of "the hall of the House of
Representatives" for Mrs. Mott for "a religious exercise." Recalling the pleasant "social intercourse" he had enjoyed in the Mott
home, Adams asserted his willingness to bring up the request for
permission for Mrs. Mott to address Congress, but stated "that
Mrs. Mott was known as a distinguished abolitionist of slavery;
that there was little difference between her opinions upon the subject of slavery and [his]," a fact that was well known in Congress.
For this reason he felt that "an application for the use of the hall"
would hardly be received favorably if presented by him.[5]

There is every reason to believe that Lucretia Mott would have made the "religious exercise" an appeal for the causes dear to her heart — antislavery, justice for women, better conditions for the working man, universal peace — as well as for a broad conception of the principles of religion. Against John Quincy Adams, however, she cherished no resentment; her high esteem for him was not abated. Indeed, as she wrote Richard Webb shortly after her failure to secure permission to address Congress, "Have you taken an interest in our Congressional proceedings this winter? Or rather will you when you hear or read how bravely our veteran J. Q. Adams is acquitting himself in Washington?"

Although she was unable to address Congress in 1842, she and her husband traveled as far as Winchester, Virginia, on her mission to voice her "heresies," to carry a word for righteousness. Public sentiment, she believed, was making a change for the better, a change, she thought she had observed "even in the Baltimore Yearly Meeting — notwithstanding its Epistle of charges against those who follow not them and its desire for 'quiet.' " As the Motts journeyed from place to place, they went to "Washington, Alexandria, Fredericktown, Sudbury, Winchester and many country places and villages — New Market, Harpers Ferry, etc etc. — in all of which," as she wrote Mrs. Chapman, "the slaveholders not a few gave audience." Reports of these speeches are missing. Perhaps, as she again wrote, "They heard patiently — but carefully avoided in any of their public notices making mention of that part of what they heard. Probably the Papers would not have admitted faithful report." [6]

In contrast to the harmony prevailing in the early meetings of the Woman's Rights Movement, the National Anti-Slavery Society was threatened with dissolution almost from the first days of its organization. As the ideas of the members ranged from theories of gradualism to proposals for immediate freedom of the slaves, even at the price of destroying the American Union, the meetings often resolved themselves into occasions of endless discussions on slavery and subjects offered as allied to slavery. It was in these arguments that Lucretia Mott showed her clarity of thought as she protested the introduction of extraneous subjects into the programs of the meetings.

In 1852, the Pennsylvania Association spent much time in argument as to the possibility of good emerging from evil. Protesting that this question should have become a part of the Proceedings Lucretia Mott asked of the group two pointed questions:

Is it not better to speak of evil as evil, not deducing from it any consequences which do not strictly belong to it? Does it not tend to weaken our abhorrence of wrong? There is nothing easier than to quote texts of Scripture in favour of any theory, as every sect supports its faith by such texts. I am not willing to admit that Harriet Beecher Stowe was moved to write Uncle Tom's Cabin by that law; if she says so, I think she mistakes the influences which have moved her. I believe, rather that it has been the moral sentiments and truths promulgated by the *Liberator*, the *National Era*, and the public discussion of the subject, upon her pure mind exciting it to feel for the oppressed. If you point to the progress of our cause through persecution as evidence that the efforts of its enemies have helped it on, I have as good a right to say that but for these impediments, Slavery would have been abolished before now. I hope the Society will instruct the striking out of these passages of the Report.[7]

On this point, however, her objection was unsustained, the Society preferring to endorse Miller McKim's more logical proposal that Mrs. Stowe's statement should be preferred to Mrs. Mott's unsupported opinion. At this meeting also she was forced to bear another defeat in the rejection again of her resolution endorsing Free Produce.

At the next year's meeting of the same society James Mott gave a glowing account of the conditions of the Negroes settled in Canada. Fearful lest these words should be received as a support of Colonization, Lucretia voiced the warning that the aim of the abolitionists was not to bring an end to slavery by colonizing the slaves in Canada or elsewhere, but by means of the abolition of slavery to destroy the evil in its stronghold.[8]

Later, at the Second Decade meeting of the American Anti-Slavery Society, Lucretia Mott appealed again for limitation of the topics of discussion to the practical issues at hand, without wasting time in "elaborate arguments and researches into Scriptures, to prove a self-evident truth." She declared,

It is enough for us now to affirm that slavery is a sin, that the slave has the right to his freedom, and that it is no less the duty of the slave holder instantly and unconditionally to emancipate him. . . . We should stand simply and singly upon the inherent rights of man, on the self-evident truths that have been declared before the people, and which, being so self-evident, need no proof. We have advanced, we are willing now, in a great measure, to stand on the immutable principles of justice and right. . . . Plenty of Bible will be found in support of Freedom as soon as it becomes a little more popular.[9]

In tracing the history of the antislavery movement, she referred to the number of methods that had been advocated at different times for securing the aims of the Society. Among other plans she recalled the recommendation that was made to include "weekly or monthly concerts of prayer," as aids specifically to make the "cause religiously popular." As to public prayer she proposed the "recommendation of Jesus to 'pray in secret,' to enter our closets and there pray . . . to work as the effect of that prayer, to show that we are watching and working and saying our prayers in secret." Above all, she warned the Society that there was no danger of setting "too high a value on good works," on "practical goodness, practical righteousness." The danger rather was, she thought, in forgetting "the beautiful sentiments of Jesus — 'By their fruits ye shall know them; for of thorns men do not gather grapes, nor of thistles gather they figs.' "

In offering the recommendation that discussion should be limited to the essential issues, she did not, however, place free thinking under the ban of proscription. And to the charge of infidelity she was indifferent, for each, she felt, should be privileged to be faithful to his own convictions. A protest to these views on religion was raised by Wendell Phillips who believed that the latitude of Lucretia Mott's religion could offend many who worked in the antislavery cause. Sharp words were passed, but at length oil was poured on the waters by Garrison's proposal that breadth of policy should be followed in the adoption of measures. Then Lucretia Mott calmly put an end to the dispute by stating that she had made no mention of specific religious or sectarian doctrine, her only concern being the need of caution in order to avoid the adoption of doctrines calculated to strengthen the hands of the slaveholder.

Finally, as the Report reads,

Lucretia Mott urged attention to that portion of the Declaration of Sentiments, which relates to our giving preference to the products of *free labor* over those of slave labor. She begged the friends to consider also, whether they did not compromise their principles by aiding in the purchase of individual slaves, thereby enabling the slaveholder to buy two fresh slaves in the place of the one sold.

But this appeal for the Society's endorsement of Free Produce again fell on deaf ears.

When the American Anti-Slavery Society held its regular Annual Meeting in New York in May 1854, Lucretia Mott again rose to protest the charge of irreligion leveled against members of the organization. Again she declared that the antislavery idea was not an expression of any system of religion, that "allegiance to God" was amply shown in the "defence of the rights of man," and that a program of singing and praying was an irrelevant innovation. "The Meeting," she thought, "should be held to business and . . . the praying should be done at home." The faith of the Society, as she thought, should be proved "by its works."

At this same Convention the question of dissension with the slaveholding ranks was brought to a climax by a formal resolution, introduced by Garrison, in these words:

. . . that the one grand vital issue to be made with the Slave Power is, The Dissolution of the Existing American Union.

The Resolution was about to be "unanimously adopted," but just before the vote was taken Lucretia Mott, ever alert in her ability to foresee the influence of accepted theories on action and at the same time to recognize the implications of commercial interests among antislavery men in the North, reminded those assembled that if the Resolution were passed, "the Society would be pledged to no union, politically or religiously with the slaveholders, and thence to no union in commerce or manufactures."

Trade, of course, could have been maintained between the Northern and Southern states even if the two sections were divided as separate countries. But so concerned were the members of the Anti-Slavery Society with their financial interests in the South, that they were unwilling to take a step that threatened even remotely any risk to the trade between the North and the South. Because of Lucretia Mott's warning the Society remained adamant and refused to pledge itself to "Dissolution of the Existing American Union."

Again the subject of Dissolution came before the Society on October 16, 1856, at the Twentieth Annual Meeting of the Pennsylvania Anti-Slavery Association, being held in Norristown. At this meeting a letter was read to the organization from William Lloyd Garrison. In this communication Garrison protested support of the Free-Soil Party because, as he claimed, this party seemed to conserve Western territory free of slavery while it did nothing to abolish slavery in the South. He also noted that it was absurd to assert that the Union must be preserved, a Union that was a theory only "between the free and slave states."

The reading of this letter gave rise to lengthy discussion on the issue of the Union. Henry Grew declared that it was "better to separate than to be involved in this system of iniquity." Parker Pillsbury said that there was nothing less sacred than the American Union. Oliver Johnson's opinion was that the abolition of slavery called for a Separation of the North from the South, confessing that he himself was "more than ever, if possible, a disunionist." At length Lucretia Mott made an extremely long speech, in which, however, there was no direct reference to the issue of disunion. Her aim seemed to be to prevent friction in the Society while she stressed the need of strict adherence to the principles of the organization. Mary Grew also made an eloquent defense of the antislavery cause, emphasizing the importance of principles of righteous actions and the need of courage and steadfastness of faith. Garrison she eulogized for his vision, his endurance of privation, and his unselfishness. But neither Mary Grew nor Lucretia Mott advocated, opposed, or even mentioned disunion. The secretary, however, made it a part of her record that Lucretia Mott "was clear-eyed as to the menace confronting the organization, she was sympathetic and patient with those who were slow of understanding, buoyant and brave with those who lacked courage." [10]

At the Twenty-fourth Annual Meeting of the Pennsylvania Anti-Slavery Association, held at Kennett Square on October 25, 1860, the organization considered a Resolution designed to limit trade with Southern slaveholders. Mrs. Mott was reported as believing that abolitionists should have "no union with slaveholders politically, religiously, or commercially." It was her conviction, the Secretary continued, that the purchase of "slave-grown productions" furnished "the slaveholder with motive and the means for continuing his system."

In his objections to the Resolution, Miller McKim protested his unwillingness to adopt the measure because he felt that as long as the South purchased Northern manufacturers and antislavery tracts, he could not denounce a trade that, while bringing profit to the North, produced money to serve the cause of freedom. Other leaders in the Anti-Slavery Society used similar arguments against the proscription of products from the slave states, but Lucretia Mott unfailingly advocated the principle of no trade with slaveholders, accepting no compromise. That she was doomed to failure did not alter her belief that concerted abstinence from the purchase of the products of slavery would eventually destroy slavery. [11]

Throughout the years of her connection with the antislavery

associations, she had been unable, except with the women as organized in the Philadelphia Female Society, to make a successful protest against trade with the South. As a member of the Business Committee she had managed to keep the Resolution on the agenda, but she was powerless to convince the groups to outlaw commercial relations with slaveholders. Indeed, as late as the very eve of Emancipation she proposed a Resolution protesting, but again in vain, the use of the products of slave labor. The failure of the National Anti-Slavery Society to adopt a program of proscription against the use of the products of slavery was one of the evidences of a strong divergence of opinion in the organization; and it was Lucretia Mott, in company with some other members of the organization, who maintained an unwavering attitude against trade with slaveholders.

While Lucretia Mott was in the Middle West in 1853, attending the Woman's Rights Convention in Cleveland, she accepted an invitation to go to Kentucky. Although she had been assured a cordial reception in Maysville, it required courage to speak in a section so hostile to her principles and ideals. Believing that her sincerity was protection from incivility or violence, she went into the hostile territory, referring only casually to the visit: "having traveled from Masillon — To Maysville tomorrow, remain over 1st day." [12]

As the news of her approach reached Kentucky, hostility as well as sympathy was stirred. A protest by one signing himself "A Slaveholder" appeared in the *Maysville Express*. This writer stigmatized Lucretia as "a bad woman," "a foreign incendiary," "a female fanatic," who had been allowed to use the "Court House for the profanation of her infernal doctrine." He warned his fellow-citizens that "this treason against God and her country" might be "the prelude to a heavy loss on the part of the slaveholders of the county, as a score or two of the blacks were present to behold and hear "this brazen infidel." [13]

Similar opinion was expressed in certain Northern journals. But one Southerner, the Maysville correspondent to the New York *Tribune,* under date of October 18, 1853, sent in to his paper a long account picturing the tense expectancy in the large crowd held "enchained" by the "mild, winning and attractive manner of the speaker." Continuing, he wrote that Lucretia's views were "bold, startling at least to this community, original," that "no crying evil of the day escaped exposure and condemnation," that "slavery was presented as a curse to the master and the slave and as a stain upon the honor of the Republic." And he was just as enthusiastic in his description of the address on Woman's Rights she gave in the evening.[14]

Liberal sentiment in northern Kentucky doubtless stood Lucretia Mott in good stead; but any effort to account for this indulgence she met in Southern territory must take into account not only the existence of a spirit of tolerance in a reputedly unfriendly neighborhood but the force of Lucretia Mott's convictions, tempered by her gentleness and lack of aggressiveness.

When the Pennsylvania Anti-Slavery Association held its sixteenth Anniversary Meeting at Norristown in November 1853, Lucretia gave her own account of her Southern visit. Most of all, she stressed the courtesy that had been shown her in Maysville, declaring that on no occasion had her Northern speeches been listened to with closer attention than had been accorded her in the Maysville Courthouse. It never occurred to her that her reception in the South emanated in part from her own humility, displayed in a magnetic gentleness of speech and manner. In her unfailing optimism she said she believed that her visit merely marked the "awakening of thought and earnest reflection in the South on the question of anti-slavery." This faith was unsupported by facts. "With what delight," wrote Sarah Pugh, "did I listen to Lucretia Mott detailing in her animated way her meetings in Kentucky, and watch the joyful play of her countenance at the thought that in a slave state she had been able to declare the whole counsel of the gospel of freedom."

In 1852 the Hungarian patriot, Louis Kossuth, came to America to arouse sympathy for his suffering fellow countrymen. But this reformer felt that any interest he himself might show in the problem of American slavery would hurt his own cause. Such aloofness from the great social problem of the United States aroused the American Anti-Slavery Society to such an extent that it directed its president William Lloyd Garrison and the secretaries, Sydney Howard Gay and Wendell Phillips, to call the attention of Kossuth to his inconsistency. A letter from the Anti-Slavery Society reminded Kossuth that American slavery had been censured by other foreigners — O'Connell, Wilberforce, Thomas Moore, Clarkson, and George Thompson — without their losing thereby American support to their causes. The appeal to Kossuth was unavailing; not only did he avoid mentioning America's slavery as an example of injustice, but his indifference went so far that he gave a wide berth to American abolitionists.

When Kossuth visited Philadelphia he refused an invitation to the Motts' home. But Madame Thérèse Pulszky, Kossuth's sister, was less diplomatic. She not only accepted Lucretia's invitation, but, in her account of the American visit, written in collaboration with her husband Ferencz Aurel Pulszky, included a delightful sketch of Mrs. Mott:

I have seldom seen a face more artistically beautiful than that of Mrs. Lucretia Mott. She looks like an antique cameo. Her features are so markedly characteristic, that if they were less noble they might be called sharp. Beholding her I felt that great ideas and noble purposes must have grown up in her mind, which have a singular power of expression in her very movements. Her language is like her appearance, peculiar and transparent. . . But though she so positively pronounced the views at which she has arrived by self-made inquiry, yet she mildly listens to every objection, and tries to convince by the power of her arguments, untinged by the slightest fanaticism. She expressed her warm sympathy with the cause of Hungary, and her admiration of the genius of Kossuth; yet she blamed his neutrality on the slavery question.

"But how can Kossuth, the champion of liberty, not raise his voice," Lucretia had protested to Madame Pulszky, "in favor of the oppressed race? To argue is surely not the same thing as to interfere." Madame Pulszky's final note on the visit was that although she could not accept Mrs. Mott's conviction "that the abolition of slavery should be preached in season and out of season by the defender of the rights of nations," she herself felt so strongly "the charm of [Mrs. Mott's] moral superiority" that she wished she could spend hours in "the attractive circle" of the Mott home.[15]

Notwithstanding Lucretia's adverse criticism of Kossuth, she proposed that the Pennsylvania Anti-Slavery Association appoint a committee "to prepare an address to Kossuth" expressing the sympathy of the Association for Kossuth's "sentiments of Liberty" and a statement of the Association's "own principles and aims."

Lucretia Mott never wavered in her effort to limit the subjects of debate in the antislavery meetings to the issues of slavery; the discussion of religion she particularly rejected. She urged again and again the significance of the principle of free produce, and she rejected Colonization as a solution of American slavery. On more than one occasion, she let it be known that assisting fugitives was not, strictly speaking, the dedicated aim of antislavery endeavor. As she reasoned, the number of fugitives escaping into Canada and the number of liberated Negroes emigrating to Liberia, all told, were infinitely fewer than the number of infants born into slavery each year. Yet she supported the Underground Railroad; and the home of James and Lucretia Mott was a harborage of sympathetic aid for the fugitive slave. One case that touched her was that of Henry Brown, a slave in Richmond, Virginia, who succeeded in having himself freighted in a box and consigned to Miller McKim in the antislavery office in Philadelphia. Writing to the Dugdales on March 28th, 1849, Lucretia said,

And here I must tell you what an exciting fugitive case we have had the last week. A citizen of Richmond, Va. called at the Office and told Miller and Cyrus that a slave in that City was meditating his escape, by being placed in a box, as goods, and coming in the cars — Adams' Express line. He was told of the great danger of suffocation, as well as the risk of detection — but was not deterred . . . one or 2 mornings at 3 o'clk — a telegraph at length, apprized them of his approach. The box was recd. at the Depot — more carefully handled, than it had been before — safely desposited at the A.S. office, where a trembling tap and "all right?" from Miller, was responded to "all right Sir," from the pent up man. The lid was removed as quickly as the hoops cd. be loosened, when he as quickly rose with a "good morng. gent." Miller says we can hardly conceive the relief and excitet. to find the man alive — and the poor fellow's happiness gratitude — singing a hymn of praise etc.[16]

She concluded the narrative with a summary of the last incidents of Henry "Box" Brown's stay in Philadelphia: how the fugitive was taken to Miller McKim's house for a bath and breakfast, how he was then brought to the Mott home where he talked to the group of friends assembled there, and how he was dispatched further on his journey. Her last reference in this letter to the escape of Henry "Box" Brown ends on a prophetic note: "This and the Crafts' — as well as Isaac Brown's and others not a few, will tell well in history sometime hence, in the days of freedom, oh!"

A few years after the escape of Henry "Box" Brown, Lucretia Mott assisted in the rescue of a Negro slave, Jane Johnson, and her ten-year-old son. These slaves had come to Philadelphia in the summer of 1855 with their owner, John H. Wheeler, the American Minister to Nicaragua. When the woman was informed, on her arrival, of Pennsylvania's antislavery laws, she immediately betook herself and child away from the custody of Mr. Wheeler, leaving the slaveholder deprived of his property and apparently without redress. However, the American diplomat did not submit tamely to what he considered an attack on his rights. Legal action therefore was brought against several men, among whom were Passmore Williamson, an Orthodox Quaker, and William Still, author of *The Underground Railroad*.

In the United States District Court, presided over by Judge John K. Kane, an indictment was secured against the men accused of "conspired effort" to induce the woman to run away; the indicted men were imprisoned and later put under bonds. Williamson's refusal to admit that he knew the whereabouts of the runaways after the escape brought him into trial for contempt of court. When the case was called, it was considered wise by the defense to have Jane Johnson testify in her own behalf. According to Still's account, Mrs. Mott, together with several other Philadelphia women, accompanied Jane Johnson to court, remained throughout the sessions of the trial, and then took the acquitted woman to the Mott home on North Ninth Street. In Lucretia's words, written to Martha,

. . . she [Jane Johnson] . . . was brot. here in the morng. & a carriage sent for us. Her testimony was very clear & satisfactory. We didn't drive slow coming home. Miller, and officer — Jane & self — another carriage followg. with 4 officers for protection — and all with the knowledge of the State's attorney — Miller & the Slave passed quickly thro' our house, up Cuthbert St. to the same carriage — wh. drove around to elude pursuit. I ran to the store room & filling my arms with crackers & peaches, ran after them & had only time to throw them into the carriage — & away they drove to Broad & Coates, where the Hallowell boys were ready to receive her with our carriage & horse & conveyed her to Miller's — & lest she should be pursued there, he took her that eving over to Edwd's. & the next day they sent her to Plymouth & 7th day they ventured to take her to Norristown Mg. where she told her story well & made a good impression. It was a hazardous step, to take her to Court.

Passmore Williamson was an Orthodox Quaker; but, in Lucretia's belief that his fate called for action unhindered by the restrictions of creeds, that more was demanded than the futile efforts of one or two indignant persons, she went out to Moyamensing Prison to see the accused man. Further, convinced that the time was at hand to disregard sectarian bonds in the greater need for united strength to preserve what she considered a man's integrity of conscience, she took a line of action indicative of her disregard at heart for any force of sectarian differences. In her words to Martha,

I am going round to Orthodox and Hicksite Frds. to try to induce them to act in some way against the miscreant Judge Kane, & for Passmore. All our Mo. Mgs. occur this and next week — 7 in all, & it will be too bad if they all separate, as if such an outrage had not been committed. . . . Still Judge Kane is upheld by a large number of Merchants in this city." [17]

All escaping slaves did not try to reach Canada. To many of these fugitives life on the orderly farms of Pennsylvania was such a happy experience from existence in the swamps of the rice fields or in the sugar plantations, that settlements scattered beyond the Northern border were unrealistic goals of shadowy promise. But the transplanted farmhand, however industrious, responsible, and thrifty he might be in his new environment, lived always under the shadow of the Fugitive Slave Law. One such worker was Daniel Dangerfield, sometimes referred to as Daniel Webster. In 1859 this industrious man was seized on a farm near Harrisburg and brought into the Philadelphia courts for trial as a runaway slave. Lucretia Mott, with Sarah Pugh, Mary Grew, and Mary Earle, came to this trial and remained throughout the all-night court proceedings. Shortly after daybreak they had the satisfaction of seeing the ex-slave released. The acquittal rested on a technical error in the writ of accusation concerning Dangerfield's height. As Alfred Love observed on April 6, 1859: "The trial closed here Daniel was found to be 5.10 in his boots and without them 5.7 to 8 inches." [18]

Years later, at a meeting of the Historical Society of Pennsylvania, the Unitarian minister, William H. Furness, presented a picture of Lucretia Mott at this trial. As he recalled the incident,

I went once to the Commissioner's Court, which was in session in the basement of the Philosophical Society's building, when a poor, ragged Negro was on trial for his liberty. In the close, crowded space, by the side of the ragged fugitive, the only woman present stood in her pure Quaker garb like an angel of light, Lucretia Mott. She uttered never a word, caused no interruption, and no picture by an old master of saint or martyr could be more impressive than that scene.[19]

In the dragnet thrown out for fellow conspirators of John Brown, many abolitionists, besides those specifically named as connected with the plot, were suspected of complication in the Harpers Ferry raid. To escape vengeance, many advocates of antislavery went into hiding, certain well-known abolitionists fled the country, and suspicion imposed guarded speech and action upon all who were known or even suspected as being opponents of slavery. Among the letters of Lucretia Mott that have been preserved, less than a half dozen stem from the fateful autumn of 1859, and these few record no word concerning the tragedy of Harpers Ferry. But she was not speechless. Deploring at all times the use of "carnal weapons," she could not and did not endorse John Brown's method; any type of war was abhorrent to her, but she heartily accepted the principle that had led to the bloodshed.

Following the conviction of John Brown, the wife of the condemned man stopped in Philadelphia on her way to reach Harpers Ferry just before the execution of her husband. In an unsigned letter to the *Anti-Slavery Standard* of December 3, 1859, a letter regarded as being from the hand of Miller McKim, Mrs. Brown is portrayed as living in "a home near Philadelphia." In this home the writer speaks of himself as having been "an inmate," for the better part of a week. It has been held that this "home near Philadelphia" was Roadside, the residence of the Motts.

Writing to his wife, John Brown expressed satisfaction that she was "under Mrs. Mott's roof" and then added, "I remember the old lady well; but presume she has no recollection of me . . . I am glad to have you make the acquaintance of such old Pioneers in the Cause." [20]

At "the immense gathering in National Hall" held in Philadelphia after Brown's execution, Lucretia Mott, in company with Dr. Furness, Theodore Tilton of New York, and Mary Grew, was one of the speakers. As the keynote of her address Lucretia took the subject of slavery, asserting that it was the great sin beclouding the light of America, and that the consequences of this wrongdoing must be "the sword and bloodshed." The Philadelphia *Press* reported her as saying that she was no preacher of "the milk and water passive resistance to wrong" type, that she never flinched before error and that she had only censure for those giving tacit approval of slavery by supporting the Constitution. Hisses as well as applause greeted this speech.

Shortly after the execution of John Brown, the Pennsylvania Anti-Slavery Society adopted a Resolution expressing satisfaction in the wave of sympathy for him that had pervaded the North. This Resolution was especially approved by Lucretia Mott in that, as she emphasized, it carried no sanction of Brown's action, which was in contradistinction to the pacific principles of the American Anti-Slavery Society. After repeating the Declaration of Sentiments of 1833 — at need she would quote verbatim from the historic document — she declared that, in her opinion, John Brown was to be praised for his moral heroism and to be honored as a martyr. She reminded the Society that his weapons, "drawn from the armory of truth," were the weapons of "hope and faith and love," "of moral indignation strongly expressed against wrong." She concluded with these words:

Robert Purvis has said that I was "the most belligerant Non-Resistant he ever saw." I accept the character he gives me; and I glory in it. I have no idea, because I am a Non-Resistant, of submitting tamely to injustice inflicted either on me or on the slave. I will oppose it with all the moral powers with which I am endowed. I am no advocate of passivity. Quakerism, as I understand it, does not mean quietism. The early Friends were agitators; disturbers of the peace; and were more obnoxious in their day to charges which are now so freely made than we are.[21]

During the 1850's Lucretia Mott led an almost superhuman life under the burden of her causes. That they were causes of her own choosing lessened in no way the toll exacted. When a trip to New England in the summer of 1856 did not bring the benefit expected of it, the family realized that other measures must be taken for Lucretia's restoration to health, something, at least, to protect her from the relentlessly recurring demands for her public appearances. After a family counsel, the decision was made to take Lucretia away from the storm and stress of her Philadelphia life.

Chapter Fourteen

A WOULD–BE RESPITE

To "Roadside," a rambling country house on the York Road, the old highway between New York and Philadelphia, the Motts moved in the spring of 1857. Days of "overseeing workmen & cleaners at Roadside & occasionally lend'g a hand," as Lucretia described the moving, marked the family's getting established in their changed surroundings. Although "dustpan after dustpan" had to be filled and emptied, and carpenters made "clean dirt — plumbers and masons unclean ditto, painters daub'g everywhere," a tranquil atmosphere in the new environment was eventually achieved. Then the Motts began to settle down and enjoy Roadside — its gracious sitting room, ample veranda, even its irregularity of structure and style. Sheltered by a grove of towering oak trees that partially obscured the busy highway, Roadside was secluded yet not isolated from the hum of men. This new home was a far cry from the dwelling where the Motts had lived for wellnigh fifty years. At Roadside was serenity in the comfort of a country home not too far from the city. At Roadside, also, there was adequate room for a garden, something that was out of question in the narrow strip of yard behind the Philadelphia home.

As spring passed into summer, the out-of-door mornings spent in the gathering of early peas and currants and strawberries, and in the leisurely occupations of the quiet household brought renewed vigor to Lucretia Mott.

But from the beginning certain aspects of life at Roadside repeated, though on a quieter scale, the days in the city. Wherever the Motts lived — at 136 North Ninth Street next to Edward and Maria Mott Davis, at 338 Arch Street for a five-year sojourn, or out at Roadside — there was the atmosphere of a friendly home. Moreover, the leisure of the suburban life provided all the more time for vigorous, unorthodox thinking, and thence for discussion on social issues; thought and discussion led to sympathy for suffering humanity, and eventually to renewed activity in reform. Too little time could Lucretia actually garner for relaxing with her family, for reading and writing letters, for sewing and knitting.

Soon it came to pass that the resident of Roadside began to come from her suburban home into Philadelphia for religious meetings, for assemblies for "causes," and for social gatherings. Eventually, she was again in the center of the public program of reform.

In May 1857, scarcely a month after the Motts had settled at Roadside, Lucretia wrote to Martha that she had "A party in preparation." The guests were:

Eliza Rodman from New B., the Wisters, one Wm. Fisher perhaps, McKims, Browns, Abm. & Sally Becker, Denses, and all this filling our parlor. . . Yestery. also was delightful. . . They had also a concern to go to Longwood Progresse. and as I was going they were glad of a wing. . . . The Mg. was interestg. so crowded that it couldn't be so orderly as ours — as many standing outside as were seated inside 1st day. Garrison spoke admirably well, so that Wm. Fisher couldn't help praisg. him. . . For the rest — see Report.

A few days later she spoke of having received a hundred callers in the few weeks that had passed since she came to Roadside, but added immediately that this number of visitors was "notg. to Phila."

While making her friends feel at home she kept her fingers busy, knitting between spells of winding and rolling scraps into carpet balls when she was not occupied in darning carpets. Darning and fitting ingrain carpets to rooms she found an occupation less irksome than working with stiff Brussels carpets and straw matting, a task she admitted she would "rather have done." This routine of labor with carpets she found a pleasant occupation, "as thou my sister dost not," especially when there was a gathering of friends to sit and talk in the progress of the work. "I only wish," as she concluded this letter, that "you were near eno' for me always to go in and help thee at such times, as well as be with thee at many other times." Shortly afterward, she informed Martha that the family was engrossed in Tennyson's "Princess," "Charlotte Bronte's Life," and *Aurora Leigh,* between readings of the *Edinburgh Review,* the *Westminster Review, Harpers, Putnam's,* the *Woman's Advocate,* and the daily newspapers. She sums up this news of her reading by adding "Maybe I shall have time before I die to read the 100 books that I have resolved to. Our book case is not yet cleared out nor my lots of papers assorted."

Her alert mind kept her acutely interested in public affairs. "Our men say," she wrote toward the end of 1857 that,

. . . business begins to revive a little & are avail'g themselves of any improve't they say there may be in unhealthy reaction. What the thous'd exasperated people will do, who are thrown out of employ't is a fearful quest'n. . . But can David or any other say where rightful interest ends & Usury begins? Where legitimate trade ends & gambling begins? Where self-protection ends & injustice & oppress'n begins? Wouldn't you like at times to see all swept off and the world begin anew? It was a natural conception — that flood of ancient time when "Capt. Noah weighed anchor" when the wickedness of men had become so great. But modern science teaches that "our own backslidgs. reprove us" & the penalty is "the fruit of our own doings." So we may expect a heap of fruits. Much will have to be traced to America's slavery — even tho the panic is felt North & east first. The counterbalance of good thou anticipates, must be in our "learn'g obedience by the things we suffer." "When the judg'ts of the Lord are in the earth," the habits thereof learn righteous's. This, just as true, as if by special Provid's & far more reasonable & philosophical.

William Evans, an English liberal identified by Lucretia Mott as "a friend of John Bright" and "a defeated candidate for Parliament," declared on visiting America in 1865 that he was astonished at Lucretia Mott's knowledge of the English reformers, Foxton, Colenso, and "the English essayists."

The McKims paid cherished visits to Roadside when, as Lucretia described it, they would "sink the strop" and omit the topic of antislavery. Actually the stream of guests was unbroken until Lucretia at length resumed her journeying to Philadelphia.

"Four days of last week we were in town." Thus begins a letter to her daughter, Martha.

Freeman & A.S. Mgs. & one night up at Holly. . . We had a pleast. visit from Wm. L. Gar'n, Miller & Sarah, Wm Furness & Sarah P. & Abbey Kimber to tea on 6th day. . . I went in to the Fem. A.S. Mg. that aftern. but reached home soon after they came. Sarah & Abbey stayed the night. Thos. & Maria came & all seemed to enjoy it. We think Garrison will give up his lectur'g tour & be the agent for the Freedmen's Union & perhaps be sent to Eng. by them — which seems better to be gettg. up lectures on his own account. . . We have been interested in S. B. Anthony's articles & in the acct. of her visit to you.

Now I pray that beyond Auburn, Boston or Roxbury, Medford & Orange (including Anna B.) any correspondence may cease. . . We can't boast such constant comp'y as thine a week ago, but 2 or three times since I came home we have had 17 in fam'y a night & part of 2 days — & yester'y 9 & last night 20 — countg. Liz. to tea. The 2 Parrish & wives — Mary Cav'r, Isaac T. W., Willie D., Anna M. can come only rarely. She has been so busy darn'g carpets.

She went to the Fair Circles, to weekday Quaker Meetings, to gatherings of the Temperance Society, the Equal Rights Association, and the Peace Society. Frequently she was in Philadelphia to attend lectures. In December 1858 she heard Emerson, of whom she said:

We have been greatly pleased with listening to R. W. Emerson. His lecture on The Law of Success is full of gems. Collier heard him for the 1st time & was carried away with delight. He remembd so much yestery that we quite enjoyed hearg it over. I spoke to him (Emerson) after the lecture — thanked him for it — he replied, "I got some leaves out of yr. book" — addg "from yr. New Bedford Freds." I remembd that his mind was enlightened beyond his Pulpit & Ordinances about the time of the enlightened Mary Newall's (new light) com'g out & I doubt not she had some influence on him. The only objection to his philosophy the other evg. was his makg Nature utilize everything — the bad as well as the good. That may be in the animal economy — but in morals, I told him, wickedness works only evil & that continually & the only way was to destroy it with unquenchable fire.

She emphasized her belief that there should be a constant antagonism between good and evil,

Eagleswd. essays, last winter, made good and evil — right & wrong no longer antagonistic, but running in parallel lines. . . Buckle calls free will a metaphysical while predestn. is a Theological hypothesis or dogma. It was revolting to my moral sense years ago when I heard Dr. Tyng at a Coloniz'n Mg. say that with all the cruelty of the Slave trade, the horrors of the middle passage, the evils of Slavery in this country, he was prepared to say that Slavery & the Slave trade wd. yet be a bless'g to Africa. At this time Liberia was held up as a great civilizer & evangelizer to that Nation. I don't understand this & want no such quietus to the conscience.[1]

In the early days at Roadside, she wrote the Webbs many informal letters, budgets of news of her family and friends, which also affirm her independence of thought and throw light on her reading. In this correspondence the subject of Blanco White's *Life* recurs more than once. "And didn't I rejoice after reading Blanco White that we saw so exactly eye to eye," she asks Richard Webb,

It certainly was the most interesting work of the kind I ever read. It has not been reprinted here, for it is more anti-sectarian than Unitarians can bear, and more religious or devotional than Infidels would respond to "if there are any such which I sometimes doubt"; so we

stand no chance of a wide circulation of that "holy book." I am lending our copy constantly.

She also read with unrestrained eagerness the writings of
Cardinal Newman, Joseph Barker, and Henry C. Wright — men
whose reflections on the Scriptures, man's spiritual nature, and
religious dogma influenced them to reject orthodox assumptions.
The views of such men, she wrote Richard Webb, were not popular with American publishers who were "all too conservative to
reprint Barker's life or that of Blanco White."

Commenting on Webb's column in the *Anti-Slavery Standard*,
comprising letters on the subject of reforms and reformers in Great
Britain, Lucretia declared that she found these writings "vastly interesting." Then she added a word on the happiness she experienced in realizing that there were so many fine and good people in
the world. "I am constantly combating," she said, "the human
'depravity' doctrine & preach in its stead, the innate purity of man."

Referring again to the fact that Richard Webb had renounced Quakerism, she deplored his inclination to place upon
his own shoulders the burden of guilt. It should, she said, "rather
have been for the reason of the declension in the Society, while
thou hast been makg. progress on the true Quaker principle —
obedience to the conviction of thy mind." As to her own convictions, she added, "we are not prepared to yield our right & yet
we are nearly weaned from our Mother Church as it now is — no
longer a nursing Mother to new born reformation."

This group of letters [2] closes with a note introducing Miller
McKim to the Webbs and bringing these friends of hers up-to-date
on some of her personal concerns: Sarah Pugh had started traveling in Europe; Martha, the Motts' youngest daughter, had married George Lloyd of New York; Edward M. Davis, in spite of Lucretia's half-hearted approval, had recently purchased a suburban
home, Oak Farm.

In the fall of 1857 the traveling began again with a visit to
Columbia, Pennsylvania, which must have recalled the unhappy
riots of 1834 with the town's resentment of her outspoken denunciation of its lawlessness and guilt. The passing of the years had
evidently softened the anger, for a "very large audience," according to the *Columbia Spy*, "assembled on Thursday evening, at
Odd Fellows Hall and gave a most respectful and interested attention to an admirable discourse from Mrs. Lucretia Mott." The
newspaper noted that, although Mrs. Mott's opinions were abso-

lutely unorthodox, and opposed to "the opinions and prejudices of her hearers," she was listened to with respect. "We have seen the day," concluded the report, "when she could not have found an audience in a public hall in Columbia, that would not have interfered to prevent the expression of unpopular sentiments and views. It would be no compliment to those assembled last night to say that they were most orderly and attentive; we expected nothing else." [3]

In September 1858 Lucretia Mott went to the little town of Yardleyville, Bucks County, Pennsylvania. There she gave one of her most significant sermons, speaking at length on man's inheritance of the divine gift of the Holy Spirit. For her text she selected a sentence from the New Testament "The Kingdom of God is within us," adding in her own words, "a testimony of one of the modern writers: 'Christianity will not have performed its office in the earth until its professors have learned to respect the rights and privileges of conscience, by a toleration without limit, a faith without contention.' "

In the development of this text, she made a strong plea to man to accept the divine spiritual gift, the power transcending creeds and dogmas; to walk uprightly; to act righteously, to be just, to be faithful. "I would not set a high opinion on the Catholic Church," she stated, "the Episcopalian, Presbyterian, Methodist, Quaker, or any other. They all have their elements of goodness, and they all have their elements of bondage; and if we yield obedience to them, we become subject to them, and brought under bondage. If we acknowledge this truth, and bow to it, we shall dare show our dissent."

No compromise, as she urged at Yardleyville, should be made with any form of injustice: the wrongs suffered by women and slaves, the assumption of the right to force observance of a "Sabbath," and the evil of war. But, though she imposed upon all a degree of general guilt in a passive acceptance of national wrongs, she was by no means pessimistic as to the future. Her final note bespoke her faith in humanity. "The people flock more to hear moral discourses," she said,

. . . than to hear the preaching from the pulpit. This would not be the case were the preaching of the pulpit like the preaching of Jesus. There is a quick understanding in the fear of the Lord among the people, and I will trust the people. I have confidence in their intuitive sense of right, of the good. It is this great heart of the people we are to preach into, to proclaim liberty and truth, justice and right into; and let it be done.

Two points she mentioned specifically: the perversion of the Scriptures that assumed total depravity, and the degradation of men's natural instincts. In her opinion one of these errors led to the other.[4]

With the abolition of slavery legally proclaimed, Garrison with many other members of the Anti-Slavery Society felt that the purpose of the Anti-Slavery Society had reached a triumphant end. But, despite her admiration for Garrison's talents and sincerity, Lucretia Mott, guided by her own convictions, did not accept his belief that the Anti-Slavery Society should be disbanded. On this issue she found herself in accord with Wendell Phillips, who did not believe that the object of the Anti-Slavery Society had been accomplished. Another rift in the ranks became apparent as state and local societies took opposing stands in arguing the question of dissolution. At the meeting of the Pennsylvania Association held in Franklin Institute on November 28, 1866, expression of opinion on the subject of dissolution naturally followed. Some thought that the work of educating the recently emancipated slaves by supporting the effort of the Freedmen's Aid Society seemed the immediate, the practical solution; others, including Robert Purvis, Edward M. Davis, and Lucretia Mott, emphasized the importance of the ballot.

"We have all been surprised at the marvelous progress which has been made," were Lucretia Mott's words on the question of dissolving the Anti-Slavery Society,

. . . but, on the other hand we have watched the accounts that have been furnished — some in the daily papers, and some in letters and communications directly to us, and in personal visits, of the cruelty that has been practiced in the South; and those accounts have come to us with the expressed desire that we should keep on and not resign the organization. They have told that the time has not come, while the slave in so many instances is only nominally and legally free, while in fact the almost unlimited power of his oppressor continues; and that in many parts of our Southland large numbers of families of slaves are still actually held in bondage, and their labor extorted from them by the lash, as formerly; that while, so far as the law is concerned, they may no longer be publicly bought and sold, yet they have been actually sold and transferred from place to place. All these facts show the necessity of our cause, and the continued existence of the

Anti-Slavery Society, notwithstanding the legal abolition of the ac-cursed system. All this has kept us on the watch, and has kept our interest alive in the great cause.

Although emphasizing the incompleteness of the labors of the organization, she included a word of satisfaction with what had been accomplished:

Even while we mourn that so much wrong yet exists, we are all astonished and wonder at the advance in our land so far above our most sanguine calculations, for the most sanguine anticipations of the Abolitionists never reached what has been realized within a year or two. I want, therefore, in the beginning of our anti-slavery meeting, that we should be affected in our hearts so much as to offer the silent thanksgiving of praise to Him who is greater than we, whose power is mightier than all, in that so much has been affected through us more than we could hope for.

At the close of this meeting of the Pennsylvania Anti-Slavery Association, the Business Committee offered Resolutions endors-ing the need of the ballot for "the legally emancipated slaves," the support of Anti-Slavery Societies as "the only organizations in this country which uncompromisingly demand suffrage for the Negro," and "the impeachment of Andrew Johnson, President of the United States." Lucretia Mott was one of the five members of this committee.[5]

Chapter Fifteen

"ALL THESE REFORMS"

After the very first years at Roadside, Lucretia Mott was challenged by a flood tide of demands for her voice to aid the promotion of social reform. Despite her sufferings at this time from chronic dyspepsia and the relentlessly "bad throat," she was able to answer many of the calls. Marching in the van of the Woman's Rights Movement and absorbed in efforts to destroy slavery, root and branch, she found it no effort apparently to lend enthusiastic support to "Whole World Temperance" and "Universal Peace." And there were always the urgent calls of her Meeting.

From time to time, Lucretia Mott, while criticizing illiberal theories and practices among the "hierarchy of Friends," had refused to take part in another division of the Society. This view she again maintained in 1853 when certain liberals organized a group which made a signal effort to express their religious convictions in the practice of broad principles of democracy. Among these men and women were Samuel J. May, Theodore Parker, Whittier, Garrison, Thomas Garrett, a resolute abolitionist of Delaware, and John and Hannah Cox, Pennsylvania Quakers. As events proved, Lucretia endorsed at heart the liberal aims of the Progressive Friends; many of her co-workers were a part of the organization; and, without technical membership, she took active participation in the yearly conventions of the new group.[1] But the anguish she suffered as a result of the Quaker Separation of 1827 kept her from becoming a formal part of another branch of Quakerism.

Shortly after the organization of the Progressive Friends, New England became the center of an upsurging religious agitation. Not a criticism of the tenets or practices of any one sect nor a plea for democracy, this unrest was rather a confession of lack of faith in the adequacy of existing religions to meet the spiritual needs of man. Consequently, many leaders among Unitarians, Universalists, Transcendentalists, Congregationalists, avowed radicals, and men of no sectarian affiliation whatever were found among outspoken critics of religion. At length, after "some fifty or sixty gentlemen and ladies" held a conference in Boston in the winter of 1866–1867 to discuss what was given out as "the need for reform in religion," the decision was reached to call a meeting for the organization of a nonsectarian, radical group aimed to promote "pure and genuine Religion in the World — to develop a nobler spirit and higher purpose both in society and the individual." This was the aim of the Free Religious Association, and the formal organization of the movement was planned to take place in Boston on May 30, 1867.

Scheduled to appear on the program of the meeting for organization were twelve persons, eleven men and one woman. In this group was Thomas Wentworth Higginson, who after his early years as a Unitarian clergyman had become the Colonel of a Negro regiment in the Civil War. Others listed in the proposed program were Ralph Waldo Emerson; William Furness, the Unitarian minister of Philadelphia; Oliver Johnson, the New York abolitionist; and Robert Dale Owen, son of the Welsh philanthropist Robert Owen. The younger Robert Owen, an abolitionist, was a member of Congress from Indiana. Then too, there were the Brooklyn Universalist Henry Blanchard, the scholarly Rabbi Isaac M. Wise of Cincinnati, and another Rabbi from Ohio, the educator Max Lilienthal.

One woman only, Lucretia Mott, was chosen to speak at the meeting.

Although she had not signed the call for the organization of the Progressive Friends, Lucretia was willing to be grouped among the leaders of the Free Religious Association. Other women were present at this May 30 meeting; but she was the only one scheduled to address the gathering. And her presence was not taken casually. As the chairman, Octavius B. Frothingham of New York, remarked in pointing out the effort of the committee to bring together significant speakers, ". . . we sent for Lucretia Mott."

In explaining further the purpose of the assembly, Mr. Frothingham made clear the fact that the selection of the speakers from different religious groups had been made advisedly — not with the intention of binding the speaker to the tenets of his own sect but in the hope of effecting breadth of opinion. "We have therefore," he emphasized, "invited no one to speak here this morning as a representative of an organized sect; no Orthodox man as Orthodox; no Unitarian as a Unitarian; no Universalist as a Universalist . . . We ask to be heard not as disorganizers, but as organizers."

The program, thus formally explained, began with "Remarks" from the Universalist, Henry Blanchard. After noting that in his opinion the chief distinction between Universalism and Unitarianism was that Universalists accepted the principle of the Atonement, Mr. Blanchard stressed his hope that there would be among the Universalists no tendency to introduce further division among the ranks. This was his main point of emphasis.

Following Mr. Blanchard, Lucretia Mott was the second speaker. Declaring that she was not in the conference as a delegate from any branch of Quakerism, "The Orthodox portion," "the Hicksite portion, the Progressive Friends or any of these," she made a plea for the recognition of independence of mind and breadth of understanding. This independence, she thought, would not of itself offend as long as it refused to deprecate the beliefs of others. The relation of religion and liberty, she said, should be considered "the only science of theology . . . to study or necessary to be taught." Admitting advantages in organization, she pointed out that there could not "be any movement, any fellowship of anybody together without some form or some rules of government." But it was her opinion that Americans had "yet to learn something that should recognize independence of the mind and the truth that maketh free . . ." Again and again in this speech she made a plea for independence of thought and action.[2]

Among the tenets of the Society of Friends is the Testimony for Peace, "That it is not lawful for Christians to resist evil, or to war or fight in any case." Accepting from her earliest years the letter and spirit of this testimony, surely from the time when her voice was first heard in public meetings, Lucretia Mott had steadily urged the adoption of "moral weapons" in the crusade for righteousness and freedom.

Holding the Principle of Peace and living in Philadelphia, the most significant center of Quakerism in America, Lucretia Mott was well known in England as an important pacifist. When, therefore, a number of women of Exeter, England, appealed in 1842 to American women for support in an effort made by the English women to avert war between America and Great Britain, the "15 foot scroll with 1601 signatures" was addressed to the "Women of Philadelphia." The reply, sent in 1846, to this "Friendly Address," bears one signature only, that of Lucretia Mott.[3]

External evidence is lacking as to the authorship of this document. But certain ideas in the content — the allusion to a wide humanitarianism, the challenge to women to instill principles of peace in children, the plea for "the hour of human brotherhood," the stress upon "the mighty influences that cluster around the domestic hearth" and "by the wayside" — these ideas and the general simplicity, directness, and friendliness of the tone suggest the influence, if not the hand, of Lucretia Mott. And significantly, the "Women of Philadelphia" were satisfied to be represented by her signature alone.

As a vice president of the Pennsylvania Peace Society, Lucretia Mott attended committee meetings and the larger gatherings whenever her strength permitted. Attentive audiences heard her denounce the corporal punishment of children, which she deemed the genesis of man's refuge in war. As substitutes for force in the rearing of children, she advocated instructing the young in the principles of pacificism, kindness, and goodness; and she urged that heed be given to the love of peace in the human heart. To the Peace Movement, she brought the faith that had sustained her in the antislavery cause, the faith that had kept her optimistic in the struggle for Woman's Rights; and she rarely let a Peace Meeting close without pointing out the evidence of progress in righteous causes.[4]

Believing in peace, Lucretia Mott could be deemed a nonresistant. But, when her friend Robert Purvis called her the most belligerent nonresistant he had ever seen, she retorted that she was no "milk and water non-resistant" having had the conduct of the early Friends in mind who were not passive at all times. In the gloomy days of the Civil War, however, speaking from the galleries of Friends' Meetings, she had urged the implications of the Quaker Testimony for Peace. Her convictions also had been strengthened by the unhappy experiences of numbers of young Quakers seeking spiritual comfort and encouragement from her as they suffered the obdurate fetters of the draft. These experiences but strengthened her belief that war was wrong.

In the summer of 1861, however, she preached a sermon in Boston that was interpreted by the *Boston Bee* as being a defense of the war. The newspaper's statement was that Lucretia Mott had acknowledged her hope that "[the war] would be prosecuted with energy and faith since it was founded on so good a cause, [and that she] thought the greatest danger would be in listening to compromises, which would only result in again fighting the old battle." To this account of her lecture, Lucretia Mott sent a protest through the *Anti-Slavery Standard,* declaring that the charge of her indorsing the war was an "injustice to the few remarks" she had made on the subject. "I spoke," she said, "of our country and of Christendom generally not having attained to the highest mode of warfare, the weapons of which are not carnal, but mighty through God, etc., and expressed the fullest confidence in their efficiency, inasmuch as labor, begun single-handed and alone, on behalf of the suffering and the dumb, by earnest appeal and faithful protest had aroused the country from its alarming lethargy on the slavery question." She explained that she had tried to say that the War had been brought on through the guilt of the Nation in its failure to destroy slavery. To that extent it was her belief that the War was a righteous cause being the logical result of "wrong doings and atrocious cruelties." Her protest also pointed out that she had voiced the hope that although all wars were terrible this war would not be *stayed,* not brought to a conclusion by compromise that would prolong the evil of slavery. Slavery, she said, was of itself a cruel war which had endured in America "from generation to generation, with all the force of our government, the President himself Commander-in-Chief." [5]

In the renewed period of traveling in the 1860's she preached in Brooklyn, in Wilmington, and in Washington. The sermon in the Fifteenth Street Meeting House in Brooklyn, November 11, 1866, begins with the words, "The Lord is in his holy temple, let all the earth keep silence before him." In contrast to the denunciation of wrongs characterizing many of her speeches for causes, here is an expression of optimistic faith, of spiritual calm, of the kingdom of heaven within man. "True religion," as she said,

. . . makes men not gloomy. Penances, asceticism, old sacrifices, "daily crosses" — all belong to a more gloomy religion than that of the benign and beautiful spirit of Jesus. . . We know well that there are sacrifices to make in our life, in the pursuit of our duty, the attempt to lift the lowly, to spread the gospel of glad tidings of great joy to all people. We know that the right hand the right eye (to use again a figure of speech) have to be parted with at times; but always we feel the conviction that we enter into life thereby and its rich experience.[6]

This sermon breathes the spirit of peace and happiness to be found in Christianity.

Lucretia Mott's correspondence of the years 1869–1870 contains fewer references to the problems of faith and doubt and sectarianism, subjects that had filled her pages in the earlier period of her life. It is as though scant necessity remained for discussing her beliefs, the beliefs which had become matters of public knowledge. Now she referred to people, her health, her reading, and the active social life in her home. Perhaps she took to heart the advice given her by her cousin Mary Earle, who late in 1860 wrote:

I have a concern — dear Cousin L. . . that is to advise thee what should we all do. Now, do rest thyself & "go no more a roving." Thou hast certainly done thy part toward making the world wiser & better & now please confine thyself to that dear hut, thy home & to thy children & grandchildren and cousins etc. etc. These are my delightful items in exchange for thy sterling metal. But it is all I have to give thee.[7]

In 1865 the *Nation,* described by Lucretia as a "Weekly Journal Devoted to Politics, Literature, Science and Art," was founded under the joint editorship of Miller McKim and Garrison's son, Wendell Phillips Garrison. To finance the journal, its founders sought backing or assistance from American liberals; specifically they expected from the Motts a substantial contribution to their venture not only because of their known generosity but because of the warm friendship existing between the Motts and Miller McKim, Wendell Phillips, and the entire Garrison family.

Although liberal causes exerted a tug on Lucretia's heart, she did not give her financial aid to causes unthinkingly. Concerning the request to aid the *Nation,* she wrote Martha:

. . . Miller McKim is very full of this new Union Association & the Paper is to be called "The Nation" He & Wendl. P. G. to be Editors. They are collectg. money on a large scale. M . . . who never gave before was called on, gives $1000. Miller wd. like all A.S. & Freedmen's Societies to be merged in this — a Reconstruction Union. He sent an appeal to our Frds. Association. I told him it was objected, that woman was ignored in their organizn. & if really a reconstructn. for the Nation she ought not so to be — and it would be rather a "come down" for Anti-Slavery women & Quaker women to consent to be thus overlooked after sufferg. the A.-S. Socy. to "split" in 1840 rather than yield & after claimg. our rights so earnestly in London to a seat in the Convention. He was rather taken a back sd. "if there seemed a necessity for women he thot. they wd. be admitted — to wh. the impetuous reply was "seemed a necessity" "for one half the Nation to act with you" (the larger $\frac{1}{2}$ too we might say) — so many men slain. You ought to have been here — he couldnt. ask Jas. with quite so good a grace for $1000 *did* ask but I guess he will not get anything like so much from him.

Despite the fact that Lucretia Mott was subject to persistent physical illness, she would not abate her interests in the concerns that touched her heart. When her husband protested her vigorous program she responded: "It was Jack who fell down & broke his crown, but I forbear Jill may come tumbling after." But again and again, in the 1860's she felt the weight of her years. "If I had not had E. Davis' arm & swift feet coming from the Festival," she wrote in a Family Letter, "I might not have reached the hall." (But Edward Davis himself protested, "Mother trotted me along.") Continuing this letter, she said,

I only wait for the May meeting to withdraw from every office. Age infirmities are reason enough — do not think it would do for thee at thy age to cut loose. Doubtful if I have strength to go to Boston to the Anniversary . . . but I am keeping quiet lest A. or some other worthy should offer to bear me company. Dread more & more in my old age these goings from home. Reporters cunning at Conventions.

In the 1860's she suffered almost continuously from cold hands and feet, but she declared that the numbness was due to lack of exercise, not to her advancing age. Notwithstanding this brave protest, she could not deny certain effects of time. "I shrink from new acquaintances in my old age," she wrote. "I'm glad sometimes I shall not have much more to do in any of these movements."

Returning home from the Green Mountains in the summer of 1867, she stopped to visit the newly established Vassar College. Here, at Poughkeepsie in the neighborhood of her old school, Nine Partners, she could but contrast the modern institution with the restricted educational offerings of her day. She was duly impressed with the "house and grounds" of Vassar, with the quarters for the riding school, the gymnasium, and beyond all, with Maria Mitchell's observatory. But her final observation on her visit to Vassar College was: "I was satisfied not to have to listen to school exercises . . . We had good time to see all we wanted to." [8]

On April 10, 1861, James and Lucretia Mott celebrated the fiftieth anniversary of their wedding, an occasion marked by greetings from their friends and by widespread public tributes for the couple united so long by "the mutual love of truth." A scroll prepared for the anniversary reads, in part:

James and Lucretia Mott, having completed 50 years of married life, we the undersigned, assembled on the tenth day of April, 1861, to celebrate their Golden Wedding, joyfully record here our names in loving and respectful tribute to them who have given to us, and to the world another illustration of the beauty and glory of true marriage.[9]

To this statement was added a poem entitled "Fifty Years of Joy and Sorrow!"

As the years passed, Lucretia Mott evinced not the slightest inclination to relinquish her beliefs or to evade censure for her "heresies." Her convictions, she believed, were evoked by sound reasoning; her steps were taken under the guidance of the Inner Light. But though she remained unperturbed by criticism, time had not dulled her perception and understanding of the price she paid for her independence. As she explained to Richard Webb in 1867, the trials of Blanco White were not unlike her own experiences.

I could go with him in this non-conformity also, even while it has brot. down Cherry St. Anathemas thick upon me & raised quite a tempest in our teapot this winter, when the Liberals wd. have me on the School Committee. My going to the Unitarian Convention too was almost an unpardonable sin — but I must stop — James has sent up for the letters. I wanted to sum up the cheering evidence of Anti-Slavery progress, as I have in a letter to George Combe. It just occurred to me to send that letter as it contains more than I wished to say here about J. B. White. People will cry "Mad dog" when doctrines or sentiments conflict with their cherished ideas, and I'm glad to say with the Apostle "It is a small thing to be judged of man's judgment." [10]

Indeed, opposition seemed not only to encourage her to remain steadfast in her views but to spur her to strengthen the faith of others. As she had written to her cousin Lydia Mott in 1861:

And when our meetings are forbidden, & doors closed against us, it is no time to stay away, & thus yield to the enemy. We received a Paper from Utica two days ago — giving an account of Beriah Green, S. B. Anthony, & Aaron Powell being denied the Hall they had engaged. We may hope that these demonstrations are only the outbreak of the present desperate effort of the Slave powers — & that by untiring perserverance, the advocates of freedom will eventually find place among all ranks — & "Liberty be proclaimed throughout the land." [11]

The amazing thing is that, in spite of Lucretia Mott's "heresy," she continued to possess the confidence and respect of such a large number of Philadelphia Friends. Having taken upon herself the stigma of radicalism, openly critical of what she called the "Quaker priesthood" and of many forms and observances of the Society, she was, paradoxically, chosen again and again to be one of the representatives from the Philadelphia Quarterly Meeting to the Philadelphia Yearly. Notwithstanding the conservatism of many Quakers on the subject of slavery as contrasted with her outspoken liberality, she was one of "a joint committee" appointed to prepare an essay on the abolition of slavery in the District of Columbia. And when a committee was chosen to consider the advisability of revising the Discipline on the question of outgoings in marriage, Lucretia Mott, "the heretic," was a member of the committee.[12]

Writing to her friend, Elizabeth Pease Nichol of England, in the spring of 1866, Lucretia Mott closed her letter with these words:

My husband says add his loving regards. On the 10th inst. we celebrated our 55th Anniversary — & had all our children — grandchildn. & great granchn. with us. Our daughter Elish. M. Cavender, a lovely link in our circle was removed from us by death in the 9th mo. inst." [13]

This was a simple allusion to a grievous blow, the loss of one of the members of a closely united family. And before many months had passed, James Mott, while visiting his daughter Martha in Brooklyn, was stricken with pneumonia. He died on January 26, 1868.

In the light of the prominence of his wife, James Mott as a public figure tends to be overlooked; but his interests and participation in social problems of the nineteenth century inspired respect and confidence. Especially was he recognized as a man who showed always the strength of his convictions. Regardless of the popularity of causes he did his own thinking, arriving at his conclusions on principle, in a deliberate, quiet, unspectacular manner. He was always dignified but never unsympathetic to calls of distress. Many offices of trust and leadership among reformers were conferred on him. It is recalled that as an independent thinker he took the step to leave the Orthodox Friends before Lucretia could make the decision. As an Elder in the Society he was often given a Minute to call meetings when he and his wife traveled on religious visits. Prominent as a counselor of young Friends he influenced youth by his unfaltering belief that children should be taught, "by precept and example, the principles of Justice, Mercy and Truth." The Minutes of the Philadelphia

Yearly Meeting record his membership on committee after committee, and frequently he was the appointed chairman of these groups chosen to conduct the concerns of Friends.

James and Lucretia Mott were among the Friends who signed in 1861 an "Address of Some Members of the Society of Friends to their Fellow Members on the subject of Education and of the Establishment of a Board School for Friends' Children and for the Education of Teachers." [14] This appeal led to the founding of Swarthmore College, which was officially chartered on April 1, 1864. As a former schoolteacher, educated in the best Quaker tradition, James Mott maintained his interest in education throughout his life. It was no accident that he became one of the incorporators of the new college.

The marriage of James and Lucretia Mott, a union of fifty-seven years, was often referred to as the perfect example of wedded life, the complete realization of a bond welded by mutual understanding and love. "Yr. father," as Lucretia wrote once while on a visit in Nantucket, "amuses himself with long walks & rides. He seems quite as contented, & at home with my relations, as I am wont to be with his. The North Shore came within his rambles yestery." [15] In the Preface of *James and Lucretia Mott,* the author says, "As I began the work as appertaining only to my Grandmother I soon discovered that she was accompanied even in my thoughts by my Grandfather, and that it would be difficult for me to write of one without the other or attempt to give an idea of her life without presenting side by side, the complementary account of him."

At the funeral of James Mott, Rachel M. Townsend, William H. Furness, Mary Grew, Robert Purvis, and George Truman spoke. Further tributes appeared in the newspapers, one writer saying that "a few men belonging to the persecuted class, craved the privilege, which was accorded them, of bearing the remains, and assisting in any other office incident to the occasion." Writing to the *Anti-Slavery Standard,* Wendell Phillips concluded his eulogy of James Mott in these words: ". . . he had a spirit full of hope which nothing could daunt, tire or depress; one who feared not the face of man and whom nothing could move to the slightest bitterness." The memory lingers long, however, on the words spoken at the funeral by the family friend, Robert Purvis: "I thank God for such a life." [16]

When James Mott died, Lucretia was seventy-five years old. Fortunately she was left in financial competence; but bereft of the understanding companionship that had endured over the years, she felt her bitter sorrow keenly. Bowed in "resignation to the event" she took up the threads of her life, a life, however, that was less active with no new interests.[17] With the traveling of the earlier days lessened, she lived relatively quiet days and evenings at Roadside. Here she was surrounded by her close relations; and the friends of many years came and went. But complete inactivity or seclusion was not permitted her. In the promotion of Woman's Rights, Susan B. Anthony and Elizabeth Cady Stanton often journeyed out to Roadside for inspiration; for shorter or longer visits some of the others who sought out Lucretia were Alfred Love, her associate in the Pennsylvania Peace Society; Frances Watkins Harper, a Philadelphia writer; the gifted young lecturer Anna Dickinson; and Lucretia's old antislavery fellow crusader Oliver Johnson.

Shortly after the Motts moved to Roadside they rejoiced to find living in the neighborhood their friend, the Unitarian minister Robert Collyer. A native of Yorkshire, England, and a blacksmith, Collyer had been a Methodist; later he became dissatisfied with what he considered certain illiberal tenets in Methodism; but a separation from his "mother church" and from friends and associates in his church seemed unthinkable. It was Lucretia Mott, as he wrote later, who "opened her heart" to him and comforted him by relating the sufferings she herself had borne in the Great Separation which had divided the Quakers, forcing her to part with friends in order to be "true to her own soul." Moreover, it was she, "the grand-hearted Quaker preacher," as Robert Collyer called Lucretia, who cheered him in his "religious heresies." As similar experiences cemented a lasting bond of friendship between the two ministers, Robert Collyer was often found at Roadside.[18]

In 1866 she went to New York to attend the meeting which inaugurated the Equal Rights Convention, the association aimed to secure "Equal Rights to all American citizens . . . irrespective of race, color, or sex." Of the new organization, Elizabeth Cady Stanton was first elected president. But Mrs. Stanton proposed that the first president of the Equal Rights Convention should be Lucretia Mott. "Thus," Mrs. Stanton explained, "the office of President . . . might ever be held sacred in the memory that it had first been filled by one so loved and honored by all." Then, just before the meeting was adjourned, Lucretia Mott made a brief statment urging the group to remember that the progress of great achievement must be slow, must be the work of "the few in isolation and ridicule." But sincerity of action, she added, would enable the workers to "walk with angels . . . under the protection of God the Father." "As she uttered her parting words of benediction," wrote Susan B. Anthony, the Secretary,

. . . the fading sunlight through the stained glass windows fell upon her pure face, a celestial glory seemed about her, and a sweet and peaceful influence pervaded every heart. And all responded to Theodore Tilton when he said, "this closing meeting of the Convention was one of the most beautiful, delightful and memorable which any of its participants ever enjoyed." [19]

In January 1869 Lucretia Mott was in Washington for the Equal Rights Convention, of which she was still president, and also for the sessions of a meeting of the Universal Peace Union. At the Equal Rights Convention she reiterated her oft-repeated warning that the weapons to be used in the struggle for the rights of humanity were "moral weapons" and that the program of the Association endorsed suffrage for the Negro as well as for women. During the two-day sessions, according to a contemporary account, she presided with "great dignity and amiability," maintaining an atmosphere of fairness felt not only by members of the Association but by visitors not committed to the ideals of the reformers.

At the same time she did not lose sight of the need of keeping alive faith in the cause. "Take a cheerful view of the past," she said, "be hopeful for the future, and be *fair* to the present." One writer described the convention as "a brilliant gathering." By another observer the group was "set down as lunatics . . . as homely an assemblage as would well be brought together . . . large, rawboned, masculine specimens of the feminine portion of the human species." It was this writer who added that Lucretia Mott with her "refined and beautiful expression of countenance" was an exception in appearance to the group.

No speech of Lucretia Mott's life received wider acclaim than a sermon she preached at the Unitarian Church in Washington in 1869. Following the announcement of her appearance a crowd of elegantly dressed women, dignified Senators and Representatives stood side by side with plainly clad working men and women to listen to her words. "So inspired by love of humanity," wrote the correspondent to the *Lewiston Journal,* "was all she said, that each one present felt his heart throb and glow with nobler thoughts, higher inspirations and deeper love to his fellow-men, as he listened." [20] The correspondent to the *Radical* wrote of the "overflowing audience" that greeted the speaker, of her comprehensive and beautiful discourse, "as related to the duties and responsibilities of human beings." By this writer Lucretia was described as the most beautiful woman he had ever seen, "the noblest, truest and most beautiful type of womanhood" in America.

Between 1870 and 1880 more than forty references to Lucretia Mott's public speaking, either in the assembly of the Peace Society or at the Friends' Meetings appear in the Diary of Alfred Love. On November 13, 1870, Love wrote:

. . . went to Green St. Meeting. Lucretia Mott spoke freely & fluently, taking her text, "The fields are white unto harvest but the laborers are few, etc." She went on to all reforms dwelling largely on Peace. I advertised our Peace Meetings to be held this week. She went so far as to urge those forward "who even did not wear the peculiar dress of Friends & she was glad of it." She urged work and an active religion & said — "this formal waiting upon the Lord even sitting still may be abused," & then again — "active labor is better for that is waiting upon the Lord." She was excellent & to me so inspiring I own to feeling the full force of some of her remarks as though directed at me.

Unfortunately the organization of the American Equal Rights Association could not effect harmony among the members of the Woman's Rights Movement. When Lucretia Mott was president a truce was effected. As Alfred Love commented on May 14, 1868:

Then to business meetings of Equal Rights Society & there I was instrumental in retaining Lucretia Mott as President & thus saved a difficulty between Lucy Stone & Miss Anthony.[21]

Soon the Association was divided into two factions, each group sponsoring its own organ of publication. The National Woman's Suffrage Association, under the leadership of Elizabeth Cady Stanton and Susan B. Anthony published *Revolution,* while the American Woman Suffrage Association, led by Lucy Stone, Mary Livermore, and Julia Ward Howe, issued *The Woman's Journal.*

When Theodore Tilton of New York desired to bring together the divided allegiances he called a few persons to meet in the Fifth Avenue Hotel in New York to discuss the problems of the division. In replying to his plea for her support, Lucretia Mott promised to take part in the effort to reconcile the "divided ranks in the labor for woman's suffrage," but she added,

I most willingly have my signature attached, only please not place the name first; but rather far below those who have prepared the circular.

I had interviews last Fall with the active workers on both sides in Boston & New York, and plead with them, that at the then coming Convention in Cleveland they should merge their interests in one common cause, and have one universal society — This however was not done — Still I hope it is not too late for the proposed union to take place.

I had observed with regret that the anniversary meetings in New York are appointed for the same time.

I shall not be present at either — our Yearly Meeting of Friends in Philada. occurs at the same time, which will keep me here. I love the pioneer & earnest labor [sic] on both sides too well to become a partizan — and shall be glad to attend any meetings when in my power.[22]

A postscript was added by Sarah Pugh wishing that the "efforts for Union may not be in vain."

At the drawn-out gathering of "about a dozen" representing both sides, heavy arguments were presented; yet good temper was maintained. Finally, the interminably long meeting was forced to disband with no agreement reached. At the moment, Lucretia Mott, who adhered to the National Association, made a fervent plea for union. Weighing the principles urged by both groups, she could see no valid reason for a division. She felt that the supreme issue, "absolute rights for woman," should have been kept steadily to the fore, obscuring, or at least, placing in relative insignificance, less important questions. "I believe," she observed, "that the two societies should unite by such mutual concessions as each should make to the other."

But her letter home was brought to this conclusion: "I did not expect great things, & I didn't get 'em. Glad to be out of it all & never expect to join another organization."

However, when summer came, she urged her sister Martha to go to the Saratoga Convention as "E. C. Stanton will need thee & thou ought to be willing to preside. I agree with thee in a willingness for the Revolun. to *close.*" Moreover the cause of justice for women was so close to her heart that, in spite of her fatigue and the burden of her years, she urged Paulina Davis to prepare for the forthcoming "second decade" meetings about to be held in Philadelphia. She was forced to admit that she could give no active support to the reunion, but she allowed her name to be used on the circular. Then she insisted that the invitation to the "second decade" be "sent to Boston & all interested without regard to party." This decision she made although she said that "Garrison, Lucy Stone & Henry too, Wendell P. & few others [were] very set agt. workg. with S. B. Anthony, E. C. Stanton & even Paulina D." [23]

Elizabeth Cady Stanton's vision had empowered her to see that little real progress for women could be gained until women themselves had a voice in the making of the laws. Chief among the offending legal restrictions suffered by women were the stringent laws concerning divorce. Against "these fetters of degradation" Mrs. Stanton raised her protest, only to meet the argument that the subject of divorce had no place in the program of the Woman's Rights Convention. Among the advocates of rights for women, therefore, the subject of divorce aroused many disputes, while the reactionaries rejoiced, believing that lack of harmony would weaken the whole program of the cause. Undismayed by the unpopularity of her criticism Mrs. Stanton had the courage to offer, in the Convention of 1860, Resolutions providing that an unequivocal stand on the subject of marriage and divorce should be taken by the Convention. Wendell Phillips offered strong opposition to these Resolutions, even going so far as to move that they be stricken from the Minutes. The ensuing discussion was sharp and bitter. Finally, William Lloyd Garrison, while supporting Phillips' contention that the subject of marriage and divorce had no part in the program of the Convention, agreed in spirit with Mrs. Stanton by concluding his speech in these words:

No matter what any book might say to the contrary, human rights were equal, inalienable, indestructable, without reference to sex or complexion. They belonged to the constitution of every human being . . . [and] in a government like this, that they had nothing more to do than to put the ballot into the hand of woman, as it was in the hand of man.[24]

The Resolutions, though not stricken from the Minutes, were not passed.

Lucretia Mott was not reported as having been present at the 1860 Convention. On the causes of the division she said little, but she was not one to take refuge in evasions or to sidestep essential issues. Above all she was indignant that opponents of changes in the divorce laws allowed themselves to cherish personal animosity toward Mrs. Stanton. Bringing up the subject in the letter sent to Martha before the Saratoga Convention, she scored Mary Grew's criticism of Mrs. Stanton, for she felt that Mrs. Stanton's opponents were indirect, evasive, and arrogant. She herself was not willing to accept the proposal on the question of divorce, but she realized that changes in "the marriage and divine law" were imminent. On the other hand, she thought that both Mrs. Stanton and Susan B. Anthony ought to continue with their lecturing without exhausting energy and talents in combating the issue which had brought friction into the Woman's Rights Movement.[25]

Shortly after the First Seneca Falls Convention of 1848, Lucretia said,

While in Western New York, we attended two Conventions called to consider the relative position of woman in society — one held at Seneca Falls, the other at Rochester. The "proceedings" have been published in the North Star and several other papers.

The attendance and interest manifested were greatly encouraging; and give hope that this long-neglected subject will soon begin to receive the attention that its importance demands. . .

All these subjects of reform are kindred in their nature; and giving to each its proper consideration, will tend to strengthen and nerve the mind for all — so that the abolitionist will not wax weaker in his advocacy of immediate emancipation. He will not love the slave less, in loving universal humanity more.[26]

Many of the nineteenth-century reformers knew that Lucretia Mott did not regard suffrage as the paramount aim of the Woman's Rights Movement. But this belief on her part did not impair her wholehearted leadership in the cause. As Martha wrote Miss Anthony in 1853,

My sister concurs in this opinion — an unsuccessful attempt, throwing further ridicule on the movement — would be unwise. She wishes me to ask you if the requisite steps have been taken to announce to the public the Oct. Convention thro/Tribune, Women's Advocate & other papers.

And a fortnight later, Martha's words were:

My sister begs me to answer your note of Saturday, saying that she agrees with you in the opinion that the National Convention had better not be postponed on accot. of the election in the Fall, and that is certainly my opinion.[27]

Actually no reform was closer to Lucretia's heart than rights for women; but she regarded intemperance, religious intolerance, human slavery, and the wrongs imposed on women as being forms of social injustice, growing, as she put it, from warped thinking. To her there could be no peace in the world until all the evils, interlocked, were abated. Her philosophy and her religion embraced the quest for the ideal of an all-comprehending justice, and seemingly, she had the strength to pursue the many-sided ideal.

Chapter Sixteen

EVENING

"As for taking a long breath," Lucretia wrote to Martha shortly after her sixtieth birthday, "it is what I have not done since the Convention of 1833 — rather since I was born — except in days of yore, when I could sit and sew carpet rags in some obscure corner of your house." And this public speaking, which had started in the remote past of Lucretia Mott's life, seemed to continue into her very last days. Between 1870 and 1875 she paid several visits to Boston, primarily to speak at the sessions of the Free Religious Association, but also to enjoy meetings of the Boston branch of the Universal Peace Union, to attend sessions of the newly organized Radical Club, and to be with informal gatherings among those whom she described as "the cultured and learned circles of Boston." [1]

The Radical Club was an organization of thoughtful people who met at the house of Mrs. Mary Sargent on Chestnut Street. During the thirteen years of its existence, from 1867 to 1880, discussions in the Club were held on religion, science, art, philosophy, and social issues. Never taking an active part herself in the programs, Mrs. Sargent possessed the enviable talent of bringing together others who voiced their opinions on many challenging subjects. Little formal procedure hampered the conduct of the meetings; but the program consisted usually of an opening speech or essay, followed by informal discussion, called "Comment," on the subject that had been presented. Among those who appeared from time to time in the assembly were Emerson, Henry James, Whittier, Phillips Brooks, Mary Grew, W. H. Channing, W. C. Gannet, Thomas Wentworth Higginson, and Samuel Longfellow, the poet's younger brother. [2]

There seems to be no record of Lucretia's ever having read a paper before the Radical Club, but she was present at several of the assemblies and was recorded as taking part in the discussions. On one occasion, after she had listened to an address on Charles Darwin by Nathaniel Southgate, a member of the Harvard faculty, she wrote Martha that she had heard "an excellent scientific discourse on the Darwin theory." What she did not say in this letter

was that she herself took part in the Comment. Mrs. Sargent, however, remembered that at this meeting Lucretia Mott told the
club that as a result of her interest in science for fifty years, she
had welcomed scientific progress, but had "lamented" the connection of religion and theology because religion was not to be found
in "creeds and forms, [but] in clean living, in doing right, in common honesty." Continuing the discussion, Samuel Longfellow opposed Lucretia's "condemnation of theology," in that it was his
belief that theology was simply statements of great truths and that
"religion should follow theology." Lucretia's final observation on
this meeting was that she did not find the reasoning too abstruse
or the language too highbrow for her understanding, one word
only having floored her.

At another meeting of the Radical Club a paper was read by
John Weiss, the Unitarian minister. Weiss, called "one of the most
brilliant of New England reformers and transcendentalists," chose
as his subject "The Immanence of God." In the discussion following Weiss' paper, Lucretia said,

It is admirable in its methods of asserting Divine Providence and
justifying the ways of God to man. Year by year more people are prepared to accept the plain statement of these ideas. Elias Hicks long
ago taught this same doctrine and when some timid members of the
Society of Friends questioned him in regard to it, he asked impres-
sively, "Are we to go back to miracles?" The natural and the spiritual
ought never to be spoken of antagonistically. Both belong to men and
both should be recognized and cultivated so as to give the benefit of
both.[3]

Again, writing home, she spoke of the cordiality that she enjoyed in Boston, especially of the welcome she received from "several fine women." Gifts also were presented to her — volumes of
Weiss' *American Religion* and Giles Stebbins' *Bible of the Ages*.
Stebbins' book she described as a collection of "Extracts of the best
words from Pagan & Heathen philosophy — from our Bible, a little
& from the best writers — quite a good collection."

She mentioned seeing William Lloyd Garrison, Jr., happily
restored in health from serious burns he had suffered in an accident. Because of the illness of the elder Garrison and the absence
of his name from the program of the Free Religious Association
Lucretia was disturbed. Garrison, she said, should have been on
the program because Garrison was "so tho'ro'ly liberal . . . so
truly religious too without sectarian bigotry." [4]

In the early 1870's Lucretia Mott suffered the loss of three members of her family and one close friend. The first death was that of Lucretia's sister, Elizabeth Yarnall. As Lucretia wrote Richard Webb on February 24, 1870,

She was 75 yrs. old. We were like twin sisters 10 months the longest time we were ever separated. The loss is very great to me. My sister Martha Wright was with her during her illness. She is still here & a great comfort to us to dwell on her bereavet. together. I expected to go first & now so soon to follow, it may seem that at our age I might rejoice rather than mourn but all our speculations as to "What we shall be are unavailing," when the heart is torn.

> When the human drops of bitterness will steal
> Nor can we lose the privilege to mourn
> While we have left the faculty to feel.

Indeed all guesswork as to the future is so vain that we may as well content ourselves with the certainty that both here and hereafter "we are secure to be as blest as we can bear." [5]

On May 4, 1871, she sent Webb news of the death of Abby Kimber. With the passing of the decades the friendship of Lucretia Mott, Abby Kimber, and Sarah Pugh had grown ever stronger. To Lucretia, Abby's death was "a severe blow," like a broken family tie.

Shortly after her return from Boston in 1874, Lucretia Mott endured a bitter sorrow in the death of her oldest child. And this oldest child, the brilliant but modest Anna Mott Hopper, fulfilled the dearest hopes of James and Lucretia Mott. All the Mott children were innately alert. As would be expected, they possessed a keen awareness of social problems, an awareness tempered by a sense of humor; but none was more talented than Anna. With her mother and her sister Maria she was an enthusiastic member of the Philadelphia Female Anti-Slavery Society, using her imagination, magnetism, and understanding of people to make the organization successful, especially through the annual Fairs. After Emancipation she became increasingly active in broader fields of social work in Philadelphia, welcoming the challenge of new situations calling for clear thinking, power of initiative, and ability to guide others.

Perhaps the most significant recognition of the gifts of Anna Mott Hopper was her election to the Board of Managers of Swarthmore College and to the Executive Committee of that Board, a position she held from 1869 to her death. To the development of the newly established college she brought an open mind for ad-

vanced ideas of education; yet her suggestions were always practical. The Managers' Report of Swarthmore College for 1874
emphasizes specifically Anna Hopper's leadership in "organizing
and arranging the various departments" of the college.

In reply to a letter received a few weeks after the loss of her
daughter, Lucretia wrote:

I too was stricken with deep sorrow over the departure of a dear
daughter . . . a longed-for termination of a fatal malady — Death
then losing his sting. Still even thus, the tender ties of nature & affection are not severed without many a pang strong tho faith may be
in the beautiful "spirit life." [6]

In this same year Lucretia Mott was decidedly feeble in health
and, understandably, broken in spirit. As the autumn days grew
shorter, as the oaks at Roadside reddened and became bare, it was
with a feeling of desolation that she looked forward to the New
Year, formerly a happy time because of her birthday. But in this
year January 3 was saddened by the illness of Martha Wright, who
died on January 4, 1875, the day following Lucretia's eighty-
second birthday.

This blow brought to Lucretia the grief of outliving her youngest sister and of seeing the last of her generation leave her. The
years of the maturity of the sisters had witnessed the affection between them growing ever stronger. In the little line-a-day books
kept by Martha over the years, the entries begin most frequently
with "letter to Sister L." or "letter from Sister L." The secret of
this glowing affection could be the unwavering liberality of spirit
that characterized both Lucretia and Martha. Each held her own
views; each cherished her own dreams. Witty and imaginative,
shrewd in a wholesome sense, Martha Wright possessed the gift of
making sage judgments of causes and people; and she was rarely
fooled. Not believing, like Lucretia, that the acceptance of the
principle of righteousness would banish all the wrongs of the
world, Martha narrowed the scope of her labors to the practical
aim of securing the right of suffrage for women. This goal, she
regarded, not as a symbol or a principle, but as a concrete end in
itself — necessary, simple, sufficient, and just. To her, this end
was an imperative.

After Martha went to New York State to live in 1829, her association with her family, except for brief visits, was in great measure maintained by and through the "family sheets" and her own
letters. The letters written in Martha's hand are compact of fam-

ily chitchat, trenchant observations on the problems of life, and original remarks on her wide reading. Trollope and Dickens and Byron and Scott she knew virtually by heart, and her comments on her reading are delightful in their lively gaiety and wholesome philosophy. "In reading Scott's works," she once wrote to her daughter Marianna,

. . . you must not slide over them merely for the excitement of the story, but note the beauty of the style, and remember at the same time the sensation they produced on their first appearance coming after the sickening love stories of old-fashioned novels. You will feel an affection for Scott after being indebted to him for so much real pleasure as the perusal of his works affords that will make it interesting to you to read his Life by his son-in-law Lockhart when you meet with it.

And to Lucretia:

Eliza. is reading Boswell's Life of Johnson, but does not like it so well as Moore's Life of Byron. I won't wonder for Byron's letters are natural & amusing while Dr. Johnson's are the stupidest that ever were written — whole pages filled with apologies for not having written. It is the notice of contemporary writers that makes it interesting. Johnson is a disagreeable creature to read about, the contempt one feels for Boswell diminishes the interest in what he writes. I found a great deal that I liked to read however, when Marianna was reading it.[7]

In the early years of the *Nation,* Martha wrote for the periodical a forceful defense of the demands of women for suffrage.[8] Her other writings comprise book reviews, reports of meetings, short stories, including some stories for children, and her "manuscript abridgment of the Life of Jefferson." [9] Lucretia encouraged Martha to develop her unique talents, for she could not endorse what she called Martha's habit of "depreciating her talents." In Lucretia's words,

Our mother used to ask us if we were "suing for encomiums" — Now thou knows that thy ability to write "sentiment," is before that of any of our family . . . And now, much as we enjoy everyday famy. details be . . . as thy everlastg. sweepg. of rooms (too much at thy age) we still more relish thy sage comments on man's boast of supportg. woman, be she ever so equal to her lord & master, in industry & providg. for the famy. — so also thy comments on the Revolutn. & the Lucy Stone attempt to ignore our Pioneers — Stanton & Anthony — thy occasional reviews of books read, & not read — & the clerical doings of the day, far more to *my* taste than 2 pages of boat races, inasmuch as all about the Harvard & Eng. match in the papers was *skipped* by me . . . so take all the above, not as complaing. only eager for such sentiment as thy letters often contain. This last, Maria D. handed back to me, after readg., sayg., "It is a very smart letter."

In the avalanche of household duties that Martha usually viewed with jaundiced eye, her gifts, Lucretia thought, were hidden. Once Martha wrote, "I dread the care of the furnace — of the house — of the cow — of the children." And at another time, "Willy is upstairs with Susan, Frank asleep & the rest at school. What a blessed place school is." [10] But such unaffected outbursts of resentment against tasks that Lucretia found diverting simply endeared the younger sister to the older.

Holding high offices in the Woman's Rights Association, Martha was at one time the national president. Preserved in Miss Anthony's "Scraps" is this note written in long hand:

This was given me by Martha C. Wright, Auburn, N.Y. — who with Lucretia Mott, Elizabeth Cady Stanton, Mary Ann McClintock & Jane Hunt called the Convention, though they did not put their names to it.

And on another Report Miss Anthony wrote that Martha Wright's precise handwriting together with the accuracy of her notes was in great measure the inspiration for the preservation of the Records.

In a letter to Garrison, written on March 8, 1870, Lucretia Mott indicates her power to take up the thread of life even when oppressed with personal grief:

Our E. M. Davis is now in Boston. He will confer with our friends there, as to the time of holding the commemorative Mg. of the 15th Amendmt. and of the great events of few years past.

Since he left us I have regretted that I did not urge him to call on thee and ask if thou cannot, in view of so great a movement leave the things that are behind and unite with all who may be disposed to come together to celebrate the marvelous events. I called on Mary Grew yesterdy. She agreed with me in this desire, & said that Ex. Com. would doubtless send a special invitation. May we not hope that it will be accepted, and that Edmund Quincy, Samuel May Jr. & others of our long tried friends may again cooperate with us in a measure that involves no compromise? Let us not hope in vain. We have not met I think since the pleasant eveg we passed at J. M. Mc-Kim's — & thy Wendell's in Llewellyn Park.

After thanking Garrison for the gift of Samuel J. May's *Recollections of the Anti-Slavery Conflict,* she said that an account of the antislavery movement should be written by Garrison and Miller McKim, for "no others could give the movement what it deserved." Clarkson's *Slave Trade,* she added, "tho' necessarily egotistical not offensively so, could not have been written by his helpers, as by himself." [11]

She continued to raise her voice against military training in educational institutions, and she repudiated again and again the recourse to war as a settlement of differences. "We must not admit," she declared at the Fifth Convention of the Universal Peace Union held in New York, May 10, 1871, "that war can be right under any circumstances." In her pervasive optimism, she wrote more hopefully about the chances for achieving a durable peace. "Will not this terrible devastating War tend to open the eyes & the conscience to the Un-Christian — the wicked — the barbarous resort to murderous weapons? There is certainly more life and interest in Peace Meetings now than ever before. The Conventions are well attended & higher ground is taken." Her belief was that war would cease to be "a game for kings" when the people became in earnest to achieve peace in the world, "to substitute other settlements of claims & redress of grievances."

In 1870 the country became agitated over an outbreak in hostilities between two Indian tribes, the Modocs and the Clamaths. The bloodshed that followed the subsequent uprising of 1872 left years of bad feeling. When, however, the leaders of the Modocs were sentenced to be hanged, the justice of the wholesale condemnation did not pass unquestioned.[12]

In the *Voice of Peace* an account is given of Lucretia Mott's effort to obtain clemency for the condemned men:

Her memorable visit to President Grant when he was at Chilton Hills, at Jay Cook's mansion, in behalf of the Modocs will be long remembered. Hearing he was in the neighborhood of Roadside, her residence, she expressed her desire to go and see him and plead for the lives of the twelve condemned Modocs. Edward M. Davis said, "Mother, thee has no invitation, thee has not announced thy desire, etiquette demands thee to send first and see if it will be agreeable and convenient." She replied, "My spirit says go and it will not wait for etiquette. My visit is urgent! Harness the horse!" She went, and the result of that interview is well known. . . The President heard her appeal for Captain Jack and the others, and explained how he was goaded on to execute all, but leaning down and speaking low, said: "Madam, they shall not all be executed." [13]

This crisis in Indian affairs furnished Lucretia with a theme for a sermon on the power of righteousness. Recalling her experiences in the antislavery crusade, she declared that in the face of the opposition of the majority her faith in the righteousness of the cause had never wavered. This faith, she said, had its roots in the Queries of Quakerism. "If one is but assured of the justice of a cause," she declared, "one need not hesitate to embark on the path of justice, one need not fear to go forward." Quakers, she thought, had passed over the admonition against bearing arms too thoughtlessly; they were "satisfied" with the testimony but not inspired or strengthened to accept its guidance. Her conclusion in this sermon was that man's spiritual nature would be widened and deepened if the goal were kept steadily in sight. Thus would come a "fullness of faith" in the knowledge of the endurance of righteousness.

At the third annual meeting of the Peace Festival, inaugurated by Julia Ward Howe and called by her "Mothers' Day," [14] Lucretia made another encouraging speech on the subject of peace. As she dwelt on the hastening changes in the achievements of the reform movements her optimism again prevailed. In the recent past, she recalled, there were but "a few earnest men [who] endeavored to awaken an interest in this subject — John Woolman, Jonathan Dymond, Elihu Burritt and others . . . Within thirty or forty years there had been more remarkable success than ever before in all reforms."

Several years before the death of James Mott, the "Home for Aged and Infirm Colored Persons" had been established in Philadelphia. From its very beginning this Home had been adopted by Lucretia Mott. Recognition of her interest in the institution was shown by the fact that among the articles deposited in the cornerstone of the building for the Home, side by side with the Bible, the Discipline of the American Episcopal Church, photographs of the eight Bishops of the American Episcopal Church, and a copy of the *Christian Recorder,* were several photographs including one of Lucretia Mott. At the dedicatory exercises Lucretia formed a part of the program. She was a life member of the Board of Directors; but she continued to make gifts to the Home and to visit the institution as long as she was able to get into Philadelphia from Roadside. Gifts of furniture, bakery, apparel for the inmates, vegetables, fruit, and money are listed in the Records of the Home as from Lucretia Mott.[15] This donor of practical, even homely items, was the only woman sent by the American Anti-Slavery Society to the 1840 World's Anti-Slavery Convention in London, whose leadership was sought at Seneca Falls by the pioneers of the Woman's Rights Movement, and who held her listeners spell-bound as she dared to preach rationalism and independent judgment in religious thought and action.

She retained her interest in the development of Swarthmore College. At its inauguration she and her son Thomas planted on the campus two oak saplings that had been raised from acorns placed in the ground at Roadside by James Mott with Lucretia's assistance. Making an address on this occasion, she voiced her deep interest in the College and her hope that it would never degenerate into a mere sectarian school but keep its teachings free from theological bias. She made a plea for training that would enable the students to "be prepared to recognize good wherever found," but she emphasized the warning against "skepticism which sometimes grows out of the study of Science and unaccompanied by religious faith." [16]

On a table in the sitting room at Roadside, Lucretia Mott's favorite books were assembled with her knitting, mending basket, writing materials, garnered newspaper clippings, and carpet balls. Conspicuous among her books and close to Worcester's *Causes and Contentions* and Blanco White's *Autobiography,* was Henry Buckle's *History of Civilization in England.*

Though feeble under the weight of her fourscore and five years, Lucretia Mott was in Seneca Falls in the summer of 1878 to attend the thirtieth anniversary of the inauguration of the Woman's Rights Movement. At this meeting she shared the platform with Frederick Douglass and Belva Lockwood, "the woman who would be President." Described as possessing "her old vigor and activity of mind," she now appealed for the right of women to hold property, to receive wages adjusted to the performance of tasks and to enjoy higher education. Significantly, she included in her demands at this time, the franchise for women as a needed reform. If women were given equality of power, privilege, and responsibility, they would, she said, never abuse their rights but would help to purify and enable every aspect of life.

In the discussion evoked by a Resolution declaring the right of woman to form her own judgments in the principles of religion, to follow the dictates of her own individual conscience, and to use her own reason in the interpretation of the Scriptures, Lucretia Mott emphasized the necessity of "distinguishing between true Christianity and theological creed," of believing that "True righteousness and goodness were the only right for the correction of wrong," and of maintaining faith in the ultimate triumph of right. As the secretary concludes her account of the proceedings:

In her closing remarks, and just previous to her departure for the East, she said she wished to add her expression of gratitude to the Unitarian society that had so kindly given them the use of their edifice. She spoke of the fitness of this courtesy having been extended by just such a demonstration. The Convention then arose in her honor, and in behalf of all assembled, Frederick Douglass said to her "Good bye." [17]

On her eighty-sixth birthday Lucretia Mott received a rather unusual token of esteem, a letter from the "officers and employees" of the North Pennsylvania Railroad voicing the cordial relations that had existed between Mrs. Mott and the Railroad for so many years and wishing for the famous traveler "a happy continuance and peaceful ending of her long and useful life." [18]

Eventually the traveling ceased. She was unable to go into Philadelphia in November 1879 with a committee of one hundred members of the Pennsylvania Peace Society as delegates to honor President Grant. Because of the unwillingness of the Peace Society to take part in Philadelphia's military demonstration in honor of the President, the committee arranging the demonstration for the President had permitted the Society to hold a quiet nonmilitary gathering in Philadelphia's Continental Hotel. During these ceremonies a picture of Lucretia Mott was presented to the President. "I receive this picture," responded the President, "with great pleasure. The life and history of Lucretia Mott are well known to this country as well as abroad." Then, recalling, evidently, Lucretia's appeal for the Modoc Indians, he added, "I have had the pleasure of meeting her and I appreciate her devotion to the cause of peace very highly." [19]

In April 1880 she attended the Philadelphia Yearly Meeting, and a few weeks later she went into Philadelphia to be with the Executive Committee of the Peace Society. This was her last public appearance.

In the fall of 1880, Lucretia Mott grew weaker as she gradually relinquished the tie that bound the frail body to life. Never robust or strong, she seemed to take on at the end of her life the appearance of a small child.[20] Surrounded by her family and from time to time by close friends who journeyed to Roadside, she lay in peaceful quiet. In these last days, she retained her strength of conviction and independence; in the face of suffering she was courageous, but gentle and reposed. In her length of days was written the testimony of one who had endeavored to hold fast to truth, to repudiate dogmatic creeds, to quicken man's sense of justice. Above all, while cherishing the simple creed of righteousness, she had endeavored to show that the inner springs of her faith were nurtured in the groundwork of reason. Her aim had been to advocate faith and righteous action. This principle she believed to be explicit in the original faith and practices of Quakerism. Never relinquishing her convictions that man was endowed with a birthright of righteousness, she communicated her optimism to others. Transitory failure, criticism of her philosophy never weakened her position, and she inspired those whose lives she touched.

Death came on November 11, 1880. Among those making brief remarks at the funeral services held at Roadside were Dr. William Furness, who had spoken at the funeral of James Mott, the younger William Lloyd Garrison, Dr. Henry T. Child, Robert Collyer, Alfred Love, the Reverend C. G. Ames, and Deborah Wharton. The body was laid to rest in Fairhill Cemetery in Germantown, Philadelphia, a tranquil spot in the midst of but detached from a teeming business center. For the greater part of her life Lucretia Mott had lived in the hubbub of Philadelphia engaged in the crosscurrents of the city's life, but keeping inviolate her serenity, her independence, her spirituality. It seems fitting that her remains should repose in an oasis of quietness and peace within the sight and earshot of the rush and tumult of business life. Among the simple markers bearing the names of members of Lucretia Mott's family is one stone, unpretentious too like the others, which reads "Lucretia Mott, 1793–1880."

When the Philadelphia Friends' Meeting recognized the young Lucretia Mott as one that had "a gift in the ministry committed to her," honor was paid not merely to the magnetism of her speech, the power of her "silver voice," but to the unsullied uprightness of her life. Throughout the long years of this life the power of her voice, this strength of her right arm, was dedicated unfalteringly to the attainment of religious freedom, unqualified justice, human brotherhood, temperance, and world peace. While her failure to convince others never aroused personal resentment on her part, attacks on her beliefs but strengthened her faith in decisions made through logical thinking.

Lucretia Mott was a woman who maintained a gracious home, cherished warm friendships, and lent her presence to simple neighborhood gatherings as well as to those of the day's major reformers. Her independence, especially her so-called heresies, brought opposition. Yet leadership that was never sought was accorded her, as contemporaries paid homage to the vigorous mind that rejected prescribed religious dogma and ecclesiastical authority, to the inspired leader of a gospel of righteousness and peace, to the gentle woman of whom one said, "None but thyself can be thy parallel." [21]

No testimony, it seems, discloses more truly the nobility of Lucretia Mott than the words she spoke at a meeting of the Free Religious Association in Boston:

Therefore, I say preach your truth; let it go forth, and you will find without any notable miracle, as of old, that every man will speak in his own tongue in which he was born. And I will say that if these pure principles have their place in us and are brought forth by faithfulness, by obedience, into practice, the difficulties and doubts that we may have to surmount will be easily conquered. There will be a power higher than these. Let it be called the Great Spirit of the Indian, the Quaker "Inward Light" of George Fox, the "Blessed Mary," Mother of Jesus of the Catholics or Burmah, the Hindoo's God — they will all be one, and there will come to be such faith and such liberty as shall redeem the world.

BIBLIOGRAPHY

BIBLIOGRAPHY

The list of titles included in this selective bibliography has been limited to the manuscripts and printed reports actually used as source material. The specific date of each quotation from the manuscript is usually given in the text, while the notes indicate the ownership or custodian of the manuscript at the time of consultation.

MANUSCRIPTS

LETTERS

Mott Manuscripts (Friends Historical Library, Swarthmore College); William Lloyd Garrison Family Papers (Sophia Smith Collection, Smith College); Anti-Slavery Letters to Garrison and Others (Boston Public Library); May Collection (Cornell University Library); Papers of Edward M. Davis (Houghton Library, Harvard University); Weston Family Papers (Boston Public Library); Foster Collection (Worcester Historical Society); Letters of Elizabeth Cady Stanton to Lucretia Mott (Library of Congress). Other letters in Boston Public Library, Library of Congress, Haverford College Library, Huntington Library, Historical Society of Pennsylvania, Houghton Library, and Atwater Kent Museum.

DIARIES

Lucretia Mott's Diary (Friends Historical Library, Swarthmore College); Diary of Alfred Love (Swarthmore College Peace Collection); Diary of Cyrus M. Burleigh (Pennsylvania Historical Society); Diary of Edmund Quincy (Massachusetts Historical Society); Microfilm of Extracts from the Diary of Lord Morpeth (Library of Congress); Notes written in longhand by Susan B. Anthony in her Collection of Scraps (Library of Congress).

LEGAL DOCUMENTS

Transcript of Record of Births, Deaths, Receptions, Disownments, Removals Alphabetically Arranged in the Society of Friends on the Island of Nantucket (Haverford College); Real Estate Records, Nantucket (Office of Records, Nantucket); Real Estate Records, Suffolk Registry of Deeds (City Hall, Boston); Taking Books, The Census Records of Boston from 1800–1809 (City Hall, Boston); Copy of Wedding Certificate of James Mott and Lucretia Coffin (Arch Street Center, Philadelphia).

REPORTS OF ORGANIZATIONS

The Society of Friends:

Quarterly Meeting, Philadelphia, 1772–1826 (Arch Street Center); Monthly Meeting, Northern District, Nantucket 1797–1799 (Nantucket Historical Association); Monthly Meeting of Women Friends, Philadelphia, Western District, 1805–1831 (Arch Street Center); Monthly Meeting of

Women Friends of Philadelphia, Southern District, 1808–1816 (Arch Street Center) ; Quarterly Meeting, Philadelphia, 1826–1862 (Friends Historical Library Swarthmore College) ; Yearly Meeting of Women Friends, Philadelphia, 1827–1880 (Friends Historical Library, Swarthmore College) ; Yearly Meeting, Philadelphia, 1828–1861 (Friends Historical Library, Swarthmore College) ; Genesee Yearly Meeting of Women Friends, 1834–1880 (Fifteenth Street Meeting House) ; New York Meeting for Sufferance, 1868 (Fifteenth Street Meeting House) ; Memorial to Congress, Philadelphia Yearly Meeting (National Archives) ; Proceedings of the Pennsylvania Yearly Meeting of Progressive Friends for 1853 (Friends Historical Library, Swarthmore College) ; Monthly Meetings, Northern District, Nantucket, 1797–1799 (Nantucket Historical Association) .

Antislavery:

Transcript of Declaration of Sentiments, American Anti-Slavery Society, December 6, 1833 (New York State Historical Society) ; Minutes, American Anti-Slavery Society, 1836–1839 (Boston Public Library) ; Excerpt from Minutes of May 16, 1839; Minutes, Board of Managers, Philadelphia Female Anti-Slavery Society, 1833–1848 (Historical Society of Pennsylvania) ; Minutes, Philadelphia Female Anti-Slavery Society, 1833–1869, March 24, 1870 (Historical Society of Pennsylvania) ; Minute Book, Vigilante Committee of Philadelphia, 1839–1844 (Historical Society of Pennsylvania) ; Minutes, Executive Committee, Pennsylvania Anti-Slavery Association, 1856–1870 (Historical Society of Pennsylvania) ; Minute Book, Western Anti-Slavery Society, A copy (Library of Congress) .

Miscellaneous:

Report of Meeting of the Boarding School Committee held at Nine Partners, 8th or 9th mo. 1808 (Oakwood School, New York) ; Record Book (Stephen Smith Home for the Aged, Philadelphia) ; Copy of Extract from School Records (Westtown School, Pennsylvania) ; Swarthmore College Peace Collection: Letters, Diaries, Records, and other papers.

PRINTED SOURCES

REPORTS

Legal Proceedings:

Decow vs. Shotwell. *A Full Report of the case of Stacy Decow and Joseph Hendrickson vs. Thomas L. Shotwell* . . . Philadelphia, 1834.

Antislavery:

Proceedings of the Anti-Slavery Convention of 1833; Annual Reports of the American Anti-Slavery Society, 1834, 1836, 1853, 1855, 1857–59, 1860; Boston Female Anti-Slavery Society, *Report or Right and Wrong in Boston,* 1835, 1836, 1839; Anti-Slavery Convention of American Women, *Report for 1837, 1838, Report of a Delegate to Convention in 1837;* Philadelphia Female Anti-Slavery Society, *Printed Reports for 1838–1841, 1843–1847, 1849–1856, 1859–1870; Sixth Annual Report of the Executive Committee of the American Anti-Slavery Society* . . . Held in the City of New York on the 7th of May 1839; British and Foreign Anti-Slavery Association, *Anti-Slavery Reporter,* 1840 (London, 1840) .

BIBLIOGRAPHY 213

Woman's Rights:

Proceedings of Conventions: Seneca Falls, 1848; Rochester, 1848; Salem, Ohio, 1850; Worcester, 1850; Akron, Ohio, 1851; Worcester, 1851; Westchester, Pa., 1852; Syracuse, 1852; New York, 1853; Cleveland, 1853; Albany, Philadelphia, 1854; Saratoga Springs, 1855; New York City, 1859; Boston, 1859; New York, 1859; New York City, 1860; Worcester, 1861; New York, 1866. Equal Rights Convention, *Reports,* New York, 1867, 1870. Catt and Shuler *Report of Suffrage Amendments.*

Proceedings of Other Organizations:

Anti-Sabbath Convention, 1847; Free Religious Association, 1868–1881; Progressive Friends, 1852–1880; Nantucket Historical Association, 1899.

Books, newspapers, and other printed source material are indicated in the Notes.

NOTES

NOTES

Chapter One — ISLAND HERITAGE

1. Alfred H. Love of Philadelphia was one of Lucretia Mott's friends as well as a co-worker in the Pennsylvania Peace Society. For years he kept a diary in which — between 1859 and 1880 — are nearly 200 detailed references to Mrs. Mott: comment on Lucretia's sermons and other speeches, descriptions of tensions in the woman's rights movement, references to the antislavery struggle, and brief narratives of other occurrences relating to Lucretia and her life in Philadelphia. This voluminous diary, which is a part of the Swarthmore College Peace Collection, was pointed out to me by Miss Ellen Starr Brinton, Curator of the Collection, as a "possible source of comment on Lucretia Mott."

2. Anna Davis Hallowell, *James and Lucretia Mott . . .* (Boston, 1884), p. 31. Other biographies of Lucretia Mott include: Lloyd C. M. Hare, *The Greatest American Woman: Lucretia Mott* (New York, 1937); Constance Burnett, *Lucretia Mott* (Indianapolis, 1951); Homer T. Rosenberger, "Montgomery County's Greatest Lady: Lucretia Mott," *The Bulletin of the Historical Society of Montgomery County*, Vol. VI, No. 2 (April 1948), pp. 91–171, a factual monograph based on serious study.

3. "Letter of Rebecca Jones to Henry Drinker Seventh Mo. 10th, 1799," *Friends Review*, Vol. II, No. 29, Fourth No. 7, 1849.

4. Alexander Starbuck, *History of Nantucket* (Boston, 1924), pp. 1–40.

5. William M. Gardner, *Three Bricks and Three Brothers* (Cambridge, Mass., 1945), pp. 13–27.

6. Nantucket Quaker Records, 54C, Haverford College. Furnished by Miss Anna Hewitt of Haverford College.

Children of Thomas and Anna Coffin

	Births	*Deaths*
Sarah	27–10–1790	
Lucretia	3– 1–1793	
Elizabeth	22–12–1794	
Mary	20–11–1796	29–9–1797
Thomas Mayhew	19– 6–1798	
Mary	20– 3–1800	
Lydia	14– 3–1804	

7. Miss Lucy Davis of Cambridge, Massachusetts.

8. William Lloyd Garrison Family Papers, Sophia Smith Collection, Smith College.

9. Starbuck, *Nantucket*, p. 410.

10. Nantucket County Records, Vol. 15, p. 149. According to these same records, Thomas Coffin in 1799 had the means to "buy in" from his brother Paul Coffin. Paul's "Real Estate and Sheep" inherited from the father, Benjamin Coffin; and the next year Thomas made a similar purchase from his

brother Nathan Coffin. Paul's willingness to dispose of his inherited posses-
sions may have been due to his migrating from Nantucket with the group of
Quakers settling, toward the end of the eighteenth century, in Guilford, North
Carolina.

11. *Ibid.,* p. 204.

12. *The Journal of John Woolman* with an Introduction by John G. Whittier (Philadelphia, 1898) , p. 172.

13. *Proceedings, Woman's Rights Convention,* Oct. 5, 6, 7, 1853 (Cleveland, 1854) , pp. 169, 170.

14. Nantucket County Records, Nov. 4, 1800, Recorded Nov. 6, 1800, Vol.
12, p. 263.

15. Garrison Family Papers.

16. Theodore Parker, *Additional Speeches and Occasional Sermons* (Boston, 1859) , p. 397.

17. Monthly Meeting, Northern District, Nantucket 1797–1799, Nantucket
Historical Association.

18. Copy of letter among Mott MSS, Friends Historical Library, Swarthmore College.

19. Garrison Family Papers.

20. Deeds to Property in Nantucket.

21. Garrison Family Papers.

22. New York Historical Society.

23. Garrison Family Papers.

Chapter Two — BOSTON INTERLUDE

1. Advertisements of stock held by "Thomas Coffin jun." located at "5 Central Wharf" appeared in the *Columbian Centinel* for April 11, 18, 25, 1804;
Jan. 19, 26, 1805; Feb. 2, 1805; Jan. 8, 15, 22, 1806; Feb. 19, 1806; March 26,
1806; Aug. 2, 1806. Advertisements of stock of "Sumner & Coffin" located in
"No. 1 Long Wharf" appeared in the *Centinel,* March 14, 21, and April 14,
21, 1804. The advertisements specified not merely articles of stock "in store,"
but included at times "complete cargo" of specified schooners, "on landing,"
or "afloat," and the Exchange on London was advertised in the *Centinel* on
April 4, 16, 21, 1804.

2. Real Estate Records of Boston, Boston City Hall. By deed dated "December 5, 1806," "William Sutton Skinner of Boston . . . in consideration
of Five thousand six hundred dollars, paid by Thomas Coffin, Junior of said
Boston, Merchant [did] give, grant, sell and convey unto the said Thomas
Coffin junr., . . . a certain piece of land with a new brick dwelling house
thereon standing . . ." In the course of the years this brick dwelling has given
place to structures erected to conform to the mercantile needs of the neighborhood; a similar fate has befallen Lucretia Mott's Philadelphia homes. But
the timbered house built by Thomas Coffin at "Scool Street' in Nantucket
in 1797 remains standing.

3. Anna Davis Hallowell, *James and Lucretia Mott* (Boston, 1884) , p. 35.

4. School Committee-System of Public Education in Boston, 1807.

5. *Boston Directory,* 1806, p. 148.

Chapter Three — NINE PARTNERS BOARDING SCHOOL

1. During the nineteenth century differences of belief on points of doctrine engendered disputes among Quakers as to the ownership of the school's property, thus causing changes in the name and location of the institution. But after a period of time Nine Partners reëstablished itself in Dutchess County as Oakwood School. In the final settlement of the religious controversy the school was brought near its original site within view of the low hills of the Catskill Mountains and the Hudson River. Set in ample grounds, Oakwood School presents an architectural structure that is simple and friendly, dignified and poised. It is a gracious country school, progressive in the educational procedures it follows, in the broad principles of its curriculum, and in the sensible program of work and play for its students. But, although the modern school departs somewhat from the austerity of earlier days, it adheres to the solid tenets of education characterizing the beginnings of the institution. It is "incorporated by the University of the State of New York," but it maintains still the "guarded education" for youth.

2. Reports of Nine Partners Boarding School, Oakwood School.

3. *Friends Miscellany*, Vol. IX, No. 1, Eighth Mo., 1836, pp. 42, 43; Vol. XI, No. 1 (January 1838), pp. 1–28.

4. Esther Gonegal, "Nine Partners Boarding School," *Bulletin of Friends Historical Association*, Vol. X, No. 1, pp. 10–14.

5. Reports of Nine Partners.

6. Priscilla Wakefield, *Mental Improvement or The Beauties and Wonders of Instructive Conversations* (New Bedford, 1799), pp. 32–33, 75–80.

7. *Report, Pennsylvania Anti-Slavery Association for 1861*.

8. Reports of Nine Partners.

9. *Ibid*.

10. *Proceedings, Woman's Rights Convention in Cleveland in 1853* (New York, 1854).

11. Anna Davis Hallowell, *James and Lucretia Mott* (Boston, 1884), pp. 38, 40.

12. Martha, the youngest child of Thomas and Anna Coffin, was born in Boston in 1806.

Chapter Four — WIDENING PATHS

1. Monthly Meeting of Women Friends of Philadelphia, for the Southern District, 1805–1814. Arch Street Center, Philadelphia.

2. Monthly Meeting of Friends of Philadelphia for the Southern District, 1808–1816. Arch Street Center.

3. "The Kimberton Boarding School. The French Creek Boarding School for Girls was instituted by Emmor Kimber in 1817 . . . This school . . . was conducted on principles somewhat different from those of most seminaries, there being no penal laws or rules in force . . . The school stood high, was prosperous, and had many scholars from other states and the West Indies." G. Smith Futhey and Gilbert Coke, *History of Chester County, Pennsylvania with Genealogical and Biographical Sketches* (Philadelphia, 1881), p. 305.

4. *The Letters of Ralph Waldo Emerson*, edited by Ralph L. Rusk (6 vols., New York, 1937), III, 126.

5. *The Philadelphia Directory*, 1811 by James Robinson, pp. 111, 210.

6. William Lloyd Garrison Family Papers, Sophia Smith Collection, Smith College.

7. *Philadelphia Directory*, 1811, p. 73.

8. Monthly Meeting of Women Friends of Philadelphia for the Southern District, 1808–1816. Arch Street Center.

9. A copy of the marriage certificate of James Mott and Lucretia Coffin is preserved at Arch Street Center, Philadelphia.

10. Anna Davis Hallowell, *James and Lucretia Mott* (Boston, 1884), pp. 44, 45.

11. *Philadelphia Directory*, 1813.

12. Garrison Family Papers. In a letter to her sister Martha, dated "2 mo. 4th 70," Lucretia wrote "Our Mother had no faith in French Creek Works & in our father's endors'g thousands for John James, & used to beg him to quit before he was involved so deeply — but he went on till they were sadly in debt — the $9000 to be paid in 60 days — the works sold *well*, tis true, but our father's advances & acco'ts in conductg. the sales etc. were disputed by the [?] because of their inability to pay & before the referees decided our dear sufferer was removed from it all — leav'g his fam'y poor, includ'g Jas. Mott whom he had taken in as a partner in the kindness of his heart — In the wind'g up there being a deficiency & Jas. part ⅓ being $3000 — he gave his note & one of our noble mother's first acts as a widow was to destroy that note."

13. *Voice of Peace*, Vol. II (N.S.), No. 4 (July 1875), pp. 51, 52.

14. Monthly Meeting of Women Friends of Philadelphia for the Southern District, 1816–1827, Friends Historical Library, Swarthmore College.

15. Hallowell, *Mott*, pp. 53, 54.

16. *Ibid.*, p. 94.

17. Minutes of the Female Society for the Relief and Employment of the Poor [1811] [1813]. Inasmuch as this organization was eventually affiliated with the Orthodox group of Friends, the shadows of the coming Separation may have been forecast as early as 1820; and it is even possible that the ordinance of the Society restricting its membership to Quakers might have been so repugnant to Lucretia's broad principles of fellowship that she did not join the organization.

18. Garrison Family Papers.

19. Hallowell, *Mott*, p. 78.

20. Garrison Family Papers.

21. *Ibid.*

22. *Proceedings, Woman's Rights Convention* (Syracuse, 1852), pp. 91, 92.

23. Anti-Slavery Letters to Garrison and Others, Boston Public Library.

Chapter Five — REVOLT AND FAITH

1. A copy of this letter, pointed out by Miss Dorothy Harris, Reference Librarian, is in Friends Historical Library, Swarthmore College.

2. Anna Davis Hallowell, *James and Lucretia Mott* (Boston, 1884), p. 64.

3. *Hopewell Friends History 1734–1934* (Hopewell Friends, assisted by John W. Wayland, n.d.), pp. 124–125, 150, 323, 433, 458, 549.

4. Hallowell, *Mott*, p. 69.

5. Monthly Meeting of Women Friends, Philadelphia, Western District 1814–1831, 8th mo. 21st, 1822, Friends Historical Library, Swarthmore College.

6. Monthly Meeting of Women Friends of Philadelphia held 6 mo. 27th 1822. The subsequent dates are "7th mo. 25, 1822"; "29th of 8th mo. 1822"; "26th of 9 mo. 1822"; "10th mo. 24, 1822"; 11 mo. 28th, 1822"; "12 mo. 26, 1822" and "1st mo. 30th 1823," Friends Historical Library, Swarthmore College.

7. Hallowell, *Mott*, p. 69.

8. Anti-Slavery Letters to Garrison and Others, Boston Public Library.

9. *The Quaker, being a Series of Sermons by Members of the Society of Friends* (Philadelphia, 1827). See also: *An Epistle to the Members of the Religious Society of Friends belonging to the Yearly Meeting of Pennsylvania, New Jersey, Delaware and the Eastern Parts of Maryland and Virginia, Philadelphia . . . 1827*, pp. 3–20; *An Epistle to Friends of the Quarterly and Monthly Meetings within the compass of the Yearly Meeting held in Philadelphia . . . 6th Mo., 1827*, pp. 5–12; *Declaration of 1828* (signed by Samuel Bettle, Clerk), pp. 13, 14; Elbert Russell, *The History of Quakerism* (New York, 1942).

10. MS at Atwater Kent Museum. Copy given by Mrs. H. F. Gummere.

11. Friends Historical Library, Swarthmore College.

12. *An Authentic Report of the Testimony In a Cause at Issue in the Court of Chancery of the State of New Jersey Between Thomas L. Shotwell, Complainant and Joseph Hendrickson and Stacy Decow Defendants. Taken pursuant to the Rules of the Court by Jeremiah J. Foster, Master and Examiner in Chancery* (2 vols., Philadelphia, 1831).

13. Mrs. Churchill's Scrapbook. Item from the *New York Times*, Nov. 14, 1880. Friends Historical Library, Swarthmore College.

14. Minutes, Philadelphia Yearly Meeting of Women Friends, 1830–1840, Friends Historical Library, Swarthmore College.

15. John Comly, *Journal of the Life and Religious Labors of John Comly, Late of Byberry* (Philadelphia, 1873), p. 635.

16. Hallowell, *Mott*, p. 107.

17. Minutes, Philadelphia Yearly Meeting of Women Friends, 1830–1940, Friends Historical Library, Swarthmore College.

18. May Collection, Library of Cornell University.

19. May Collection.

20. Harriet Martineau, *Retrospect of Western Travel* (London, 1838), pp. 66, 67.

21. *Liberator*, Vol. VI, No. 143, Oct. 15, 1838.

22. *Liberator*, Vol. XI, No. 3, Jan. 15, 1841.

23. May Collection.

24. Anti-Slavery Letters.

25. Hallowell, *Mott*, pp. 215, 216.

26. William Lloyd Garrison Family Papers, Sophia Smith Collection, Smith College.

Chapter Six — SOCIAL REFORM

1. See National Archives, Washington, D.C.

2. Thomas E. Drake, *Elihu Coleman, Quaker Anti-Slavery Pioneer of Nantucket* (Wallingford, Pa., 1944), pp. 124–126.

3. Thomas E. Drake, *Quakers and Slavery in America* (New Haven, 1950), p. 61.

4. Ruth Ketring Nuermberger, *The Free Produce Movement, A Quaker Protest Against Slavery* (Durham, N.C., 1942) , p. 14.

5. May Collection, Library of Cornell University.

6. William Lloyd Garrison, *Thoughts on African Colonization* (Boston, 1830) , I, 57.

7. Many thought that the punishment inflicted on the young Garrison was too severe; among his sympathizers was Arthur Tappan, who came to Garrison's aid by paying his fine. But Garrison himself bestowed a gratuitous offering to Baltimore by inscribing on the prison walls two impassioned sonnets, "To Sleep" and "The Guiltless Prisoner," composed during his imprisonment. Though no great poet perhaps, he wrote verse with ease and had mastered the forms of the Elizabethan sonnet.

8. *Liberator,* Vol. XIX, No. 45, Nov. 9, 1849, p. 178.

9. *Proceedings American Anti-Slavery Society . . . 1863* (New York, 1864) pp. 41–43.

10. William Lloyd Garrison Family Papers, Sophia Smith Collection.

11. Minutes, Philadelphia Female Anti-Slavery Society 1833–1869. The recorded manuscript notes are appropriately preserved in Philadelphia among the holdings of the Historical Society of Pennsylvania. Not merely an account of the labors of the Philadelphia Female Anti-Slavery Society, these meticulously kept records are an eloquent tribute to the imagination and constructive thinking of the members. Mr. R. N. Williams, II, Curator of the Historical Society, and his assistants were extremely helpful in pointing out this material and in furnishing photostats.

12. Letters of Lydia Maria Child, Houghton Library, Harvard University.

13. Minutes, Philadelphia Female Anti-Slavery Society, 1833–1869.

14. *Proceedings American Anti-Slavery Society 1863,* pp. 41–43.

15. May Collection.

16. Benjamin P. Thomas, *Theodore Weld, Crusader for Freedom* (Rutgers, N.Y., 1950) , pp. 70–87.

17. May Collection.

18. May Collection.

19. *Proceedings, Anti-Slavery Convention of American Women, 1837.*

20. *Proceedings, Anti-Slavery Convention of American Women Held in Philadelphia May 15th, 16th, 17th and 18th, 1838* (Philadelphia, 1838) . Report of Mary S. Parker; Report of Sarah G. Buffum.

21. Houghton Library, Harvard University.

22. *National Gazette,* Philadelphia, May 18, 1838.

23. *Ibid.*

24. *The Works of William E. Channing, D.D.* "Remarks on the Slavery Question in a Letter to Jonathan Phillips, Esq., Boston, 1839" (Boston, 1903) .

25. *Proceedings, Anti-Slavery Convention of American Women, 1839.*

26. *The Non-Resistant,* Vol. I, No. 19, Oct. 5, 1839; Vol. I, No. 21, Nov. 2, 1839; Vol. I, No. 22, Nov. 16, 1839. Through Mr. Barney Chesnick, Reference Librarian of the Library Company of Philadelphia, the copies of the *Non-Resistant* owned by the Library Company were placed for my study on an Inter-Library Loan with the Library of Congress.

27. Massachusetts Historical Society.

28. Anti-Slavery Letters to Garrison and Others, Boston Public Library.

29. Library of Syracuse University.

Chapter Seven — A STEP AHEAD

1. Anti-Slavery Letters to Garrison and Others, Boston Public Library.
2. *Seventh Annual Report, Board of Managers . . . Massachusetts Anti-Slavery Society,* 1839.
3. Minutes, American Anti-Slavery Society, May 7, 1839. Duly recorded in the clear, firm handwriting of Wendell Phillips, this record is preserved in the Boston Public Library.
4. *Liberator,* Vol. XI, No. 3, Whole No. 574, Jan. 15, 1841.
5. "Letter from Wendell Phillips," *Liberator,* Vol. X, Whole No. 499, July 24, 1840.
6. Manuscripts Division, Library of Congress.
7. *Ibid.*
8. *Emancipator,* Vol. V, No. 1, May 1, 1840, p. 3. *Herald of Freedom,* May 30, 1840.
9. Mott MSS, Friends Historical Library, Swarthmore College.
10. *Liberator,* Vol. X, No. 23, June 1840, reported in the *Emancipator.*
11. *Liberator,* Vol. X, No. 23, June 1840, reported in the *Christian Witness.*
12. Frances H. Bradburn, editor, *A Memorial of George Bradburn by His Wife* (Boston, 1883), p. 171.
13. *Herald of Freedom,* May 30, 1840.
14. Anti-Slavery Letters.

Chapter Eight — "THE PROPER SPHERE OF WOMEN"

1. The basic material for this Chapter is the original manuscript of Lucretia Mott's Diary, in Friends Historical Library, Swarthmore College. This manuscrip has been edited and transcribed with notes, and published by Frederick B. Tolles, under the title, *Slavery and 'The Woman Question,' Lucretia Mott's Diary of her Visit to Great Britain to Attend the World's Anti-Slavery Convention of 1840* (Haverford, and London, 1952). My notes taken from the original Diary have been carefully collated with Dr. Tolles' transcription.
2. The first entry in the Diary is undated; it gives however, the date of the Motts' sailing from New York as "5 Mo. 7th, 1840." This entry refers to the storms, the mild seasickness, and the restrained drinking of the passengers. Her own illness on this outgoing passage is commented on in the last entry of the Diary, "4th day 26th" "Not so sick as in the voyage out."
3. Passage from a letter from William Lloyd Garrison to Edmund Quincy, Sophia Smith Collection, Smith College.
4. Frances H. Bradburn, editor, *A Memorial of George Bradburn by His Wife* (Boston, 1883), pp. 43, 44.
5. The events of Lucretia's first view of England are described in the daily entries "29," through "1st day 7."
6. Diary, "5th day 11th," Friends Historical Library, Swarthmore College.
7. Diary, "6th day 6 Mo. 12th."
8. The meeting of Lucretia Mott and Elizabeth Cady Stanton is described in Chapter III, Alma Lutz, *Created Equal, A Biography of Elizabeth Cady Stanton 1815–1902* (New York, 1940), pp. 25, 26.
9. *British and Foreign Anti-Slavery Reporter,* Vol. I, 1840, June 17, 1840, pp. 136–140.

10. Diary, "7th day 20th."
11. Anti-Slavery Letters to Garrison and Others, Boston Public Library.
12. Anti-Slavery Letters. " 'Don't shilly-shally Wendell,' she said, when her husband went into the Convention to contend for the right of the women to take their seats." Francis Jackson Garrison, *Ann Phillips, Wife of Wendell Phillips* (Boston, 1886), pp. 7, 8.
13. Diary, "6th day 6 Mo. 12th."
14. Diary, "7th day 13th."
15. Diary, "4th day 24th."
16. Referred to by James Mott, *Three Months in Great Britain* (Philadelphia, 1841), pp. 42, 43.
17. *Mary Howitt An Autobiography,* edited by Margaret Howitt (2 vols., London, 1889), I, 291–292.
18. *Liberator,* Whole No. 499, July 24, 1840, p. 119.
19. Alexander D. Penrose, editor, *Robert Haydon, The Autobiography and Memoirs, 1786–1846* (London, 1927), p. 531.
20. Anti-Slavery Letters.
21. Diary, "1st day 16th."
22. Carlyle, "Essay on Burns."
23. Diary, "6th day 3rd."
24. Diary, "2nd day 27th."
25. The letter in the Manuscripts Division of the Library of Congress, dated "Sept. 6, 1869," bears the superscription, apparently in Miss Anthony's handwriting, "From Elizabeth Cady Stanton — to the Eighth W. R. Con. held in Mozart Hall, New York — May 12 and 14, 1868 — and read by Susan B. Anthony."
26. Anti-Slavery Letters.

Chapter Nine — ONE–THIRTY–SIX NORTH NINTH STREET

1. Diary, "5th day 6th," Friends Historical Library, Swarthmore College.
2. Anti-Slavery Letters to Garrison and Others, Boston Public Library.
3. William Lloyd Garrison Family Papers, Sophia Smith College, Smith College.
4. *Ibid.*
5. Anti-Slavery Letters.
6. May Collection, Library of Cornell University.
7. Diary, "4th day 7 mo. 1st."
8. Garrison Family Papers.
9. *Dublin Weekly Herald,* as quoted by Anna Davis Hallowell, *James and Lucretia Mott* (Boston, 1884), p. 190.
10. Garrison Family Papers.
11. Sojourner Truth, *Narrative of Sojourner Truth* (Battle Creek, Mich., 1878), p. 164.
12. *Proceedings of Philadelphia Female Anti-Slavery Society,* "5 mo. 12th, 1863."
13. Truth, *Narrative,* p. 314.
14. Philip Jordan, *Singin' Yankee* (Minneapolis, 1946), pp. 94, 95.
15. Anti-Slavery Letters.
16. Mrs. Alan Valentine.

17. Garrison Family Papers.
18. A. D. Hallowell, *James and Lucretia Mott,* p. 328.
19. May Collection.
20. Garrison Family Papers.
21. *Ibid.*
22. Anti-Slavery Letters.
23. *Memoirs of John Quincy Adams,* ed. by Charles Francis Adams (Philadelphia, 1876) , IX, 302, 303.
24. *The Letters of Ralph Waldo Emerson,* ed. by Ralph L. Rusk (New York, 1939) , III, 131, 137–139.
25. *A Life for Liberty, Anti-Slavery and Other Letters of Sallie Holley,* ed. with Introductory Chapters by John White Charwick (New York and London, 1899) .
26. MS in Essex Institute.
27. Abby Kelly Foster Papers in Worcester Historical Society.
28. Anti-Slavery Letters.
29. *Ibid.*
30. *Amberley Papers,* ed. by Bertrand and Patricia Russell (London, 1937) , II, 84.
31. Anti-Slavery Letters.
32. *Friends Weekly Intelligencer,* Vol. VI, No. 37, Dec. 6, 1840, p. 295.
33. *Anti-Slavery Standard,* Vol. IX, No. 15, May 17, 1849.

Chapter Ten — "IN THE WAY CALLED HERESY"

1. These are included in the Anti-Slavery Letters to Garrison and Others, Boston Public Library.
2. Isaac T. Hopper, *Narrative of the Proceedings of the Monthly Meeting of New York . . . in the Case of Isaac T. Hopper* (New York, 1842) .
3. Anti-Slavery Letters.
4. Manuscripts Division, Library of Congress.
5. Mott MSS, Friends Historical Library, Swarthmore College.
6. *National Anti-Slavery Standard,* Vol. II, No. 18, Oct. 7, 1841, p. 70.
7. *Liberator,* Vol. XVII, No. 23, June 4, 1847, p. 91.
8. *National Anti-Slavery Standard,* Vol. III, No. 39, March 2, 1843, p. 156.
9. *The Letters of Ralph Waldo Emerson,* ed. by Ralph L. Rusk (New York, 1939) , III, 131.
10. Bradford Torry, ed., *The Writings of Henry David Thoreau, Journal* (Boston, 1906) , VI, 97. But writing from New York to her sister, "5 mo. 27th 72," Lucretia protested, "Did you see the Herald's accot. of 1st day preachg.? It was not true that my 'Bonnet was handed to sister' — a thing I never do — nor was 'a hkf. unfolded & laid over the railing' as is the way some do."
11. *Christian Register XXV,* No. 44, Oct. 31, 1846, pp. 174, 175.
12. William Lloyd Garrison Family Papers, Sophia Smith Collection, Smith College.
13. *National Anti-Slavery Standard,* Vol. VII, No. 23, Nov. 5, 1846, p. 91.
14. Anna Davis Hallowell, *James and Lucretia Mott* (Boston, 1884) , p. 284.
15. Mott MSS, Swarthmore College.

16. [Lucretia Mott] *Sermon* (Philadelphia, n.d.) , pp. 6–8. *Anti-Slavery Bugle,* Vol. V, No. 33, April 6, 1849.

17. *Proceedings, Anti-Sabbath Convention . . .* March 23, 24, 1848, Boston. *Liberator,* Vol. XVI, March 31, 1848, p. 50.

18. John W. Chadwick, "Lucretia Mott and Lydia Maria Child. A Sermon . . . Preached to the Second Unitarian Society, Brooklyn, N.Y., Sunday forenoon, Nov. 20, 1880," *The Woman's Journal,* Vol. XI, No. 51, Boston, December 18, 1880.

19. Minutes Yearly (Y.M.) Women Friends 1850. Fifth 13–17, p. 295.

20. "Discourse by Lucretia Mott at Friends' Meeting, 15th Street, New York, First day morning, 11th mo., 11th, 1866. Reported by Andrew Graham," *The Friend,* Vol. I, New York, December 1866, No. 12.

Chapter Eleven — THE LAUNCHING OF WOMAN'S RIGHTS

1. William Lloyd Garrison Family Papers, Sophia Smith Collection, Smith College.

2. Robert Samuel Fletcher, *A History of Oberlin College From Its Foundation through the Civil War* (Oberlin, Ohio, 1943) , pp. 375–376.

3. Alice Stone Blackwell, *Lucy Stone, Pioneer of Women's Rights* (Boston, 1930) , p. 61.

4. Manuscripts Division, Library of Congress.

5. Thomas Carlyle, *Letters and Memorials [of Jane Welsh Carlyle],* edited by James Anthony Froude (New York, 1891) , p. 70.

6. Anti-Slavery Letters to Garrison and Others, Boston Public Library.

7. Mary F. Thomas, "Incidents in the Life of Lucretia Mott," *The Woman's Journal,* Feb. 19, 1881, p. 11.

8. *National Anti-Slavery Standard,* Vol. VIII, No. 51, May 18, 1848.

9. Manuscripts Division, Library of Congress.

10. See Paulina W. Davis, *A History of the National Woman's Rights Movement for Twenty Years* (Journeymen Printers Cooperative Association, 1871) . Elizabeth Cady Stanton, Susan B. Anthony, Matilda Joslyn Gage, editors, *A History of Woman Suffrage, Rochester, N.Y.* (London, Paris, 1887) , V. 1.

11. Davis, *Woman's Rights.*

12. Manuscripts Division, Library of Congress.

13. *Proceedings, American Anti-Slavery Society at its Second Decade . . . Dec. 3rd, 4th and 5th, 1853* (New York, 1854) .

14. *Report of the Woman's Rights Convention Held at Seneca Falls, July 19 and 20, 1848* (Rochester, 1848) .

15. *Proceedings of the Woman's Rights Convention Held at the Unitarian Church, Rochester, N.Y., August 2, 1848* (Rochester, 1848) .

16. Manuscripts Division, Library of Congress.

17. *Proceedings of the Woman's Rights Convention, Rochester.*

18. *Report of the Woman's Rights Convention, Seneca Falls.*

Chapter Twelve — THE PATH FROM SENECA FALLS

1. New York *Herald, Morning Edition,* Thursday, Aug. 3, 1848.

2. *National Anti-Slavery Standard,* Dec. 28, 1848.

3. *The Weekly Herald* (New York), Dec. 28, 1848.
4. Manuscripts Division, Library of Congress.
5. *Proceedings, Woman's Rights Movement Held at Syracuse, September 8th, 9th, and 10th, 1852* (Syracuse, 1852).
6. *Liberator*, Vol. XXII, 42, Oct. 15, 1852.
7. *The Delaware County Republican.*
8. Elizabeth Cady Stanton Papers, Library of Vassar College.
9. Joseph B. Thompson, *Broadway Tabernacle Church Its History and Work* (New York, 1871).
10. *The Whole World Temperance Convention Held at Metropolitan Hall in the City of New York on Thursday and Friday, Sept. 1 and 2nd, 1853 . . . New York, 1853.*
11. New York *Herald*, Sept. 8, 1853.
12. *Proceedings, Woman's Rights Convention, New York, 1853.*
13. *Proceedings, Woman's Rights Convention Held in Cleveland, 1853.*
14. Manuscripts Division, Library of Congress.
15. *Ibid.* This "handsome Porcelain store" exists as Wright, Tyndale and Van Worden, on Chestnut Street, Philadelphia.
16. William Lloyd Garrison Family Papers, Sophia Smith Collection, Smith College.
17. Anti-Slavery Letters to Garrison and Others, Boston Public Library.
18. Manuscripts Division, Library of Congress.
19. Mary Peabody Mann, *Life of Horace Mann by His Wife* (Boston, 1865), I, 392.
20. The lecture, never printed, was reviewed by Evert A. Duyckink in *The Literary World*, March 9, 1850. Appreciation for a copy of this Review is due to Mr. Thomas D. deValcourt of Cambridge, Mass.
21. Lucretia Mott, *Discourse on Woman* (Philadelphia, 1850).
22. Sarah Grimké, *Letters on the Equality of the Sexes and the Condition of Woman Addressed to Mary S. Parker, President of the Boston Female Anti-Slavery Society* (Boston, 1838).
23. Catharine E. Beecher, *Woman Suffrage and Women's Profession* (Hartford, 1871).
24. Mason Wade, "Woman in the Nineteenth Century," *The Writings of Margaret Fuller* (New York, 1911).
25. *Proceedings of the Woman's Rights Convention held at Worcester, October 23d & 24th, 1850* (Boston, 1851).
26. *Westminster Review*, Vol. LV, No. II, 1851, pp. 289–316.
27. John Stuart Mill, *The Subjection of Women* (New York, 1911).
28. Manuscripts Division, Library of Congress.

Chapter Thirteen — ANTISLAVERY

1. Historical Society of Pennsylvania.
2. Weston Family Papers, Boston Public Library.
3. Philadelphia Female Anti-Slavery Society, "Stated Meeting . . . October 9, 1845." Pennsylvania Historical Society.
4. Anti-Slavery Letters to Garrison and Others, Boston Public Library.
5. *Memoirs of John Quincy Adams Comprising Portions of His Diary from 1795 to 1848,* edited by Charles Francis Adams (Philadelphia, 1876).

6. Anti-Slavery Letters to Garrison.

7. *National Anti-Slavery Standard,* Vol. XIII, No. 26, Nov. 18, 1852.

8. *National Anti-Slavery Standard,* Vol. XIV, No. 24, Nov. 5, 1853.

9. *Proceedings, American Anti-Slavery Society,* 1854.

10. *National Anti-Slavery Standard,* Vol. XVII, No. 23, Oct. 25, 1856.

11. *National Anti-Slavery Standard,* Vol. XXI, No. 25, Nov. 5, 1860.

12. William Lloyd Garrison Family Papers, Sophia Smith Collection, Smith College.

13. Anna Davis Hallowell, *James and Lucretia Mott* (Boston, 1884), p. 341.

14. *National Anti-Slavery Standard,* Vol. XIV, No. 24, Nov. 5, 1853.

15. Ferencz and Thérèse Pulszky, *White Red Black Sketches of Society in the United States* (London, 1853), pp. 194–196.

16. Mott MSS, Friends Historical Library, Swarthmore College.

17. Garrison Family Papers.

18. Swarthmore College Peace Collection, Friends Historical Library, Swarthmore College.

19. *Friends Weekly Intelligencer,* Vol. XLVIII, No. 7, Feb. 14, 1891, p. 103.

20. Division of Manuscripts, Boston Public Library.

21. *National Anti-Slavery Standard,* Vol. XXI, No. 25, Nov. 3, 1860.

Chapter Fourteen—A WOULD–BE RESPITE

1. Preceding letters in this chapter are from William Lloyd Garrison Family Papers, Sophia Smith Collection, Smith College.

2. Anti-Slavery Letters to Garrison and Others, Boston Public Library.

3. *Columbia Spy,* October 31 [1857]. Reported in *Liberator,* Vol. XXVII, 50, Dec. 11, 1857.

4. "A Sermon Delivered at Yardleyville, Bucks Co., Pa., Sept. 26" [1858] by Lucretia Mott, "Reported Phonographically," *Liberator,* Vol. XXVIII, 44, Oct. 29, 1858, p. 176.

5. *National Anti-Slavery Standard,* Vol. XVII, No. 30, Dec. 1, 1866.

Chapter Fifteen—"ALL THESE REFORMS"

1. *Inventory of Church Archives, Society of Friends in Pennsylvania,* prepared by the Pennsylvania Historical Survey, Works Projects Administration (Philadelphia, 1841–1866). *Minutes and Proceedings of the Western Quarterly Meeting, Held at Kennett Square,* 1852–1860, Friends Historical Library, Swarthmore College.

2. *Report of Addresses at a Meeting held in Boston, May 30, 1867, To consider the Conditions, Wants, and Prospects of Free Religion in America Together with the Constitution of the Free Religious Association there Organized* (Boston, 1867), pp. 94, 95, 96. See also Stow Persons, *Free Religion an American Faith* (New Haven, London, 1947).

3. Swarthmore College Peace Collection, Friends Historical Library, Swarthmore College.

4. *Voice of Peace,* Vol. II (N.S.), No. 4, (July 1875), pp. 51, 52.

5. *National Anti-Slavery Standard,* Vol. XXII, No. 9, July 13, 1861.

6. "Discourse by Lucretia Mott at Friends Meeting, 15th Street, New York, First day morning, 11th mo. 11th, 1866, Reported by Andrew J. Graham." A typed copy.

7. William Lloyd Garrison Family Papers, Sophia Smith Collection, Smith College.

8. *Ibid.*

9. Mott MSS, Friends Historical Library, Swarthmore College.

10. Anti-Slavery Letters to Garrison and Others, Boston Public Library.

11. Manuscripts Division, Library of Congress.

12. Minutes, Phila. Y. M. Women Friends, 1861, Fifth 13–17.

13. Anti-Slavery Letters to Garrison.

14. *Address of Some Members of the Society of Friends to their Fellow Members on the Subject of Education and on the Establishment of a Boarding School for Friends' Children, and for the Education of Teachers* (Philadelphia, 1861).

15. Garrison Family Papers.

16. *National Anti-Slavery Standard,* Feb. 2, 1868.

17. Homer T. Rosenberger, "Montgomery County's Greatest Lady: Lucretia Mott," *Bulletin of the Historical Society of Montgomery County* (Norristown, November, April 1948), VI, 136, 137.

18. John Haynes Holmes, *The Life and Letters of Robert Collyer, 1823–1912* (2 vols., New York, 1917), pp. 1, 143, 156–162, 164.

19. *The Eleventh National Woman's Rights Convention held in the City of New York, at the Church of the Puritans, on Thursday, May 10th, 1866, Cooper Institute, New York City, Martha C. Wright, President . . .* 1866.

20. Miss Anthony's Scraps. A clipping from the *Lewiston (Maine) Journal Weekly,* "Our Washington Correspondence Sermon by Lucretia Mott . . . Washington, Jan. 23, 1869," Library of Congress.

21. Swarthmore College Peace Collection.

22. Buffalo Public Library.

23. Garrison Family Papers.

24. *Proceedings of the Tenth National Convention, Woman's Rights Movement . . .* (Boston, 1860).

25. Garrison Family Papers.

26. *Liberator,* Vol. XVIII, No. 40, Oct. 6, 1848, p. 159.

27. Garrison Family Papers.

Chapter Sixteen—EVENING

1. William Lloyd Garrison Family Papers, Sophia Smith Collection, Smith College.

2. Mary Elizabeth Fiske Sargent, *Sketches and Reminiscences of the Radical Club of Chestnut Street* (Boston, 1880).

3. *Ibid.,* pp. 22–24, 265.

4. Garrison Family Papers.

5. Anti-Slavery Letters to Garrison and Others, Boston Public Library.

6. Mott MSS, Friends Historical Library, Swarthmore College. The letter addressed to "My dear Lydia" with the heading "Roadside near Phila. 9 mo. 1st. 74" is not in Lucretia's handwriting, although signed "Lucretia Mott."

7. Garrison Family Papers.

8. *The Nation,* Vol. III, No. 77, Dec. 20, 1866, pp. 498, 499.

9. Garrison Family Papers.

10. *Ibid.*

11. Anti-Slavery Letters to Garrison.

12. War Department, Adjutant General's Office, Washington, February 10, 1874, Official Correspondence Relative to the War with the Modoc Indians in 1872–73 . . . Executive Documents, No. 58–122 . . .

13. Alfred H. Love, *Voice of Peace,* Vol. VII, No. 9 (December 1880), pp. 143–146.

14. "The First Anniversary of Mothers' Day," New York. " 'Mothers Day' which was inaugurated in this City on the 2d. of June, 1872, by Mrs. Julia Ward Howe, was celebrated by the Woman's Social Education Society and New York Peace Association . . ." *Voice of Peace,* Vol. I (N.S.), No. 5 (August 1874), p. 78.

15. "Record Book," Stephen Smith Home for the Aged, Philadelphia. Scattered entries of gifts received: "1866 . . . one turkey, four mince pies, cabbage and turnips, Lucretia Mott. 1872, January 14, cane seat chairs, Lucretia Mott. 1874 . . . Lucretia Mott, $10. January 14, 1875 . . . 3 dozen handkerchiefs, 1 turkey, 3 chickens, 6 mince pies, basket apples, 1 basket beets, 1 basket turnips, handkerchiefs. Lucretia Mott. January 11, 1877 . . . Lucretia Mott $10.00. Fifty-five handkerchiefs, a turkey and twelve mince pies, Lucretia Mott. 1878–79 . . . One very large turkey and twelve mince pies, Lucretia Mott."

16. *Friends Intelligencer,* Supplement to Vol. XXVI, No. 52, Feb. 26, 1870, pp. 1, 2, 6, 7.

17. *The Woman's Journal,* Vol. IX, No. 30, July 27, 1878, pp. 237, 240.

18. Mott MSS, Swarthmore College.

19. *Voice of Peace,* Vol. VII, No. 3 (June 1880).

20. This description was given by Miss Lucy Davis.

21. Love, *Voice of Peace,* Vol. XII, No. 9, pp. 144–146.

INDEX

INDEX

(LM has been used to indicate Lucretia Mott)